Authentic Christianity

Volume 6

D. MARTYN LLOYD-JONES

Authentic Christianity

SERMONS ON THE ACTS OF THE APOSTLES

Volume 6

Acts 8:1–35

THE BANNER OF TRUTH TRUST

THE BANNER OF TRUTH TRUST
3 Murrayfield Road, Edinburgh EH12 6EL

*

First published 2006

ISBN-10: 0 85151 943 1
ISBN-13: 978 0 85151 943 2

*

Typeset in 10.5/13 pt Palatino at the
Banner of Truth Trust, Edinburgh

Printed in Great Britain at
the University Press,
Cambridge

Contents

1

The Growth of the Church

And Saul was consenting unto his death. And at that time there was a great persecution against the church which was at Jerusalem; and they were all scattered abroad throughout the regions of Judaea and Samaria, except the apostles. And devout men carried Stephen to his burial, and made great lamentation over him. As for Saul, he made havock of the church, entering into every house, and haling men and women committed them to prison. Therefore they that were scattered abroad went every where preaching the word. Then Philip went down to the city of Samaria, and preached Christ unto them (Acts 8:1–5).

I want to direct your attention particularly to the fourth verse of this passage: 'Therefore they that were scattered abroad went every where preaching the word.' Indeed, I am concerned to deal only with the first half even of that verse: 'Therefore they that were scattered abroad went every where . . .'

We are considering here these early chapters in the book of the Acts of the Apostles, as we have been doing for the past two and a half years.[1] We have been looking at these chapters for a very definite reason. It is because we are given here an account of the early church; we are told how the church ever came into being and what happened to it in the early days. Our object in considering Acts is very practical. It is not merely that we are historians, and history is very interesting, but that we are concerned about the extraordinary ignorance in the modern world – an ignorance that is incredible when you first consider it – as to what the Christian church is, what her message is, what she is meant to do and what she really is about.

[1] The earlier sermons have been published as *Authentic Christianity*, vols.1–5.

There is not only ignorance, but there is also terrible confusion at the present time, and this, of course, is the great tragedy because the contention of those of us who are Christians is that we have here the only message that can be of any avail to any individual or group of individuals. And yet the very church that is supposed to be the guardian and custodian of the mysteries contained in the Bible is herself partly the cause of this terrible and tragic confusion. I am concerned, therefore, about the masses of people who are outside the Christian church and who say quite frankly that they are not interested in Christianity. I believe that their position is what it is because of this confusion with regard to the primary and fundamental truth concerning what the Christian church really is and what her message is.

Now this ignorance and confusion, of course, take many different forms. It is one of my basic contentions that most people who are not Christians are in that position because their initial approach has been wrong. Of course, they say it is not that – and they bring up particular difficulties. But those are never the real source of the trouble. The real trouble is a fundamentally wrong approach, and if that approach is wrong, then you are inevitably doomed to go wrong all along the line.

It is simple: if you start on the wrong road, then you are bound to arrive at the wrong destination, and that, I suggest to you, is what is happening to so many. It increasingly seems to me that people are in trouble because they will for ever spend their time in discussing the implications or the applications of Christianity without first deciding what Christianity is: and you can waste an awful lot of time doing that. The books and the articles and the discussions are quite pathetic. The real trouble between the contestants is that they do not know the first principles. It is on the fundamentals that they have gone wrong. All this other argumentation is entirely beside the point.

There are two main causes for this fundamental failure in the whole approach to Christianity. The first is that it is regarded as just a teaching. People may say it is right or they may say it is wrong, but the point is that they approach it as just one of a number of possible teachings that are put before us. Here we are in this troubled world, and never has it been in greater trouble. We have already had two world wars in this century – and God knows what is awaiting us. So there are people who say, 'I've considered politics and I've considered philosophy and now here's a message that seems to address the world – what is it?' And they think of it as just another possible answer to the questions, an alternative solution to some of the problems. They think that the main message of the Christian church and the Christian faith is a point of view.

Now I must go on repeating this because this is what is being said. People talk about a Christian point of view on the war in Vietnam. Church dignitaries are always ready to give their opinions about this, both as individuals and in their conferences. A man, who is not an Evangelical, has recently written a most important book in which he says about such people, 'On what authority are they speaking? Where do they get their ideas from? How are they able to give these opinions?' And this is serious, because people think that these dignitaries are putting forward the Christian message, putting forward Christianity, when they are just giving their point of view with regard to the questions that are agitating the minds of people today.

Now church leaders are beginning to say quite openly that theology must be reconstructed altogether and that we must start with the world as it is. Nothing, of course, could be further removed from the New Testament position, but that is what they are saying.

And so people do not think of Christianity as something that is vital and essential to all of us, but only as a possible point of view, a possible attitude that we may take to these teeming, pressing problems that are troubling our modern world.

The second underlying cause for the wrong approach to Christianity is quite different. It is that people's approach is entirely personal. I am thinking of the large group of people who are not interested in the war in Vietnam as such. Someone from this group will say, 'I'm not a politician. I'm not interested in these things. Of course, it affects me, but that's not my big concern.' These people are not primarily concerned about the problem of apartheid and issues like that. What they are interested in is their own personal problems. They are conscious of certain weaknesses, certain failures, certain needs; and they are unhappy. This could be because of the treachery of some trusted friend, or some disappointment in life, or some besetting sin that for ever gets them down – whatever the cause, and there are many – they are troubled. So political questions do not occupy the centre of their minds at all. They are concerned about themselves and want some relief and release.

This second group approach the Christian faith along the line of their particular need, and it is offered to them as something that will help them to deal with their pressing personal problems – Jesus as your Friend, Jesus as the one who will heal you of that disease, Jesus as the one who will meet you at the point of your failure. He will give you peace; he will give you rest and quiet, and so on. This is their exclusive approach, and, unfortunately, at the end, they are often left exactly as they were at the beginning.

Now all this is important because both these approaches allow other people to say, 'Well, if that's the point of Christianity, I'm not interested. It doesn't concern me.' With regard to the first group, someone will say, 'I'm a politician and I don't have much use for these idealists who are always calling upon us to sit on the streets in protest, or to march, or to go out to Vietnam and stand or sit between the two armies. That's just a lot of nonsense. I'm a hard-headed man of the world. If people like to do that sort of thing, well, let them, but it's not for me.' And so the whole of Christianity is dismissed. Indeed, it may be regarded as dangerous on the grounds that it makes people think sentimentally and foolishly, and does not allow them to face facts with realism or even with courage.

And then there is exactly the same reaction with regard to the second group. Someone says, 'I'm not conscious of the needs these people are talking about. I know they crowd the waiting rooms of the consultants and psychiatrists in the practices and hospitals that deal with such problems. The world is full of this sort of thing. People are taking drugs and turning to drink, and others go to psychiatrists. But I don't have these psychiatric problems. These people can't adjust to life. They've been the round of the cults and haven't found satisfaction, so now they're coming to try Christianity. But as for me, I'm not interested.'

Now it is of fundamental importance to understand that Christianity is not a mere teaching, not a mere point of view, and nor is it merely something that helps us to deal with our problems. Thank God, it is these two things. It is a point of view, a teaching, and it does deal with our individual problems, but the fallacy is to start with that. And that is why so many are not Christians at the present time – because they have an entirely false idea of the Christian faith and the Christian message. And it is because this passage deals with this that I am calling your attention to it.

'How does this passage deal with these two wrong approaches?' asks someone.

Like this. Let me put it to you as a principle. My first proposition is that the Christian faith and teaching are the result of historical events and facts and actions. And that is what we are reminded of in this passage. The book we are studying is called the book of Acts; it is the book of the Acts of the Apostles. Or, as the writer himself seems to prefer to put it, it is the book of the Acts of the Lord Jesus Christ. This is how he begins: 'The former treatise have I made, O Theophilus, of all that Jesus began both to do and teach . . .' The writer of this book of Acts is undoubtedly Luke, the man who wrote the Gospel according to Luke, and he writes his second book, like the first, to Theophilus. He says that in the first book he told Theophilus about the things that Jesus began to do and teach, '. . . until the day in which he was taken up, after that he through the Holy Ghost had given commandments unto the apostles whom he had chosen.' Luke is saying: 'Having told you that, I am now going on to tell you of the things he continued to do.' So some people say that this book is not so much the book of the Acts of the Apostles, although they were the actual actors, but, rather, the book of the Acts of the risen Lord Jesus Christ, who is acting through the apostles. Others say that we should call this book, 'the book of the Acts of the Holy Spirit'.

The important thing to remember, however, is that everywhere we are given facts. Facts! Events! We are studying things that happened on the field of history. All that we are considering here belongs as solidly to history as does the conquest of this country by Julius Caesar, or the various other events that are recorded in the pages of secular textbooks.

Now I want to show you the relevance of this. I want to show you that it is fatal to start with ourselves or to start, even, with the world. One man says, 'I'm very concerned about these things that are happening in our world today.' All right. But what we say to him is this: 'Before you start looking at what is happening in the world, consider these events that happened two thousand years ago.' The other man says, 'I'm very concerned about my own troubles.' We say, 'My friend, forget your troubles for a moment and face these facts that took place nearly two thousand years ago.' That is how the Bible starts and for that reason it is different from every other teaching. It is a book that primarily calls us to consider certain facts.

What is the Christian church? Well, the Christian church is not an institution that has been founded by people. Men and women have founded many an institution and society. There are many learned societies here in London. A number of men and women holding similar views come together and decide to form a society and they may become incorporated, and so on. All right; that is the way the world does things, but the Christian church did not come into being in that way; and this book, the Bible, tells us all about it.

Here is a society of people that came into being entirely and solely as the result of certain things that happened in this world. The church is entirely historical, and if you take away the history, not only will you never understand the church, there would never have been a church. Whatever your experience may be, whatever your condition at this moment, for the time being it is, I say, absolutely irrelevant. Some of you may have terrible problems, others may be saying, 'Isn't life wonderful! Haven't got a problem in the world!' I say that I have a message to hold before you that is as relevant and urgent to you as it is to everyone else.

I repeat that this is absolutely fundamental. This message asks us all, first and foremost, to consider these facts, these happenings. It is a proclamation based upon events – it is a book of acts! What are they? Well, the great message that was preached by these early preachers, the early apostles, was a message concerning Jesus of Nazareth. There were problems in that ancient world, even as there are today. The Jews had been conquered by the Romans, and no country, no nation, and especially not a proud nation, likes to be conquered. But they had been conquered. They were being governed by Rome and they did not like it. Yet when the apostles went round preaching, they did not deal with the political and social conditions, they did not mention them. They preached about Jesus.

Now those of us who have been working through the first seven chapters together know this perfectly well. There is never any mention here of the Roman tyranny or the Roman bondage. No political issues are ever mentioned at all. The whole message is about this Jesus. The four Gospels are devoted to him and if you read this book of Acts, you will find that they are still talking about him, this extraordinary person who lived in Galilee and, having been a carpenter for many years, suddenly, at the age of thirty, burst upon the nation and spoke in a most astounding manner. Not only that, he also did the most amazing things: he worked miracles, stopped a storm on a lake, raised the dead and gave sight to the blind – Jesus! A phenomenon, a fact in history. This is what they were talking about.

And they talked about his death; they made a great deal of that – how he was nailed to a tree and died, and how his body was taken down and was laid in a tomb, and how they had all seen it. They told how a stone was rolled before the face of that tomb and then sealed and guarded by soldiers. But – and this was the whole point – he had risen from the dead. In spite of all these precautions, the tomb was empty. And he had appeared to them, and they had become witnesses of the fact that he had risen from the dead, in the body. This was their message – Jesus and the resurrection.

Now you need not take my word for this, it is all here. This is history. This is what they talked about. The apostles did not turn to people and say, 'Are you having trouble sleeping? Are you worried about that disease? Do you want a friend? Are you feeling lonely? Or what about this position in which we find ourselves as a nation? Don't you think it's about time we protested against this and that?' Nothing of the sort! Jesus and the resurrection!

And then, of course, on top of that, as we are told in the second chapter of Acts, there was the extraordinary event that took place in Jerusalem on the day of Pentecost. Here were these men – and they were ordinary men, fishermen, most of them, not men of culture, not men of learning, not men whom the world regarded as great. No, no, they were dismissed by the authorities as 'unlearned and ignorant men' (*Acts* 4:13). But something happened to these men on the day of Pentecost. They were absolutely transformed and transfigured. They were filled with a joy and a brightness and a gladness. Their faces were shining and they were able to speak in languages that they had never known before so that everybody could hear them speaking in their own language and dialect. They were a phenomenon.

And that is how the church began. That is the record that we are given here. And the crowd came and listened. And one of these men, a fisherman, whose name was Peter, stood up and preached with such amazing authority and power that his sermon was interrupted, not by opposition but by people in trouble about themselves and their souls, who cried out in agony of soul saying, 'Men and brethren, what shall we do?' (*Acts* 2:37). And Peter gave them the message: 'Repent, and be baptized every one of you in the name of Jesus Christ for the remission of sins, and ye shall receive the gift of the Holy Ghost' (*Acts* 2:38). So they did, and three thousand people were added to the church that day. This is the story.

We have been considering together the other events that followed that great sermon by Peter. But this is what is interesting: until the beginning of this eighth chapter of Acts, all these events are confined to the city of Jerusalem. But now, at the beginning of this eighth chapter, we come to a new departure. We see this Christian church beginning to spread abroad, beginning to spread throughout the regions of Judaea and Samaria. And we know that subsequently, as you find in later chapters of Acts, it began to spread even farther, throughout the then civilized world: it went to Greece, to Rome and to Spain. All those countries around that Mediterranean seaboard began not only to hear but also to receive this message, and the Christian church quite soon had her people, her citizens, in all these countries. And we know that today it has spread throughout all the countries of the entire world. Now this is the beginning of all that, and I remind you again that we are dealing here with something that is historical, we are dealing with the sheer facts of history.

I wonder how often you have considered the whole question of Christianity in this way and in these terms? Is there somebody here, somebody listening to me now, who is rather surprised that I am preaching in this way? You say, 'What's the relevance of all that to me?' Wait a minute, my friend – I will show you the relevance. The mistake you make is to ask that question at this point. You are still thinking about yourself, are you not? Or you are thinking about the war in Vietnam or the problems that are interesting to you. But that is wrong. Leave them alone for a moment. This is what you must consider: these events happened.

Now what is the significance of these words in Acts 8:1 that the believers were scattered abroad? Well, I make two immediate observations. The first is that Christianity is patently not just a Jewish religion; it is not just a local religion. The religions of the world are generally local religions. Confucianism, Buddhism, Islam, Hinduism are local religions. But Christianity has claimed from the beginning that it is the universal faith. 'There is none other name under heaven given among men, whereby we must be saved,' said the apostle Peter to the Sanhedrin (*Acts* 4:12). Jesus himself said, 'I am the light of the world' (*John* 9:5). He said, 'I am the way, the truth, and the life: no man cometh unto the Father, but by me' (*John* 14:6). Exclusive but universal at the same time. He came for the whole world of men and women; he is the Saviour of the world.

And here, of course, we are confronted by an extraordinary fact. It is the fact that the Christian faith started in a very little country – Palestine. What a small country it was and what a comparatively unimportant country at that particular time! And here was a man who was a carpenter. Yet they asked this question about him: 'How knoweth this man letters, having never learned?' (*John* 7:15). He had never been to the schools, he had never attended the lectures of the great philosophers in the academies and porches of Greece, he was not even a Pharisee. Unlettered, untutored! Jesus, a Galilean peasant, and yet he was the one out of whom Christianity came – this little country, this kind of person. And then there were these men who carried on after he had gone. They had nothing to commend them; judged by human standards they were absolutely hopeless. These were not the people who form royal societies, or great academies and institutions of culture and learning. No, no, the exact opposite. And yet the simple fact is that this message has spread throughout the whole world. And here in Acts, I repeat, is the beginning of that.

But I make a second observation, and this, again, is a sheer fact of history. Whatever you may think of Christianity, you have got to grant this – that it has been the most potent factor in world history. There is no doubt about this. Fairly soon – you will find it later on in Acts – people began to describe the apostles as 'these that have turned the world upside down' (*Acts* 17:6). And Christianity has, of course. Let us for a moment forget everything but just this fact of history, this phenomenon by which we are confronted. It is a fact that by about AD 325, the beliefs of this little group of people had become the official religion of the great Roman Empire. How do you explain the history of the world? My contention is that the really big movements in history are only explicable in terms of the history of the Christian church.

This is the way to approach Christianity. Forget all your personal problems, forget your views on any other general question, just start to consider this fact, this great phenomenon. Read your secular history books and see the place that has been occupied, the part that has been played, by this Christian message. What was it that saved a modicum of culture when the Goths and the Vandals and the other rude hordes came down and sacked imperial Rome? It was this Christian church that preserved the little culture that was left, and preserved it for centuries to come.

Whether or not you are a Christian, you have to agree that the Protestant Reformation was one of the great turning points in history: nothing has been the same since. And that came out of this message. What happened to Martin Luther was that he began to understand the teaching of the New Testament. It had been hidden from him, as it had been from most people, by the falsity of the Roman Catholic doctrine. But the man was suddenly enlightened and saw what it all meant. He turned, and he turned the world also, as it were. Protestantism! Look at its impact, not only upon literature and art and music, but also upon political issues. Secular historians are prepared to agree that the whole idea of democracy and of liberty in this country came directly out of the Protestant Reformation.

Now this is a fact, it is a phenomenon of history, and I could elaborate at great length – I have often done so! The Poor Law system came out of the Christian church. When nobody else was thinking about help for the poor and suffering, the church practised it. Hospitals came from Christianity – Rahere, who founded St Bartholomew's Hospital, the oldest hospital in Britain, was a monk – and so have all the greatest and most beneficent movements. Take education – you young people who are enjoying the benefits of education today, have you ever stopped to ask how it has come to you, why education is no longer the prerogative of a chosen few but has become so free? Well, you will find your answer not only in the Protestant Reformation but also in the further work of the Puritans, and still more in the Methodist revival and reawakening of two hundred years ago and all that that led to in the nineteenth century. You just do not understand your modern position apart from the Christian church. History is not explicable apart from it.

So forget your personal problems, forget your aches and pains, in a spiritual sense, forget all your ideas about the condition of the world today. I ask you just to stop and consider and ask: What is this message? What is this teaching that began to spread at this point in Acts, and has had such an effect upon the whole story of the human race? And, I repeat, these five verses that we are considering really give us the answer.

In response, then, to the two wrong approaches to Christianity, my first principle is that it is founded upon actual historical events, events that changed the world. So I come to my second principle, which is that the meaning and significance of these events can only be understood in terms of a great spiritual conflict. That is what I find here in these five verses, as I have already found it in the previous chapter, in the account of the persecution and the martyrdom of that first Christian martyr, Stephen. In chapter 7 we read how Stephen was defending himself before the great court, the Sanhedrin, and this is what we are told:

When they heard these things, they were cut to the heart, and they gnashed on him with their teeth. But he, being full of the Holy Ghost, looked up stedfastly into heaven, and saw the glory of God, and Jesus standing on the right hand of God, and said, Behold, I see the heavens opened, and the Son of man standing on the right hand of God. Then, they cried out with a loud voice, and stopped their ears, and ran upon him with one accord, and cast him out of the city, and stoned him: and the witnesses laid down their clothes at a young man's feet, whose name was Saul. And they stoned Stephen, [as he was] calling upon God, and saying, Lord Jesus, receive my spirit. And he kneeled down, and cried with a loud voice, Lord, lay not this sin to their charge. And when he had said this, he fell asleep. And Saul was consenting unto his death. And at that time there was a great persecution against the church which was at Jerusalem; and they were all scattered abroad throughout the regions of Judaea and Samaria, except the apostles . . . As for Saul, he made havock of the church, entering into every house, and haling men and women committed them to prison. Therefore they that were scattered abroad went every where preaching the word. Then Philip went down to the city of Samaria (Acts 7:54—8:1, 3–5).

What is the explanation of this persecution? The gospel spread because of it, but why did it occur? This is a vital question. Does it not astonish you to read that people should be treated in this way? Why was it? This kind of thing does not happen to teachers of philosophy. Oh, I know the philosophers, they can vilify one another, with ink, on paper; they can be very sarcastic as they go for one another. Yes, but that is a little bit of play-acting. Here is something real. This is men and women being stoned to death, dragged out of their houses, thrown into prison, thrown to the lions in the arena – terrible persecutions.

So why does persecution happen to this message and to these people? Here is something that we must consider. Why the violence? Why the bitterness? Now if you really want to deal with your own personal problems and the problem of Vietnam and the whole problem of the world today, this is the way to do it. The question is not what we can do about Vietnam but why we ever get a Vietnam. Why is there such a thing as war? Why do people behave in this manner?

Why is there heartbreak? Why is there adultery and divorce and separation, and little children breaking their hearts – why all this? Those are the questions. Before you begin to talk about what to do, find out the cause, and here we are given the only answer. Let me show it to you in its context.

What happened to these early Christians, of course, was nothing but a repetition of what had happened to the Lord Jesus Christ himself. This is what you must face if you want to understand life and want to understand yourself. Look at the Gospels: here was the very Son of God standing amongst men and women. He had left the glory of heaven and had come on earth. He had humbled himself, abased himself. He had taken the form of a servant. Why did he do it? Did he come to do harm? Did he come to create trouble? Did he come to blast us? Did he come to make life impossible for us with the standard he set in the Sermon on the Mount? Why did he come into the world?

You know the answer. He went about doing good. Never has anyone done so much good in this world in speech and in action. He was the friend of tax-collectors and sinners. He healed the sick and the afflicted. He brought peace and happiness and joy. He said, 'The Son of man is come to seek and to save that which was lost' (*Luke* 19:10). He said: I have come to help you. I have come to redeem you. I have come to tell you about God. I have come to put you into relationship with God.

But how did they treat the Son of God? You know the story, do you not? If not, it is about time you did. Here is the history that you must get familiar with. Here is the history you must understand. You cannot understand what is happening in your modern world until you understand this history. Here is the key to it all. Why did the world deal with him as it did? Why the opposition? Why the malignity? Why the bitterness? They tried to stone him. Why did they lie about him? He never did anybody any harm – he did nothing but good – yet the leaders and the people finally shouted out, 'Away with him! Crucify him!' And they did: they killed him. Why did they do it?

And when you come to this book of Acts you find the same treatment given out to these followers of his. Peter and John healed a lame man at the Beautiful Gate of the temple, a man over forty years of age who had never walked in his life. Everybody had tried to do everything they could but nobody could help him. Then Peter said, 'In the name of Jesus Christ of Nazareth rise up and walk' (*Acts* 3:6). And he did. For that they were arrested, thrown into prison, put on trial, treated abominably. They went on doing things like that and the authorities went on putting them in prison.

And then you come to the great story of Stephen, a man filled with the Holy Spirit. What had Stephen done? He had done no harm. Again, here was a man, who was preaching good news, showing people a way of salvation, doing good; yet he was stoned to death and they 'gnashed on him with their teeth' (*Acts* 7:54). What was the matter with them?

Then look at this man Saul of Tarsus. We know about Saul, do we not – that he was an outstanding genius, with an exceptional brain, that he was capable of deep emotion: we know all this as we read his later epistles. He was not suddenly given brains when he was converted; he had always been a profound thinker, always a man of deep feeling. Yet here he was, making havoc of the church, dragging men and women out of their houses and throwing them into prison. Why did he do this kind of thing?

And why has such persecution continued throughout the centuries. Why have people always thought it clever to denounce Christianity and persecute Christians? Why do they still do it? Why is this message being treated as it is in the modern world? You remember what Hitler did, you know what Communism is still doing in many a country. Why the bitterness? Why the spite? Why the vituperation? Why the readiness to kill Christians?

Now we have evidence for saying that even Stalin, in the last war, had to admit that the best workers he could find in his munitions factories in Russia were these Christians whom he despised and reviled. He confessed that they were the best people in the country, the most reliable, the most dependable, and he relaxed his laws against them. Yet the persecution came back. How do you explain this?

And opposition is not confined to governments and systems; you find it amongst individuals. You see bitter hatred; you hear people saying about their own children, 'I would sooner see them dead than become Christians.' Now you have got to explain this. These people are able people; in other respects they appear to be rational. They are people of education and culture and understanding. Yet they ostracize their own children, have nothing to do with them and vilify them because they have become Christian. Why is this?

And there is only one answer. This persecution is but a manifestation of a tremendous spiritual conflict. This is the great message of the Bible. You find it beginning back in the third chapter of the book of Genesis. When Adam rebelled and sinned against God and fell, God came down and, in effect, said, 'As the result of this sin, there shall be war perpetually between the seed of the serpent and the seed of the woman.' And there is. It is what the apostle Paul says in the sixth chapter of his epistle to the Ephesians: 'We wrestle not against flesh and blood, but against principalities, against powers, against the rulers of the darkness of this world, against spiritual wickedness in high [heavenly] places' (*Eph.* 6:12). That is the only explanation. We are not dealing with mere men and women; there is something behind them. A man like Saul did not persecute Christians by instinct or by nature. No, no, he was in the hands of another power; he was being driven; he was being pressed.

So the only explanation both of this persecution recorded here in Acts and also of the state of the world today is that there is this mighty warfare between God and the devil, a war for the souls of men and women. This world is under the dominion of an alien power, the power of the devil, the power of hell. There are 'evil spirits', 'sorcerers', evil forces and powers. The world, of course, is too clever to believe in this, is it not? And that is exactly where it is fooled. It behaves as it does because it is under the power of these evil forces, but it does not know it and it does not understand.

People in and of themselves do not behave in such an utterly irrational manner or become mad against the beneficent message of the gospel. No, no, they are the victims, they are the tools, they are the dupes, the instruments, of this power of evil that hates God and does its utmost to ruin his universe. Unseen spiritual forces are manipulating men and women. Here is the essential message.

It is a spiritual battle: that is the only adequate explanation. The physical battle, the material battle, is only a manifestation of the real battle that goes on in the realm of the spirit, working in us without our conscious awareness, making us act in this extraordinary manner. Look at this man Saul – he, of all men, behaving like this!

But, thank God, I do not and I must not stop at that. I must bring you to my third and last principle, which is this: the events that we have recorded here are, in terms of the gospel, simply an account of the outworking of God's plan and God's way of conquering these enemies, and giving salvation to men and women. Let me put it like this – I am only giving you a general message now but it is the message of the whole Bible – the world is as it is because it has listened to the devil. Adam listened and fell; everybody following him has done the same thing. All your troubles today are due to this and to nothing else. You can educate, it does not make any difference. You can improve the way in which society is ordered, it does not make any difference. People will still drink and gamble and indulge in sex and perversions, exactly as they have always done. In spite of your much vaunted advances and developments, there has been no change, and it is because man in his heart is governed by evil. And the story of Christianity is the story of God's activity to deliver us out of that. It is God acting for our salvation.

What is God doing? Well, what I read here in verse 1 is this: 'At that time there was a great persecution against *the church*.' What is the church? It is the people of God. The church is the people of God as gathered out of this world; the men and women who have been rescued by God; the men and women who have been separated by God from this evil system, this evil power, this dominion of sin and of Satan. That is what the church is. The whole story of the Bible is the story of God's deliverance. God comes down and announces that he has a plan and that he has a way: the seed of the woman shall bruise the serpent's head (see *Gen.* 3:15). There it is. There is the great promise. The rest of the Bible is the unfolding of this promise.

So how has God carried out his promise? Well, here is a bird's-eye view of the Old Testament. God calls a man named Abraham (Stephen has said all this in his great speech recorded in chapter 7), calls him out of the paganism of Ur of the Chaldees, reveals himself to Abraham and produces a nation out of him. God's people! Abraham and the nation of Israel. A separate people! Separated from the world, living a new way, a holy way, like the way of God. Of course, they are not perfect, but God intervenes on their behalf and saves them time and time again. He sends teachers, prophets. That is the Old Testament. It is the story of God working out a people for himself, setting up his own kingdom, a kingdom of light against the kingdom of darkness; the kingdom of God against the kingdom of hell.

Then we come to the New Testament and we read that 'when the fullness of the time was come' Jesus appears (*Gal.* 4:4). Who is this? He is the Son of God! He is the focus of it all – God in the flesh! And what has the Son of God come to do? He has come to fight these enemies of humankind. Look at him for forty days and forty nights tempted of the devil in the wilderness, and tempted at other times, too. What are his activities? Casting out devils, healing the sick and afflicted. What is all this? Oh, this is only dealing with the consequences of evil; this is setting men and women free from that which enslaves them and makes them behave in this irrational manner. That is what he does. That is the account we have of him in the Gospels. He again, you see, never delivers a political protest – never. He is not interested in social problems as such. No, no, he goes down to the depth, the root cause, which he realizes is in the soul, not merely in the mind and intellect. And he deals with the radical problem in a radical manner.

And supremely he deals with it, of course, upon the cross. It is the machinations of the devil, through evil men, that have sent him there; men actually work the deed, but there is something deeper in it. What he is doing on the cross, says this Saul of Tarsus later, as the apostle Paul writing to the Colossians, is this: 'Having spoiled principalities and powers' he is making 'a shew of them openly, triumphing over them in it' (*Col.* 2:15). Where they think they have got him, he defeats them, and he proves it in the glory of the resurrection when he rises, having even conquered the last enemy, and ascends into heaven, from where he sends down the Holy Spirit, adds to the church, and calls out his people.

But God's people are not left alone. Though the devil is defeated, he is not finally routed and destroyed, and he goes on working. He works in Saul of Tarsus, he works in the Sanhedrin, he works in the Jews, and through the centuries he has tried to destroy God's people, even working through a corrupt church. That is the message. It is all here in embryo in these verses in Acts. What is happening here? Oh, it is just the devil trying to exterminate the Christian church because it is the people of God whom God has separated unto himself and whom he is preparing for the final glory and the great kingdom that is to come, the kingdom that is to cover the whole universe from shore to shore.

And, thank God, I end on this note: God's triumph is absolutely certain. The most wonderful word in this text is this first word in the fourth verse: '*Therefore* they that were scattered abroad went every where preaching the word.' These members of the Sanhedrin thought that they were going to exterminate the church, and in this cruel persecution designed to that end, do you know what they were doing? Spreading the gospel! 'Therefore'! They were taking it out of Jerusalem, sending it throughout Judaea, sending it unto Samaria. They were doing the exact opposite of what they intended. 'Therefore'! The effect of their attempt to destroy it was to spread it.

You notice another word that is used in verse 4: 'Therefore they that were *scattered abroad* . . .' The Greek word that is translated here by 'scattered abroad' is the very same word that is used for a farmer sowing seed into the ground. They did not have drills in those days. The farmer put all his seed in a basket or a pan and then he took handfuls of seed and just threw it, 'scattered it abroad'. And that is how he got his crop.

So what did the persecution do? Oh, it just 'scattered abroad' the word of God. The persecution had the effect of sowing the seed of the word. This is most marvellous. Just before his ascension, our Lord spoke to the disciples and told them to wait in Jerusalem until they had received 'power from on high'. Then he said, 'After that the Holy Ghost is come upon you: and ye shall be witnesses unto me both in Jerusalem, and in all Judaea, and in Samaria, and unto the uttermost part of the earth' (*Acts* 1:8). That was his prophecy.

How was his prophecy fulfilled? Through the persecution perpetrated by these cruel, maddened opponents of the Christian faith. Or take another great prophecy of our Lord. He said, 'And this gospel of the kingdom shall be preached in all the world for a witness unto all nations; and then shall the end come' (*Matt.* 24:14) – and here is the beginning of the end. The gospel is spreading, the kingdom is gathering in men and women from all nations and tribes and languages.

'Therefore'! And the meaning of the 'therefore' is the power of God. The teaching is that God rules over all, even over his enemies. He permits much to happen that we do not understand. Why did he allow this persecution of the first believers? I do not know. All I know is that he used it. Look at Saul of Tarsus, this man who was converted on the road to Damascus and became the mighty apostle Paul. Why did God allow him to behave as he did at this point? I do not know. All I know is that God has his time for us all, so Paul only went on until God's determined hour had come, and then he was subdued. God permits much, he is permitting much in the modern world. He is allowing scepticism, materialism, infidelism, all these things. But as certainly as he allows it, he is behind it all, he is controlling it all, he overrules it all. 'Therefore they that were scattered abroad went every where preaching the word.'

God's victory is certain, the destruction of all his enemies is already fixed. Though people rise up in anger, and with vituperation and violence try to destroy his work, they cannot. Their final discomfiture was at the resurrection, and here is a repetition of it, and it has gone on throughout the running centuries. There have been times when the Christian church has been moribund; but then suddenly God has arisen, raised up a Luther, and the dead church has come to life and gone forth scattering abroad the word.

I therefore finish with a simple question: Have you faced these facts? Have you faced the fact that the Son of God has been in this world, and that he died on a cross, that he was buried, and that he rose again? Have you faced the question as to why he did that? Can you not see that there is only one explanation and it is that 'all have sinned' (*Rom.* 3:23), that all the world is guilty before God (*Rom.* 3:19)? You who came into this service thinking and worrying about Vietnam, you have never worried about yourself, have you? You have never thought of the fact that you have to die and stand before God in judgment– and you have never thought of that because you have never faced these facts. And you who came in with your psychological and personal problems, have you faced the fact that the Son of God came into this world and died on a tree and was buried and rose again? Have you ever asked why? The answer is that he came not that your body might be healed, though it might be, but that your soul might be healed and that you might be reconciled unto God. Have you ever considered these facts? And have you ever realized their relevance for you?

This is Christianity; you are involved in this cosmic, spiritual conflict, and though you may never have acted violently against Christianity, if you have just ignored it, you are equally its opponent. Not to consider it, not to consider that it is vital, not to see that it is everything, is to reject it, and to reject it is to reject God, the power of God, and the purpose of the manifestation of the power of God. It is to reject the coming again of this same Jesus to judge the world in righteousness, to condemn and to banish all evil, and to set up his glorious kingdom of light and of knowledge and of truth and of love and of peace and of joy.

My dear friend, do you belong to the church or to those who are set against the church? If you are not in, you are out; if you are not for, you are against – whether violently or politely and quietly. And not to be in the church is to be lost. Moreover, it is not only to continue in your present misery for as long as you are in this evil, miserable world, but it is also to remain in that utter misery and hopelessness for ever and for ever. The church! Do you belong to her? Do you glory in her? Do you see that she consists of the people redeemed by the power of God through his blessed Son, our Lord and Saviour Jesus Christ?

2

Samaria and the Modern World

Then Philip went down to the city of Samaria, and preached Christ unto them. And the people with one accord gave heed unto those things which Philip spake, hearing and seeing the miracles which he did. For unclean spirits, crying with loud voice, came out of many that were possessed with them: and many taken with palsies, and that were lame, were healed. And there was great joy in that city. But there was a certain man, called Simon, which beforetime in the same city used sorcery, and bewitched the people of Samaria, giving out that himself was some great one: to whom they all gave heed, from the least to the greatest, saying, This man is the great power of God. And to him they had regard, because that of long time he had bewitched them with sorceries. But when they believed Philip preaching the things concerning the kingdom of God, and the name of Jesus Christ, they were baptized, both men and women (Acts 8:5–12).

I am calling your attention to this incident in Acts chapter 8 because it is a wonderful and perfect picture of how the gospel, the Christian message, came to the people living in the city of Samaria. I also call your attention to it in order that through it I may direct your minds to the question of listening to the gospel and, indeed, our whole approach to the gospel. As I have tried to say on many, many occasions, it seems to me that the most urgent problem confronting the human race at this very moment is that it does not listen to the gospel.

Now the whole meaning and explanation of the existence of the Christian church is to present this message. If I did not believe that, I would not be in this pulpit. The Christian position is that the only hope for the world is to be found in this message, but we are confronted by the fact that as far as this country, at any rate, is concerned – and, indeed, it is but typical and representative of every other country, though in some there may be a superficial display of something that looks like Christianity – the vast majority of people are not interested in this message. They will not even listen to it; they denounce it, dismiss it, and feel that it is entirely remote and completely irrelevant to their present situation.

Now the trouble lies, as I have said, in the whole matter of the approach to the gospel. It is my contention that people who will have nothing to do with it are in that position because their whole attitude towards it is entirely wrong. That is the tragedy of their situation. And my one concern is that if there is anybody like that in this congregation tonight, I may disabuse your mind and bring you to a realization of what this gospel really is.

It seems to me that so many people are talking about 'the application of the gospel' to the current situation without first of all discovering what the gospel is. As we saw in our last study, Christianity is something historical. It is not just a point of view, it is not just a teaching. It is initially a proclamation of certain things that happened in history. It is concerned with facts, and the meaning of those facts, and the relevance of those facts to our whole situation. And we saw, furthermore, that you do not begin to understand the problem of the world today until you realize that it is a part of a great spiritual warfare between the forces of God and persecuting, malicious forces. An evidence of this spiritual conflict is the case of Saul of Tarsus, who later became the apostle Paul. Here in Acts we read: 'As for Saul, he made havock of the church, entering into every house, and haling men and women committed them to prison' (*Acts* 8:3). And we also read: 'There was a great persecution against the church which was at Jerusalem; and they were all scattered abroad throughout the regions of Judaea and Samaria, except the apostles' (*Acts* 8:1).

Now that was the point at which we arrived at the close of our last study and, of course, we ended by pointing out that in spite of all the efforts of the powers of evil, God triumphed. The effect of all this persecution was this: 'Therefore they that were scattered abroad went every where preaching the word' (verse 4). And now we are reminded that a part of that scattering was that this man Philip, who was an evangelist – you read about him in Acts 6 –

'went down to the city of Samaria, and preached Christ unto them'. And so we are given a picture of Philip arriving in this place where the gospel had not been heard before, and we are told what happened there. And I call your attention to this because it gives us, first, a perfect description of the condition of the people in Samaria before the Christian message came to them, and, secondly, an account of the effect of the gospel upon these people.

Now this brings us face to face with another difficulty that confronts a large number of people. I am thinking now of the people who denounce this gospel and even say that it is an insult to 'the modern man'. If you ask them for their reasons, they will tell you something like this: 'Our difficulty is that the Christian message is quite incapable of dealing with the problems of the world. It is a fairytale that speaks only to the individual condition and is all right for certain people who have got a kind of religious complex, but it is not for us. We are the practical people who want to put the world in order.' But the whole difficulty with these people is that their understanding of the problems of the world is so inadequate and so superficial that they cannot possibly hope to deal with it. The fact that they think they can is one of the great fallacies of the age in which you and I are living. And I want to show you this terrible failure and tragedy at the present time.

Now I am thinking of people who seem to give the impression that the only trouble in the world today is wars, and all they talk about is Vietnam and the problem of this war and other conflicts in the world. I have to go on repeating this because that is what is being said. I am speaking to the times, I am showing you the relevance of the Christian message. These people give the impression that if only the war in Vietnam could be stopped and the problem of apartheid could somehow be solved, they would have nothing more to say – those are their only problems. And, indeed, there are many in the church who give exactly the same impression. You will hear reports on the wireless or on the television of some church dignitary who has been preaching, and you can take it for granted that he will be preaching either about Vietnam or about the colour problem. Again, you feel that if these problems were solved, then they would have nothing to say. The whole gospel message has to do with these issues. And these church leaders give the impression that the problem is almost entirely intellectual, and the only solution is more education, more knowledge, more understanding. The case of these people has always been that ignorance is the cause of all our troubles. All you need to do, therefore, is multiply your educational facilities and then you will solve all your problems.

But I am here to say, in the light of this incident in Acts 2, that all that talk just indicates one thing, and that is that there is a complete and tragic failure to realize the world's problem in depth and to see the real situation of humanity.

We have already touched on this. I have said that the question to be asked is this: Why does anybody persecute this Christian message? It is a message of salvation, a message that gives hope, a message that gives great joy. I read here that after the preaching of the gospel, 'There was great joy in that city' (verse 8), yet this is the very message that people in the world damn and blast and persecute and blaspheme. Why do they do this? And I showed you that there is only one answer: it is that there are powers, evil powers, that are governing them and controlling them, blinding their understanding and leading them to behave in this terrifying manner. Now we must go farther into this matter. So far we have simply looked at it in general, but we must come to details because people are very reluctant to believe this explanation. There are people who say, 'Surely, you don't mean to tell us that today, in 1967, you believe in the devil? You can't possibly believe in evil spirits! Not in an enlightened, scientific age like this!' So I cannot leave it in the realm of generalities. I must come down to specific illustrations, the very thing that we have here before us in the story of Philip going to preach the gospel for the first time amongst the Samaritans.

What was the position of these Samaritans? There is no difficulty about this – we are told about them elsewhere in the Scriptures. They were a curious mixture. The Samaritans, in a sense, were neither Jews nor Gentiles but were partly Jews and partly Gentiles, in terms both of physical descent and, still more, in terms of their intellectual understanding. There were amongst them, originally, a remnant of Jews, so there was Jewish blood and Jewish teaching, there was Jewish influence. The Samaritans still used the first five books of the Old Testament, the Pentateuch. They had none of the rest of the Old Testament, but they did have those first five books, and they believed them and taught them, though, of course, they perverted them and gradually changed them, as the years passed, in order to suit the other side of their teaching. Moreover, as we learn from the woman of Samaria, they were looking forward to the coming of a Messiah, a Deliverer, so they had a kind of messianic hope (*John* 4:25).

That was one side of the Samaritans, but it was not the only side, for there were also many pagan influences amongst them. If you read the history of these people in the Old Testament, you will find that a remnant of Jews was left in that part of the world, but then a whole host of Gentiles came in, and they were all mixed up. A man once summed them up, very accurately, in this way: 'The Samaritans were a kind of halfway house between Judaism and the Gentile world.' They had a belief in God, a certain amount of right and true teaching, but then included a terrible admixture of pagan teaching, pagan ideas and a pagan outlook.

Now my reason for drawing your attention to this is that I feel that this is a perfect description of Great Britain today. If you analyse the constituency in Great Britain, you will find that the vast majority of our people have some vague belief in God. I can prove that to you. I read this last week, as you probably did, some statistics that say that many people who never go to a place of worship at all are anxious for religious instruction to be taught to their children. We know that many still send their children to Sunday schools, though they never go to a place of worship themselves.

Now why is this? Well, they have some belief in God. They sometimes say their prayers: if they get into trouble, they always say their prayers; when things go wrong, they say their prayers. And they go to church occasionally. A wedding! A christening! A burial! Perhaps Easter Sunday morning. Perhaps harvest thanksgiving. So there is a background of a vague belief in God and the supernatural, but mixed up with it all is an entirely alien teaching from a different background. I think you will agree that this is not an unfair assessment of the mental outlook of the vast majority of people in this country. They are a sort of hybrid, a halfway state between being religious and being irreligious, as the Samaritans were a halfway house Jews and Gentiles.

Now it was to people like that that Philip went and preached the gospel. And it is to a people like that that the gospel comes today. And what I am trying to show you is that I do not expect anybody to believe in this gospel until they have realized the need of the world. These two always go together. No one is going to believe this gospel until they have seen a need of it. Oh, I know that people think they come to Christ for many reasons, but they do not come to him aright unless they come as paupers, unless they come as desperate people, unless they come in utter helplessness. It is the only way to come: 'Just as I am, without one plea'.

What, then, is the condition of this modern world? I want to show you that it is perfectly represented in this brief paragraph about these people in Samaria. The world is in trouble, is it not? It is a world of war, a world of pain, a world of sorrow; it is a world of evil and of sin. Just go over in your mind the things that have happened during the last week, the events that have hit the headlines. We are in a very troubled world, my friend! It is not only the accidents that take place, but also the evil, the suffering, the pain, the confusion – the famine at one end of the scale, and then, at the other end, the luxury. That is the world. There are people who are starving tonight; there are people who are throwing excellent food away. Perhaps wheat and other foods are still being thrown away. Get rid of surplus: the country's economy requires it. Here it is – this is our world. And it is a world of toil, a world of labour, a world of sweat.

Now there is no argument about this; this is the world in which we are living. Of course, this world itself is at last admitting this; it recognizes it even in its art. There was a time when cinema and the theatre used to be romantic and gave people an escape. But not any longer. 'Kitchen sink'! 'Things as they are'! This is the whole tragedy, and it is terrible, is it not? Everybody against everybody else, blasting, blaspheming, cursing . . . There it is, the world itself is admitting it.

There, then, is the picture in general. But you cannot stop at that; there are particular manifestations. They are of great importance, and I must call your attention to them. We read: 'The people with one accord gave heed unto those things which Philip spake, hearing and seeing the miracles which he did.' Then, 'For unclean spirits, crying with loud voice, came out of many that were possessed with them: and many taken with palsies, and that were lame, were healed.'

'Well,' you say, 'what has that got to do with us?'

The answer is: everything! Notice, to start with, that Luke, the author of this book of Acts, draws a clear distinction between 'unclean spirits', and 'many taken with palsies, and that were lame'. And Luke adds that this second group 'were healed'. Now remember that Luke was a physician, and he proves that here. To him it was a matter of interest that not all the people who were in trouble were healed; some were devil-possessed, inhabited, he says, by 'unclean spirits'.

Why does Luke draw this distinction? He does so because it was a simple fact. It was, and still is, a medical fact. It is becoming increasingly obvious in this modern world that, as the influence of the Christian faith and the Christian message – I do not mean personal influence but the general influence in society – as that begins to wane and to be forgotten, there is a recurrence of this kind of phenomenon that had virtually become unknown – unknown in this country, at any rate. It was not unknown in China, or in India, or in many countries where there had not been a Christian culture and Christian teaching, or even a very general education. In such places they have always had cases of demon-possession.

But now in the Western world demonology is once more a matter of serious scientific study and enquiry. There are people who do not even claim to be Christian who are now increasingly prepared to admit that they must recognize the fact of demonology, the fact that we are living in a world where there are unseen spirits that can affect people and inhabit people. This is a very vital part of Christian teaching. We talk about the Holy Spirit, do we not? We say that the Holy Spirit dwells in Christians. Why do we call him the *Holy* Spirit? The answer is that we want to show that he is eternally in contra-distinction to these other spirits – 'evil' spirits. It is an essential part of the whole of the biblical teaching that the world is surrounded by 'powers and principalities' that can enter into men and women, take up their abode in them and take possession of their personalities, so that when you listen to a person speaking, you are hearing, not the person, but an evil spirit speaking through that person. These spirits are unclean. They are vile in their language, they are vile in their thoughts, they are vile in their imaginations, and they cause men and women to do terrible things.

Now in Samaria there were people who were devil-possessed. They were beside themselves. They were doing things that they did not want to do but had been made to do. They were under the influence and the control of spiritual powers greater than themselves; and it led to untold unhappiness and misery. Read the Gospels for yourselves and you will find the accounts of many, many such cases – think, for example, of the boy taken to the disciples at the foot of the Mount of Transfiguration (*Mark* 9:14–27). Our Lord spent much of his time in casting out devils. As Philip did here in Samaria, our Lord drove out these evil spirits that were ruining not only the lives of the wretched people who were possessed, but also the lives of their relatives and all who knew them. And now devil-possession is being manifested in many, many ways in our modern world. I suggest to you that a man like Hitler cannot be adequately explained except in these terms. There was something beyond man there. There was a positive evil force and power.

But then Luke goes on to say that in addition there were many taken with palsies, and many who were lame, and these were all healed. Now this, you see, is not devil-possession, this is illness. They were suffering from well-recognized diseases. And there are such diseases still. We are in a world of disease, a world of pain and suffering, and, on top of it all, death. We are in a world that manifests all the wretchedness that was there in Samaria. Just look at life – just examine it!

Now it is not only the people outside Christianity who fail to diagnose the depth of the problem of the human race. There are many Christian people who have been brought up in such a sheltered atmosphere that they know nothing about what is happening in the world, and have very little contact with it. But a church that simply inbreeds, a church that simply turns in a circle round herself, is a church that is failing. The world at this very moment is as these people in Samaria were, and we must all realize this.

But let us look at a second aspect: the false remedies that are offered to such a world. Here it is quite plainly in Acts 8:

There was a certain man, called Simon, which beforetime in the same city used sorcery, and bewitched the people of Samaria, giving out that himself was some great one: to whom they all gave heed, from the least to the greatest, saying, This man is the great power of God. And to him they had regard, because that of long time he had bewitched them with sorceries (verses 9–11).

This world, which is in pain, in agony, under the influence of alien powers, suffering from diseases and sickness and death and sorrow, is being offered false remedies. And they are all typified in this man Simon, generally referred to as Simon Magus.

Now what we have here, of course, is the counterfeit. The New Testament teaches us that this is something that has always happened. The world has always had these counterfeits: evil forces always produce them. These powers know that it is no use telling us that everything is all right. No people who are sane believe that. It is only people who are half drunk or deluded who say, 'Everything is all right; everything in the garden is lovely.' A man or woman who is sober, who thinks and reasons and faces facts, knows that everything is not all right. But the devil is very clever and he says, 'Of course things are not all right, but we can put it right.' So he produces his counterfeits. The Bible says that towards the end of this age in which we live, before the Son of God returns into this world, we must expect a great recurrence of this kind of thing. It says that there will be 'strong delusions', and that people will be ready to believe a lie. This is how Paul puts it:

Then shall that Wicked be revealed . . . Even him, whose coming is after the working of Satan with all power and signs and lying wonders, and with all deceivableness of unrighteousness in them that perish; because they received not the love of the truth, that they might be saved. And for this cause God shall send them strong delusion, that they should believe a lie (2 Thess. 2:8–11).

God allows people to listen to these lies and to be deceived. Why? Because they have rejected his offer of salvation that is in his own Son, in him crucified, dead and buried, and risen again and reigning. That is the very teaching of Scripture.

But now this is most interesting, is it not? In this world there are always false remedies. And what a perfect description we have here in Acts 8 of the world today and the false remedies to which it is paying such attention in its blindness and in its rejection of the Christian faith. Look at the characteristics of these false world healers. How perfectly they are represented in this man Simon. We are told that he had 'bewitched the people of Samaria, giving out that himself was some great one' (verse 9). Can you imagine a more perfect representation of the quack physicians in a spiritual sense in this modern world of ours?

Simon had set himself up – always the characteristic of such people. He gave out that he was some great person. He was a thinker, who understood what nobody else did. He saw through everything, and he had a simple solution! So he spoke with dogmatism, with arrogance and with self-confidence; he had an inflated opinion of himself. And the city of Samaria took him at his own valuation. The world always does this. A man stands up and says, 'Listen to me. I'm a great man. I know what I'm talking about.' And the world rushes after him, listens to him and hangs on his words.

Was this, I wonder, ever more true than it is at this moment? Look at the adventurers who do well in this world. They just set themselves up. What is their authority? What is the source of their power? The world does not trouble to enquire: it takes them at their own estimate of themselves. A fraud, a rogue, can always do very well for a while in a world like this because of his arrogance, because of his false self-confidence, his inflation of himself: 'Giving out that himself was some great one'. Such people speak about creation as if they were there when the world was created! But they just do not know. The theory of evolution is based on nothing more than arrogant, dogmatic assertions. But because it is stated with authority and assurance, and with a kind of power, it is listened to and accepted.

But I do not stay with this because I am anxious to examine the remedies that are being offered to us, the solutions and cures that humanity is holding on to and believing as it rejects the Christian faith. These people in Samaria put their faith in this man Simon, and accepted his remedies. There were the problems – devil-possession, unclean spirits, diseases, paralysis, death, sweat, labour, toil, unhappiness – and here was a man who said, 'Listen to me, I can deal with this.'

What were the remedies? Well, they are all here before us. 'There was a certain man, called Simon, which beforetime in the same city used sorcery, and bewitched the people of Samaria, giving out that himself was some great one.' His remedy boiled down to sorcery. Before we look at what this means, let me tabulate the remedies to which the modern world is prepared to pin its faith. Look at some of these men who claim to be great thinkers, the philosophers, the men who say that they have thought in depth. People listen to them and say, 'This is a great man, he has a great brain, he's always telling us that he's a thinker.' Books are brought out under that very title: 'The Thinker's Library'. The *Thinker's* library! Of course, Christian people do not think, they just sing hymns; but these are thinkers, so they have 'The Thinker's Library'. Here are the men and women who really can fathom the depths and analyse a situation – the thinkers. What have they to offer?

Perhaps the greatest of all the thinkers today is a man called Bertrand Russell, a man on whom people pin their faith. They say that he is a great man, a mathematical genius, the greatest living philosopher. What, then, has he got to offer men and women to enable them to live a moral, decent, pure life? What has he to say to them about conquering sin and temptation? What has he to say to them about death? What has he to say about the whole world? He admits that the whole situation is entirely hopeless. I am not saying that. He himself is honest enough to say it. And yet people turn to this man and to similar men and rely on them.

Then there are others who say that the position is not quite hopeless. What we need to do, they say, is turn to some of the great religions of the world. Take, for example, the late Mr Aldous Huxley, who undoubtedly was a genius and a magnificent writer. For much of his life Aldous Huxley believed in science and in knowledge and in education, and pinned his faith to them, but towards the end of his life he changed completely and said that he now believed that there was only one hope for the world and that was mysticism. He therefore became a Buddhist – Buddhism, he thought, being the best kind of mysticism. Here was a man who gave up pure thought and ended as a Buddhist. And today there is a revival of Buddhism in this country. There are able people, people in high positions in the law and elsewhere, who have become Buddhists, and say that Buddhism is the only hope for the world.

A third approach to the problems of the world is described here as 'sorcery'. This is a mixture, a strange mixture, of philosophy and superstition and magic. It has a kind of intellectual aspect and it often comes to us in terms of some wonderful intellectual teaching; but you will always find that there is a strange admixture here of the eerie, the superstitious, and that which is frankly magical. Now anybody who thinks that sorcery was confined to the first century is just ignorant of life. Sorcery is back in this world today, it is in this very country of ours, and it is on the increase.

I am referring here to what people call 'occultism'. Have you noticed how more and more people in this educated, sophisticated, advanced, developed society to which we belong are now dabbling in the occult? Astrology has become very popular; people are reading their horoscopes; they go to fortune-tellers; they believe in charms and spells; they are governed by superstitions such as Friday the thirteenth; they are turning back to witchcraft and are re-introducing devil worship. Now you need not take my word for all this. You can read about it in the papers and it has even been the subject of television programmes. These practices are coming back. There was a case in the courts last week about this very thing.

And all this is quite apart from Spiritism, which has been going for some time and is obviously on the increase. People turn to it for hope, for comfort, for consolation and for healing. Then there is yoga; this is being taken up by 'the wise man of the East', who will teach you how to relax and how to think and meditate. These practices, too, are flourishing.

Then there is something still more sinister, and that is, of course, the increasing turning, not only to drink, but also to drugs. You read about it in your papers, do you not – the soft drugs, and the hard drugs. You read about LSD – did you know that this has become a major problem in the USA where it is increasing in severity from week to week? There is an LSD cult in the States and even a League for Spiritual Discovery, centred on taking LSD, which meets regularly in Greenwich Village in New York. A leading US authority on these matters and on psychiatric problems said recently that the use of hallucinogenic drugs has reached 'near epidemic proportions' in California. Now here is a man who gives a factual account in a newspaper of an attendance at a meeting of this LSD cult in Greenwich Village. He writes that he found 'hippie-type' people sitting around on the floor, barefooted, meditating or listening to lectures. 'The air,' he said, 'is stifling with incense, oriental music is heard in the background, and statues of Buddha and other non-Christian deities are observed and watched.'

Now I am not romancing. I am here just to let you know that the preacher is not a man who lives in a glasshouse. I am in the real world. And these meetings are attended by all sorts and kinds of men and women. This is the world in which we are living, and these are the things to which they are turning. As this man Simon got his following in Samaria, so these cults and practices have their big followings today and they are on the increase. And let us be clear about this: Simon was able to produce results – he would not have lasted long if he had not.

Read Paul's second epistle to Timothy, chapter 3, verse 8, where Paul talks of Jannes and Jambres, who withstood Moses. There are people today, as there were in Samaria, who are doing something similar. Who were Jannes and Jambres? Well, they were two of the sorcerers and magicians of Egypt. We read in the Old Testament that when Moses was sent by God to deliver the children of Israel, he gave signs of God's power, but these magicians and sorcerers gave similar signs – up to a point (*Exod.* 7–8).

I say again that we are in a world where there are evil spirits as well as the Holy Spirit, and they have power, they have ability, they can do things. There are evil forces that can heal people's bodies and make them speak in tongues; there are evil spirits that can counterfeit to an amazing degree the very actions of the living God. It is part of the teaching of this New Testament. They get their results, I repeat, up to a point.

The next thing I want to note from this passage in Acts 8 is the pathetic credulity of these people in Samaria: 'To whom they all gave heed, from the least to the greatest, saying, This man is the great power of God. And to him they had regard, because that of long time he had bewitched them with sorceries.' But I want to emphasize this. Did you notice, 'from the least to the greatest'? How significant and important that is! There are people who say, 'Of course, I understand what you are talking about. I know that primitive, unintelligent, uneducated people are very ready to go in for sorcery and this kind of thing.' But notice here – 'from the least to the greatest'. Then – and now!

Who are the people who are taking LSD? Are they the 'least'? If you read your newspapers, you will find that there are many in Oxford, in the University of Harvard in the United States and in Berkeley University in California. They are found among the thinkers, the gifted, those who have had the advantage of the best education the country can offer. Very little LSD is taken by the common (ordinary) people: there is a little, but their problem is more likely to be drink. It is the intellectuals who are out for experience, something that will give them deliverance, a spiritual experience.

We are told that Simon 'bewitched' the people of Samaria, with the result that they were amazed by him. They said, 'This man is the great power of God' (verse 10), literally, 'the power of God which is called great'. They said, 'This man has got something, he can really lead us.' Do you know that it was actually a professor who had once belonged to Harvard who led this movement in the taking of LSD in America? This professor had come to the end of thinking. Reaching the same conclusion as Aldous Huxley, he said, 'We must get to another dimension.' And he said, 'Here it is, this drug can give us experiences.' And people are out for that; they pin their faith on it; they are credulous and ready to follow.

Can you not see that what we read here about these people in Samaria and their condition is nothing but an account of the world in which you and I are living? But here is the vital question: What is the cause of this credulity? How does it come to pass that any people could believe in a man like Simon Magus? How could the people of Samaria have been deluded and bewitched and astonished, and have extolled him as a great man who had something of the divine in him? How could they have revered him as a teacher, and listened to him, and followed him and abandoned themselves to him? What explains this?

And what explains the way in which men and women today, even those who are among the best in terms of culture and knowledge, are turning to drink and drugs and the occult, and the eerie and the odd? What is the explanation? There is no difficulty. If you believe this book, it is quite simple, and to me it is very significant. I am going to say something that will astonish some of you: the worse the world gets, the more I am filled with hope. What is utterly impossible to deal with is smug satisfaction and contentment. What is really impossible is polite superficiality. But once men and women really see the teeth of the devil, and the vileness and the power and the horror, it will soon bring them to their knees, it will soon cause them to turn to God. But, oh, the tragedy that God should have to permit this kind of thing! He does, you know. I can read to you many statements in the Scriptures that say that. God has to permit it because men and women will not listen to him; they spurn his 'voice divine', and reject his Holy Spirit and his power. So in order to awaken them, God abandons people to their folly and blindness.

Why is the world so credulous? Why can a man like Simon Magus succeed today? What is the explanation of it all? What is the difficulty with this present generation? I am not condemning them. I trust I am preaching out of a heart of sorrow. It grieves me to think that there are young people, with their lives before them, throwing them away, wasting them, getting demoralized by these terrible drugs, squandering their lives, throwing them away with both hands. It is a matter that should make us all weep. I trust we are all full of sympathy towards them. If you merely condemn these people, then you are not a Christian. We must face the facts, we must realize what the position is, but we do not do so as Pharisees. We say, 'There but for the grace of God go I.'

Why are they like this? Well now, you see, here is the answer – and the people who are always talking only about Vietnam and apartheid and so on, they do not begin to face the problem – it is because of the terrible uncertainty of life. This was true in the first century in Samaria, and it is true in this century to which you and I belong. We have had these two major world wars, and we realize that the whole of life is uncertain. It has always been uncertain, of course, but there are times when people seem to be more aware of it. Life was equally uncertain a hundred years ago in the halcyon days of mid-Victorianism. But they did not realize it. There had not been the calamities and horrors that we have known in this century; there were no bombs, for example. People today are asking, 'Where is the world going to? Where is it all going to end? Is there any point in anything? Look at the piling up of these bombs; look at the mounting problems; look at the horrors that face us. Is there any sense in it all? Is there any purpose in life altogether?'

These are the questions people are asking and they are bound to lead to unhappiness. Not only that, we want to know the future. Is the future going to be better? Is it going to be better for me? If somebody says that they can tell us our future, we rush to them. We want to know; we cannot wait; we must have some hope. We cannot live for the next minute unless we know that there is something – and the sorcerer tells us that the future is going to be marvellous and we believe him because we want to believe him. That is how these things happen. But it is all a terrible admission, not only of the bankruptcy of our thinking, but also of our unhappiness, the emptiness of our lives, the insecurity, our utter blindness.

And then we all have within us a feeling that things ought to be better; even the worst people have the feeling within them that the world should not be as bad as it is and that they should be better. They do not understand why it is not. And this longing, this craving, for something better will not go away. Of course, the motives may be quite wrong, they may be purely legalistic, or simply a delight in pleasure, but still there is this feeling that things ought not to be as they are.

And then, on top of all this – this is something that is increasing and it is here that I begin to see a glimmer of hope again – there is a consciousness and awareness in men and women that there is something beyond man. We have come to the end of man, and that is something, that is a great achievement. The tragedy of the foolish late-Victorians and the Edwardians was that they had supreme confidence in man. We have seen through that. Look at our attitude to politicians now as contrasted with that of fifty or sixty years ago, and our attitude to most other public figures as well. There is a sort of cynicism.

And, of course, when we hear of these distances in outer space, we feel we are nothing. But this is accompanied by a feeling that there is something outside – fate, perhaps, something unseen, powers that we do not understand:

> *There's a divinity that shapes our ends,*
> *Rough-hew them how we will.*
> William Shakespeare: *Hamlet*

And we feel so small, and so finite. Now humanity, you see, in its trouble and in its tragedy, has always tended to think in this way; they were doing that in New Testament times. Read the account of Paul's visit to the city of Athens in the seventeenth chapter of this book of Acts, and you will see that Paul makes this judgment on them: he found the city to be 'too superstitious', there were too many gods, too many temples. What was the meaning of all this? Oh, this was the meaning: great philosophy had come up against a blank wall and the people had said, 'No, no, there are other powers; a god of love, a god of war, a god of peace; these spirits, these evil powers,' and beyond them all, 'the unknown God'. There is something there and they were trying 'if haply they might feel after him, and find him' (*Acts* 17:27).

Similarly today, here are people at the end of their tether, so they have 'a League for Spiritual Discovery', and they say, 'This drug will give it you; it knocks out the rational part of your nature but it releases your spirit, and your spirit makes discoveries in the realm of the spiritual. Take the drug and you will get out of your difficulties. You will see things with a new clarity.' Ah, it is just this feeling that somehow, somewhere, we are inadequate and that beyond us there are forces and powers. So modern men and women in their agony and pain, and in their disillusion, clutch at anybody and anything that offers them a little ease, a little deliverance, a little tranquillity, a little solution to their problems.

They will believe anything, even a lie, even a fraud, even a deceit, even as these people in Samaria had believed, not only what Simon had said about himself but also what he offered to them as his patent remedy.

The world knows that it needs a leader, it needs authority, it needs power. It needs something that can take hold of it and renew it and deliver it. In its agony it cries out entirely unconsciously in these various ways. And there is only one answer: it is the answer that Philip took to Samaria. I am going to consider this with you, God willing, on subsequent Sunday evenings. The people of Samaria believed Philip's message: of course they did, because they had nothing. They would find temporary satisfaction: drunk for the moment, or under the influence of sorcery or a drug, your problems are forgotten for now, but back they come, and then back again. And you go down and down and feel worse and worse, until, at last, the authentic message comes announcing that 'God so loved the world, that he gave his only begotten Son, that whosoever believeth in him should not perish, but have everlasting life' (*John* 3:16) – not theory, not trickery, but facts!

Jesus of Nazareth, a man, yet truly God, speaking as the light of the world, living a life that can conquer the devil and evil and sin and all the unseen occult powers. Jesus of Nazareth, who speaks as one who has looked into the face of God and can tell us about his holy purposes; yea, one who does not batten on our ignorance and our superstition and our evil, but has so loved us that he has not only taken his place by our side, but has assumed human nature because we are human. He did not come as a God, he came as a man: '[He was] made of a woman, made under the law' (*Gal.* 4:4). Not only that, but he also took our sins upon him: 'Who his own self bare our sins in his own body on the tree, that we, being dead to sins, should live unto righteousness: by whose stripes we are healed' (*1 Pet.* 2:24).

He has risen again. He has conquered all our enemies – evil spirits, unclean spirits, the devil himself, death and the grave, everything that is against us. He has conquered them all literally, historically, factually. And having risen, he has sent down his Spirit upon all who believe in him. They receive the deliverance and the grand salvation. This is truth, not sorcery and lying. We are saved by the power of God, not the power of the devil, or of unclean spirits or of hell. This is fact. This is history. The only way that you will ever get peace and satisfaction and understanding and joy and victory in this world is to believe this message concerning the only begotten Son of God who left for a while the Courts of Heaven in order to deliver us from sin's foul bondage, and the tyranny of these evil powers that manipulate us for their own pleasure, and cast us on the scrap-heap to all eternity.

That is the need and this is the only answer. Have you believed it? Have you received it? Do you have the great joy that became the possession of these people in Samaria? I ask nothing of you but, just as you are, believe this message and you will find it to be true, and you will begin to know something about the glory of salvation.

3

The Word

Therefore they that were scattered abroad went every where preaching the word. Then Philip went down to the city of Samaria, and preached Christ unto them (Acts 8:4–5).

As we have been considering these verses in Acts chapter 8, we have been realizing the similarities between the people of Samaria and men and women in our own modern world. In Samaria, the people were victims of sorcery, magic and astrology. They did not realize their true need and thought they could deal with their own problems – all just like the people of today.

But there is something further, and that is the terrible confusion we see today with regard to the message of Christianity. If only everyone who begins to express an opinion either in a private discussion or in a public debate on Christianity were compelled first of all to put down on paper an answer to the question, 'What is Christianity?', I think you would avoid a lot of talk. I know there would be less entertainment on the television, but you would avoid much waste of time, because although people are all talking about Christianity, what it should do and what it is not doing, and saying that they are against it and have no use for it, they do not know what it is. They have never really studied the Word; they do not know what it stands for. And as this is such a serious matter, and as we are told here that the gospel is spread and the church expands as the result of 'preaching the word' (verse 4), it is essential that we should be absolutely clear in our minds as to what this really is.

Now we are told here that Christianity spread from Jerusalem as the direct result of the preaching of these people who had been scattered because of the persecution in that city. And then we are told about this man Philip, the deacon, that he 'went down to the city of Samaria, and preached Christ unto them'. So what is this message that we have to preach? What do we have to say to the world in its agony, in its tragedy, in its drug-taking, its drink, its final futility – and all the marching and the protesting and the shouting and the crying and the violence and the robbery and the shooting and the war – what do we have to say to it? Well, this is what we are told here in Acts – and this is our only authority, so I simply expound it.

I start with this expression, 'the word': 'Therefore they that were scattered abroad went every where preaching *the word*.' This is one of these vital first matters that we must be absolutely clear about. It is a term that is used very frequently in the New Testament itself. We are told that the last letter the apostle Paul ever wrote was his second letter to Timothy. And one of the last things he says to Timothy is, 'Preach the word' (*2 Tim.* 4:2), the very expression that we have here. What did these people do? Here they were, ordinary Christians, persecuted, scattered abroad, and wherever they went they preached the word. Now it is very important that we should understand this because of the common misunderstanding as to what it means.

Notice, then, negatively, that these people, when they were scattered abroad like this, did not just go everywhere recounting their experiences. I have no doubt that that may have come in, but that is not what we are told. We are told that they preached the word. In other words, they did not talk primarily about themselves, they talked about that which had made them what they were. They did not just go and say, 'Now look here, we've become very happy, and would you like to be happy? We can tell you how you can be', and then talk about their experiences, and say what they used to be and what they now were. No, that is not what we are told.

Why am I making a point of this? It is because many people seem to think that that is how Christianity spreads, and that that, in a sense, is the Christian message. But it is not. If you really want to know the essential difference between the Christian faith, the Christian message, and the cults that are so popular in the world today, this is it. In the cults people are always talking about themselves and their experiences. That is how the cults spread. 'I used to be like this,' someone will say, 'couldn't sleep, always worried. But now that I've taken up this teaching I sleep like a log; no troubles; no anxieties. You can get it. Here it is, ready for you . . .' That is the characteristic of all the cults. They spread by this mere relation of personal experiences.

But these Christians in Acts 8 preached the word, and did not talk about themselves. I repeat that this is absolutely of vital importance. There are clever people today who say they are not Christians because they can explain the whole thing in terms of psychology. They say, 'It's quite simple; we've no objection to your being a Christian if you want to be, but don't try to make us Christians. We can see through all this. Of course, if it helps you, have it. Take up any teaching that makes you happy. Nobody should be miserable if they can be happy.' And they say that, of course, Christianity has been very useful to many people in this respect, but it is all just a psychological trick, a kind of brain-washing or conditioning. You are familiar with these modern attacks upon the Christian faith.

There is only one answer to that, and it is this: the Christian's position does not depend upon experience; it depends upon the Word, it depends upon the truth. So these first believers and Philip did not talk about themselves but told the people the facts about our Lord – like Paul, they were preaching 'Jesus and the resurrection' (*Acts* 17:18). They were witnessing to great, objective, historical facts.

I remember once being in a ministers' retreat at which these various matters were being discussed. At one point a man got up to say something that he thought would be of great value and help to his brethren. He said, 'You know, I don't care what the critics may prove. I don't care what history may say. Nothing can ever rob me of the experience I have had.' But that is no defence of Christianity. That is giving the whole case away. No, no, no! What matters is not primarily my experience but this: Have these things happened? Who is Jesus Christ? What are these historical events and what is their relationship to me? That is what these people in Acts spoke about. They had certainly had an experience, and it had been such that they were ready to suffer for it, to be persecuted and to be driven out of their homes rather than deny it, but that is not what they talked about. They talked about that which had made them what they had become – the word! It is not just experience, so you cannot dismiss it in psychological terms. We are standing on historical events; we have truths.

But, secondly, you notice that the message was very definite and very particular. These Christians preached 'the word', and that 'the' is a limiting term, is it not? They had a particular word. They did not merely talk vaguely and in an ill-defined and uncertain, nebulous manner about some odd something they had felt, or something that they were trying to grasp. Not at all! 'The word'! It was definite. It was fixed. It was defined.

Again, this is very important. There is an old saying – one does not hear so much about it now because it has revealed its own folly – but I remember very well how at one time some people used to be very fond of saying that they were 'seekers and searchers after the truth'. These people were generally attackers of orthodox Christianity, and especially the evangelical presentation of it. They were intellectual people, and they were anxious to improve the world and to get satisfaction themselves, so they were out on this great quest for ultimate truth and reality. They were dwelling in the rarefied, intellectual atmosphere of the heights, and they were seeking and searching for truth, this great big thing.

But that is the very opposite of what we have here. We are not told that these Christians, when they were scattered abroad by the persecution of Jerusalem, said, 'Now, then, we'll go to other cities and try to find people there who can join us in the quest for truth and in the search for ultimate reality. We are seekers and searchers. There are probably others, so let's find them and say, "Let's go on together. We've never met you before but you are out for the same thing. Let's see if together we can arrive at some understanding."' Not at all.

But there are many today who still feel that the Christian is a person who is seeking for truth. Only last week I read an article in the paper by a high dignitary in a church in this country who was making this very point. A certain section of the church in America decided this last summer that there is no such thing as heresy. They said that 'heresy' is a term that must be abolished, and this man was justifying that point of view. He said, 'Heresies will not emerge until there has been much more logical reconstruction, until the explorers' tracks in what so often seems a theological jungle have become a much more reliable network of roads than they are today.'

Do you follow it? All right – that is out of an article written by a bishop, and you see he says that we are in a 'theological jungle'. We do not know where we are and there are no roads. He says that you cannot say that one is right and the other is wrong, you cannot talk about heresy, until these explorers and road constructors have had a little more time and have made some proper roads and tracks through this theological jungle. So what is our position? Well, according to this article, the Christian church today is seeking for the truth; the pioneers, the prospectors have gone ahead, these great leaders, but they are in the jungle and they do not quite know themselves what the truth is or where they are. So how can we know, therefore?

You see what an utter travesty this is of Christianity? Here is the truth: 'They went every where preaching the word.' They were not looking for anything; they were telling people what they had found. They were not explorers, they were men and women who had arrived and knew exactly what they had found. Now this is emphasized everywhere in the New Testament. A church is not a society in which you seek for truth. The church is a society that proclaims the truth, declares the truth and heralds it. And if she does not do that, she is not a church, no matter who she is, or how old she is, or who belongs to her. The idea that a Christian is someone who is seeking for salvation, or seeking for truth, is an utter lie, a contradiction of the very basis of the gospel.

There is no vagueness in the New Testament. It is absolute certainty; it is blazing assurance. The apostle Paul is constantly warning people not to listen to certain dangerous teaching. Why? Because it is heresy. He does not hesitate to say that. He puts it in very strong language. Listen to him writing to the Galatians: 'But though we, or an angel from heaven, preach any other gospel unto you than that which we have preached unto you, let him be accursed' (*Gal.* 1:8). Listen to him again writing to Timothy:

'Remember that Jesus Christ of the seed of David was raised from the dead according to my gospel' (2 *Tim.* 2:8). What is this? 'My gospel'!

I remember once reading a sermon in which it was maintained that Paul's words in 2 Timothy 2:8 meant this: 'It is my gospel; it may not be yours, but that does not matter.' That preacher turned the meaning to make the gospel just a matter of experience. He said, 'The great thing is that you are able to say, "My gospel". Now it does not matter that it differs from mine or from somebody else's, the great thing is that you should have a personal experience. If you do, hold on to it; it does not matter what people may say about it or how they may criticize it.'

But that is the exact opposite of what Paul is saying. Paul says, 'Remember that Jesus Christ of the seed of David was raised from the dead according to my gospel.' He is not talking about his experience, but about the facts concerning the Son of God. This is the sort of intolerance that you always get in the New Testament. I do not apologize for that intolerance. Let me put it like this to you – I would not be in this pulpit if I did not have an intolerant gospel. If I were not certain that this and this alone is the Word of God to you, my friend, I would not be in this pulpit. I am not here to express my hopes, my fears, my anticipations, my thoughts, my desires. No, no, I am here to proclaim to you, to tell you. It is because I am certain of it, not because of my experience, but because of what it is, that I am standing here and commending it to you.

But I want to go on. 'They went every where preaching the word', and that means it must have been an essentially simple word. Did you notice who we are told these people were? We are told, 'There was a great persecution against the church which was at Jerusalem; and they were all scattered abroad throughout the regions of Judaea and Samaria, except [apart from] the apostles.' The leaders remained in Jerusalem. Who, then, were these people who were scattered? They were not apostles, they were not deacons, they were not prophets; they were just the ordinary members of the church. These were the people who went everywhere preaching the word. Now this, again, is an important point. It tells us at once that this word, whatever it is or is not, is obviously not some great abstruse philosophy. Do you listen to the pundits and authorities when they speak about these matters on the television and everywhere? Let me ask you a simple question: Can you understand them? Can you tell from the majority of them what the Christian message really is? All that happens is that we do not try to understand them. They are very learned men, and who are we to listen to such great men! We are like the poor elderly woman attending a service in St Giles Cathedral in Edinburgh. As she was going out of the service, a man turned to her and said, 'Did you enjoy the service? Were you able to follow the preacher?' And her reply was, 'Who am I to follow such a great man?'

Now that is the opposite of Christianity. 'The common people heard him gladly' (*Mark* 12:37). If a poor old woman in her rags cannot follow it, it is not the gospel. These people went everywhere preaching the word. It is not some great philosophical position that only men who have had some special training and culture and education can follow and comprehend. That is not it; thank God, it is not. 'For ye see your calling, brethren,' says the apostle Paul to the Corinthians, 'how that not many wise men after the flesh, not many mighty, not many noble are called: But God hath chosen the foolish things of the world to confound the wise' (*1 Cor.* 1:26–27) – 'the common people'. This message is something that an ordinary person can understand.

There are some who say that this text of mine should be translated like this: 'Therefore they that were scattered abroad went every where gossiping the word.' Preaching, here, does not mean standing in a pulpit as I am doing now. That is what Philip did in the next verse. In the Greek there are two different words here. Our word 'preaching' translates one Greek word in verse 4 and a different word in verse 5. Two English words should have been used to translate the two Greek words: 'They went every where gossiping the word', and, 'Philip went down to the city of Samaria proclaiming Christ.' These people were scattered abroad and they arrived amongst strangers and were welcomed into their homes and sat down and had something to eat and to drink, and they began to tell the people in ordinary conversation about this wonderful message that they had believed and that now meant so much to them.

Whatever else may be true about it, this is a message, then, that is essentially simple, and do you know why? It is, again, for the same reason: it is because it is about facts. It is not a wonderfully constructed philosophy or point of view. It does not bandy magical terms that only the initiated can understand. No, no, it is facts! It does not matter how unlettered and how untutored we are, we can report facts, can we not? And that is what these people did. This is the essence of the Christian message, and that is why ordinary people, as Isaiah says: 'Wayfaring men, though fools, shall not err therein' (*Isa.* 35:8); it is because they are dealing with facts all along, and for that you do not need great cleverness. Thank God, you do not!

Here, again, is the thing that once and for ever differentiates this gospel from all the mystical religions. Buddhism and Hinduism, and all these other beliefs, are a whole-time job. You have to segregate yourself from the world, and read books and grapple with philosophies, in the hope that at last you will get there. That is not Christianity. Thank God, it is not. 'The word'! 'The common people heard him gladly.' 'God hath chosen the foolish things of the world to confound the wise; and God hath chosen the weak things of the world to confound the things which are mighty . . . and things which are not, to bring to nought things that are' (*1 Cor.* 1:27–28).

But it would be wrong of me just to leave it at that. That is only one way of looking at this gospel. I must start with that, and I am glad to do so. You may be in this congregation, my friend, and you may never have read a book in your life, you may not even read a newspaper. But here is a message that you can receive and believe because it is a message that tells you about something that God has done for you and about you and that can put you right to all eternity. It postulates nothing in you except failure, need, hopelessness, despair. But that is not the whole truth about it. There is another side to this gospel, another aspect to it: 'Philip went down to the city of Samaria, and proclaimed Christ unto them.' Now this is different. It is right to start by saying that the gospel is essentially simple, but you must not misunderstand that. Do you know that in this gospel there is all the wealth of the mind of God? 'Howbeit', says Paul, again to the Corinthians, 'we speak wisdom among them that are perfect: yet not the wisdom of this world, nor of the princes of this world, that come to nought: but we speak the wisdom of God in a mystery, even the hidden wisdom, which God ordained before the world unto our glory' (*1 Cor.* 2:6–7).

Oh, yes, let me make this clear, this to me is the glory of the gospel. This is a word that can save a child, an ignoramus, and yet it is so great and so vast that the mightiest intellect in the universe and all the intellects of all the ages cannot encompass it. They cannot surround it, they cannot grasp it, they are still trying to understand it. So there is the element of proclamation also. It is the biggest, the largest, the deepest, the highest, the most glorious thing that men have ever considered. It is the wisdom of God! So it is both, you see – 'gossiping the gospel' and proclaiming it, teaching it, expounding it, holding it forth.

You know, my friends, I am in my thirtieth year in this pulpit and I am beginning to feel that I am only just beginning to understand this gospel. It is much more thrilling to me tonight than it was when I came here in 1938. Oh, how big it is, how great it is, and how short time is! There is not time enough to tell you about all the glories of this gospel as expounded in the epistles of the apostle Paul – 'the breadth, and length, and depth, and height; and to know the love of Christ, which passeth knowledge' (*Eph.* 3:18–19). Here it is: I am in it. And I look at it and I am more and more amazed.

Here it is, then, but it is still 'the word'. Thank God that I was able to preach it when I came here. I think now that that was very poor, but it was all right at that time. And you, too, can start just as you are, in utter simplicity, and then you will go on and on and on seeing its illimitable heights and depths. And you will go on learning from it as long as you live, and through the countless ages of eternity.

So this word is obviously a word that can be stated. These early Christians did not just sit down and raise theories and questions and have arguments and disputations; they told the people, they preached the word, they 'gossiped' it, they declared it. And as the apostle Peter says later on, you must 'be ready always to give an answer to every man that asketh you a reason of the hope that is in you' (*1 Pet.* 3:15). And every Christian can do this. If you cannot tell me why you are a Christian, I will tell you that you are not a Christian; if you are only hoping to be a Christian, you are not a Christian; if you are trying to be a Christian, you are not a Christian. A Christian man or woman *is* a Christian, and they can tell you why they are. They must do, they are bound to 'give a reason for that hope that is in [them]'. You do not depend upon feelings, you do not depend upon experiences and sensations. No, no, you have heard something, you have believed it, as these people in Samaria did. It is this 'word' and you can tell others about it.

Shall I put it to you like this: Would you like to know for certain whether you are a Christian at this moment? Here is my test. Imagine that when you are at home tonight, somewhere round about 10 o'clock, there is a ring at your front door bell. There is someone there with a message for you. A man whom you know very well has unfortunately had a very serious accident and is in hospital, dying – the doctors say that there is very little hope for him – and that man is asking to see you. What is the test? Well, it is this: What will you say to him? Suppose you have often talked to this man about religion, about Christianity, and have tried to persuade him to come to a place of worship, but he would not come. There was always something about him you liked. He did not live a very good life, poor fellow, but still you liked him. You said he was a good sort, he had a good heart. You could not leave him alone. You were always glad to meet him and you generally talked about these things, but he would not listen, he would have nothing to do with Christianity. But now this poor fellow is dying and he knows he is, and he is afraid to die. He suddenly thinks of you because you are a chapel-goer, because you have always said that you are a Christian and have tried to persuade him to become one. He wants to see you; he is in trouble.

It is a big thing to die. It is all very well to talk when you are young and hale and hearty, but on your deathbed, going out of this world, you do not know where – oh, it is a tremendous thing! And the man has come to himself, as the prodigal son did, and he sends for you. So you must go. You arrive at the hospital and there you are, looking at the man dying on that bed, and he is looking into your eyes as only a dying man can look. He wants to be helped. He wants something. What have you got to say to him? Have you something to give him? Will it help this man if you turn to him and say, 'Well, you know, my friend, you remember I told you about that marvellous experience I had' – is that going to help him? No, your experience cannot help him.

I wonder whether it will help him if you turn to him and say, 'Now, of course, you have become concerned about this, why didn't you listen to me? I always told you that you should give up your kind of life and live a good, clean, moral life as I've been living.' Does that help him? No, no, that just puts him into hell while he is still alive. It is utter condemnation. It is useless. Or will it help him if you turn to him and say, 'My friend, you are now, of course, in this death agony looking, seeking, searching for truth, and so am I. For years I've been grappling, trying to understand. I'm reading the philosophers and listening to the men who are exploring the theological jungle. I also am seeking.'

What is the value of that to a man who will be dead before midnight? No, no, a Christian is someone who can speak the word to him and can tell him the one thing he needs to hear – that for him who now realizes that he is a sinner there is a way of salvation. You can tell him the facts – that there was once in this world one called Jesus of Nazareth; that he was the Son of God; and that he came into the world in order to die for men and women, even a man like himself who has left it to the last minute. You can tell him the facts, the word about Christ, who has borne our sins in his own body on the tree, who is ready to receive all who turn to him in their helplessness and hopelessness, and cast themselves upon him. That is it! 'They preached the word', and it is a composite, it is a whole, it is distinct, it is discrete, it is clear, it is essentially simple at its beginning, but it is enough. And that is what these people in Samaria did. So remember 'the word'.

Let me say just something about this word 'preaching'. Unfortunately, as I have said, this is not a very good translation. All the lexicons are agreed in saying that the word translated 'preaching' means, 'telling everybody about the good news, or the glad tidings'. Of course, my illustration has just brought it out, has it not? This is the preaching that is emphasized everywhere in the New Testament. So what is this 'word'? What is the Christian message? Let me say it again in order that your mind may be disabused once and for ever, of any misapprehensions. Christianity is not just a protest. These wretched men give the impression that this is what it is – a protest against the war in Vietnam, a protest against bombs. But if it is a protest, it is not 'good news'. Where is the good news in that? Neither is Christianity just an exhortation to people to live a better life. Where is the good news there? That is the preaching of the law, and it condemns. So by definition the gospel is not a perpetual protest against things, and nor is it merely an exhortation to rise up and to put our backs into the effort to be moral and clean and good. What is the use of saying that to a drug addict, or to a man who is in the grip of an evil spirit or paralysed?

No, no, this is glorious good news, and everything you read about this word in the New Testament always introduces it in that particular way. Read again even the very beginnings in the early chapters of the Gospels according to Matthew and especially Luke. Listen to how Luke tells us about the archangel whom God sent to Mary, the mother of our Lord: 'The angel came in unto her, and said, Hail' – Greetings! – 'thou that art highly favoured, the Lord is with thee: blessed art thou among women' (*Luke* 1:28). Why? Because of this child who was going to be born of her, this 'holy thing'. He would be a deliverer, a Saviour, the promised Messiah. He was coming!

And this message did not only come to Mary. Even poor old Zechariah, the father of John the Baptist, was given the same good news. This is how it came to him: 'Blessed be the Lord God of Israel; for he hath visited and redeemed his people, and hath raised up an horn of salvation for us in the house of his servant David' (*Luke* 1:68–69). Good news!

The announcement of our Lord's coming was couched in language of great joy and happiness. And you remember what happened when he was born: the shepherds in their field, watching their flocks by night, suddenly heard heavenly music. And what words did they hear? 'Glory to God in the highest, and on earth, peace, good will toward men' (*Luke* 2:14). 'Unto you is born this day in the city of David a Saviour, which is Christ the Lord' (*Luke* 2:11). The angels proclaimed it:

Hark! the herald angels sing
Glory to the new-born King.
Charles Wesley

This is Christianity! Not your miserable moralisms and ethical programmes and protests and negativities. Oh, may God silence those who thus conceal from the people this great and glorious message of salvation and deliverance and joy! 'The people that walked in darkness have seen a great light' (*Isa.* 9:2). This is Christianity – preaching, telling forth the good news, the glad tidings of salvation.

And right from the beginning the result of this preaching has always been that people are filled with joy. I read this, after Peter's sermon on the day of Pentecost: 'And they, continuing daily with one accord in the temple, and breaking bread from house to house, did eat their meat with gladness and singleness of heart, praising God, and having favour with all the people' (*Acts* 2:46–47). This is the great characteristic of Christian people at all times and in all places; and that is what made these people, wherever they were, gossip the word.

It had filled them with joy, and they wanted everybody to hear about it. They knew the condition of people, they had been in that position themselves. They could see the people in Samaria half worshipping Simon Magus, deluded by his sorceries and his chicanery, allowing him to batten on their ignorance and darkness, treating him with adulation. 'Oh,' they said, 'we must tell these people!' And they did tell them. And that is how Christians feel in this world. They look out upon it, they have their eyes open, they see the tragedy, the sadness, the evil, the foulness, and they know that there is only one solution, only one way of deliverance, and they want to tell everybody about it.

What, then, is the message? I merely start now and give you the headings. It is summarized in what we are told about Philip: 'But when they believed Philip preaching the things concerning the kingdom of God, and the name of Jesus Christ . . .' (verse 12). Here is the essence of this message. It is a message about 'the kingdom of God'. And this is absolutely vital for us: it is our only hope.

The Word (8:4–5)

Our Lord started his public ministry by preaching the kingdom; he said, 'The time is fulfilled, and the kingdom of God is at hand: repent ye, and believe the gospel' (*Mark* 1:15). He was always talking about some great kingdom. If you read the Gospels you will find that he was always talking in parables and many of the parables were about the kingdom. 'The kingdom of God', he said, 'is like this'; 'The kingdom of heaven is like that.' What does this mean? Well, the kingdom is the essence of our Lord's message. Negatively, it is not a message about reforming the world or improving it or banishing war. Our Lord never said that. He never said he would make the world better. Indeed, he said this, 'And as it was in the days of Noe [at the Flood], so shall it be also in the days of the Son of man' (*Luke* 17:26). And he said, 'Likewise also as it was in the days of Lot . . . even thus shall it be in the day when the Son of man is revealed' (*Luke* 17:28, 30).

Of course, I know that people who pervert this gospel maintain the exact opposite. They say that our Lord came to reform the world and that Christianity will put an end to war and turn the world into Paradise. But not only did our Lord never give that teaching, it is found nowhere in the New Testament. Again, you find the exact opposite: 'Evil men and seducers shall wax worse and worse' (*2 Tim.* 3:13). 'In the last days perilous times shall come' (*2 Tim.* 3:1). There it is, an exact prophecy of our world as it is today. No, no, the gospel is not a message of world improvement.

What is it, then? It is this: that God is setting up another kingdom in this world, the kingdom of God. This is it, prophesied in the Old Testament and started through the Jews. God called those people and made them into a nation and gave them laws in order that he might have his own people to proclaim his message and his way of life. Then came Christ; he preached this kingdom. The apostles were sent out, they preached the same message – 'the things concerning the kingdom of God' (*Acts* 8:12; 19:8). Our Lord himself said, 'My kingdom is not of this world' (*John* 18:36). Why not? Because it is a spiritual kingdom; it is the kingdom of God, the kingdom of heaven.

This world is entirely different. Here are 'the kingdoms of this world'. This world is the kingdom of Satan; it is the dominion of the devil, who is the god of this world, 'the prince of the power of the air; the spirit that now worketh in the children of disobedience' (*Eph.* 2:2). And the kingdoms of this world are characterized, as we have seen, by darkness, by evil, by slavery, by shame, by sin, by failure, by helplessness, by hopelessness, and the worshipping of charlatans. And this message tells you that God is forming another, entirely opposite, kingdom. It is the kingdom of truth, as over against the lies of men; it is the kingdom of light, as opposed to darkness, the light of the holiness of God. 'God is light, and in him is no darkness at all' (*1 John* 1:5) – and God says he wants citizens who are like him. He says, 'Ye shall be holy: for I the LORD your God am holy' (*Lev.* 19:2).

And blessed be the name of God, it is a kingdom that has power in it to deliver us out of the kingdom of darkness and of Satan, as it did to these very Samaritans. The kingdom of God means the rule and the reign of God and of his Christ over us as against the god of this world, the prince of the power of the air. The message? It is that God is still concerned about this world, because it is his. He made it. But man rebelled against him, following the rebellion of the devil who has become the god of this world and governs its peoples. But God will not allow him to be victorious. God has started a great movement, the great work of redeeming man out of the clutches of the devil and all his evil and his darkness and his foulness – and that is what is meant by the kingdom of God. You have it in the Jews, you have it in the Son of God, you have it in the apostles he sent out, and you have it in the church. Here it is.

What is God's method of bringing this about? His method is to deal with us as individuals. The apostle Paul, in writing to the Galatians, reminds them of what happened to them as the result of this gospel:

Grace be to you and peace from God the Father, and from our Lord Jesus Christ, who gave himself for our sins, that he might deliver us from this present evil world, according to the will of God and our Father: to whom be glory for ever and ever. Amen (Gal. 1:3–5).

Or, as Paul puts it in writing to the Colossians:

Giving thanks unto the Father, which hath made us meet to be partakers of the inheritance of the saints in light: who hath delivered us from the power of darkness, and hath translated us into the kingdom of his dear Son (Col. 1:12–13).

That is it! By birth, you, and all of us, are in the kingdom of the devil, in darkness, sin, lust, passion – with all the vileness and the foulness of our imaginations and our actions and deeds, everything that was true of these Samaritans. But in his Son God has a power and a way of delivering us out of that darkness, and he translates us out of it 'into the kingdom of his dear Son'. So that while we are still in this world we become citizens of the kingdom of heaven, the kingdom of God, and we say, 'Our conversation [citizenship] is in heaven', though we are still living on earth, and 'we look for the Saviour, the Lord Jesus Christ: who shall change our vile body . . .' (*Phil.* 3:20–21). Now the kingdom is spiritual; then it will be visible.

And that was the message that these people gossiped and Philip proclaimed – that God in Christ can deliver us from the thraldom and the slavery of sin and evil and Satan. He can change us and give us a new heart and a new life and a new hope and a new understanding. He can put a power into us that can make us more than conquerors. He is separating us unto himself. He is preparing for a future glory when his Son will come again and gather unto himself all who have believed on him. You can enter his kingdom at this moment, but one day it will be external and visible and will spread over the whole cosmos. And then:

Jesus shall reign where'er the sun
Doth his successive journeys run;
His kingdom stretch from shore to shore,
Till moons shall wax and wane no more.

Isaac Watts

My dear friend, are you in this kingdom? Has this word come to you, either from a pulpit like this, or as someone has spoken to you? Do you know it? Have you realized what it means to you that 'God hath visited and redeemed his people'? He sent his own Son to deliver you from sorcery and drugs and drink, and all the works of hell and the devil, and at this very moment, unless you are already in it, you can be translated from the kingdom of darkness into the kingdom of God's dear Son.

And what is demanded of you? Nothing! Only that you acknowledge your need and confess your sin and helplessness, that you believe this word and act upon it and give yourself to him. And he will receive you, and you will begin to know something of the gladness that these people had, who had been scattered abroad by the persecution, and the gladness that was experienced by the citizens of Samaria when they believed this message as they heard it from Philip.

My friend, do you belong to the world or do you belong to God? It is one or the other. Under whose power, under whose authority, are you? Who are you living by? Who are you listening to? How are you living? Is it the devil? Is it darkness? Is it sin? Is it shame? Or is it light and glory and truth and gladness and joy? I repeat, you have nothing to do but to believe this word. Surrender yourselves to him, and ask him by his Spirit to make the message of this kingdom plain and clear to you in such power that you will know that you are a new man or woman in Christ Jesus, a citizen of the kingdom of God, and an heir of the glory which shall be revealed when Jesus Christ, the King, shall come again and take unto himself the kingdoms of this world; and the kingdoms of this world shall have become the kingdom of our God, and of his Christ. Where are you?

4

The New Birth

Therefore they that were scattered abroad went every where preaching the word. Then Philip went down to the city of Samaria, and preached Christ unto them . . . But when they believed Philip preaching the things concerning the kingdom of God, and the name of Jesus Christ, they were baptized, both men and women (Acts *8:4–5, 12).*

We are now continuing with our consideration of that twelfth verse of Acts 8, in which we read that Philip went down to Samaria and proclaimed 'the things concerning the kingdom of God' – God's plan for this world, God's purpose for this world, God's way of delivering this world from the devil and his powers and all the consequences of evil and of sin. And we have seen that God has done this supremely in the person of Jesus Christ of Nazareth. So Philip 'went down to the city of Samaria, and preached Christ unto them'. He told them how our Lord came and lived and died and rose again in order that we might be forgiven, and reconciled to God. And we saw that we receive this forgiveness as helpless paupers. We can do nothing. We deserve nothing. It is the free gift of God.

That is what Philip preached in Samaria, but he did not stop at that, and neither must I. There are many who do stop at that point and so there are many who think that Christianity is a message of forgiveness and nothing more. They think that the gospel tells men and women that it does not matter how much you have sinned: if you go and confess it to God, you will be forgiven. Well, so far so good, but if you stop there, it is all wrong. And even there you must be very careful to ensure that you realize that you can only get this forgiveness because the Son of God has himself taken your sins and your guilt upon him, and has borne the penalty and died your death.

Forgiveness is the first essential, and if you have not realized your need of forgiveness, there is a sense in which all I am going to say now is wasted on you. If you have not seen your utter, absolute need of being forgiven by God and being reconciled to him, then your whole position is wrong and you have no right to consider anything else.

'But,' you say, 'I'm concerned about living in this world.'

Let me answer you. You have no guarantee that you will be alive this time tomorrow – none at all. We can cure many diseases but there are many we cannot cure, and there is death. Do not presume. No, no, the first great question that each of us must settle for ourselves is: How can I know that my sins are forgiven? And the first great message that we hear is that forgiveness is in Christ Jesus and him crucified, and in him alone. You have got to go out of this world, and the old world will go on after you have left it. But now here you are, you have come into it, you are passing through, you are going out. Here is your question: How can you face God and face eternity?

That is the first question, but I say again that it is not the only one, and we must not stop there. For if this message stopped only at forgiveness of sins, it would leave us as we are with regard to our natures and our make-up, and with regard to what we do. So we are still left in a terrible position, still subject to the world, the flesh and the devil, to all the tyranny of sin and of Satan. A salvation that only gives me pardon and forgiveness and leaves me at that, is an incomplete salvation. God made human beings perfect, and salvation is not perfect unless it restores them to that original perfection. And blessed be the name of God, this Christian gospel proclaims that very restoration.

John in his first epistle puts it very well in these terms: 'For this purpose the Son of God was manifested, that he might destroy the works of the devil' (*1 John* 3:8). Now that is a very great and comprehensive statement. The Son of God, Jesus Christ, came into this world that he might destroy, undo, nullify, negate, all the works of the devil. This is what Philip preached when he went down to those Samaritans. This is our salvation, and thank God it is because if you consider for a moment our state by nature, then you will begin to see our need for this gospel. The world does not see their need of it. People do not believe in Christ, they do not believe in the Christian faith. Why not? Because they have never faced themselves; they have never seen themselves. The blind people in this world today are all those who are always looking out at some problem outside themselves. Oh, I know it is very comforting to do this. We all like denouncing other people's sins and failures, do we not? It is easy to criticize governments, and much that is happening in the world today. And, of course, while you and I are doing that, we are all right, we are not considering ourselves. But this gospel is primarily personal and it comes to us individually, and it gets us to face ourselves.

I have often said this, but let me say it again. If I had no other reason for believing this book called the Bible, I would believe it for this reason: it is the only book I know of that tells me the plain unvarnished truth about myself – the only one. Nothing else does. The world around me tells lies to me about myself. It always tells me that I am really a very good fellow. If only the world were a better place, if only other people were all right and behaved decently, especially governments, what a perfect fellow I should be. What a lie that is! I know that the trouble is not so much in the world as in myself. All right, Shakespeare said it:

> *The fault, dear Brutus, is not in our stars,*
> *But in ourselves, that we are underlings.*
>
> William Shakespeare: *Julius Caesar*

Have you realized that? This is one of the reasons why the Son of God had to come into this world. He came to undo all the works of the devil. The first work of the devil is, as we have seen, to put me out of accord with God, to put me under his wrath, and I must be delivered from that.

But, then, here I am. I am forgiven. But look at me. What is my condition? It is described in many places in this Bible. Take the passage in Ephesians from chapter 4:17 to chapter 5:16. That is a sheer, accurate description of what men and women are like apart from this gospel. It is the stark, real truth about every one of us by nature. There are other descriptions, too. Paul has put it in a very brief compass in a passage in his first epistle to the Corinthians, in chapter 6 beginning at verse 9: 'Know ye not that the unrighteous shall not inherit the kingdom of God? Be not deceived: neither fornicators, nor idolaters, nor adulterers, nor effeminate, nor abusers of themselves with mankind' – you know what that means? Those are perversions that are now legal – 'nor thieves, nor covetous, nor drunkards, nor revilers, nor extortioners, shall inherit the kingdom of God.'

You thought Christianity was sob-stuff, did you not? It does not sound like it now, does it? You say you are a realist and have no use for Christianity, that you do not believe in drawing down the blinds and singing hymns. Are we doing that? My dear friend, this alone is truth, this alone is realism, this alone tells us the truth about ourselves and shows us the world in which we are living. What does it tell us?

First, with regard to our spirits, this gospel tells us that we are 'dead in trespasses and sins' (*Eph.* 2:1), and that means that by nature we are completely dead to the life of God, dead to the spiritual realm. I need not waste your time in proving that, you need only listen to people on the television. They cannot understand, they cannot see, the truth. They do not believe it. Their philosophical arguments and all their propositions are so learned, but what are they talking about? They just do not know. Spiritually dead!

Not only that, people are dead to their own souls. They trot out the old catch questions and they really think this is clever. A man was doing it the other night, but he was only repeating what Sir Arthur Keith said over forty years ago! I remember very well when he said it. Sir Arthur Keith was a great anatomist and he said that he had dissected so many thousands of bodies and had never yet come across an organ called the soul. And people still ask the same question: Where is the soul located in the body? But nobody has ever said that it is located anywhere in the body. What the Bible says is that there is such a thing as the soul, there is that in man which is immaterial, but it is bigger and greater than the body, and it goes on when the body dies. And, of course, I could give you scientific evidence to support this. There are people who, at times, owing to illnesses, are aware of themselves, as it were, apart from their bodies. This is the soul, something that links us with eternity, something that makes us know and feel within our very bones that we are bigger than the whole universe, something that makes us cry out for 'an ampler ether, a diviner air', something that makes us such that the whole universe cannot satisfy us. But to the natural man this is nothing. He wants exactness but, of course, he does not have it anywhere. There is no such thing as exactness and precision.

Well, you say, you must be scientific. But what does that mean? What is science? The science of today denounces the science of the past, and that denounces the science before it. Where is truth? Human beings have never found it, and they never will. In this Word alone is there truth.

There, then, is the spirit. And then you come to the mind, and you should notice what Paul said about the mind – and he certainly had a mind. If you have a superfluity of intellectual ability and agility, then take my advice, begin studying the apostle Paul. That will give you something to think about and it will keep you occupied for a considerable length of time. Paul wrote: 'This I say therefore, and testify in the Lord, that ye henceforth walk not as other Gentiles walk, in the vanity of their mind, having the understanding darkened, being alienated from the life of God through the ignorance that is in them' (*Eph.* 4:17–18). And how true that is! 'The understanding darkened'! What understanding do men and women have of themselves and of life in this world? What do they know about death? What do they know about the greatest things, the only things that really matter? They do not understand; they are darkened.

And then when you come to people in the world and tell them that the Son of God has entered into time and into this world, that he has humbled himself and taken on human nature, having divested himself of the insignia of his eternal glory, they say, 'What are you talking about?'

'But the natural man', says Paul again, 'receiveth not the things of the Spirit of God: for they are foolishness unto him: neither can he know them, because they are spiritually discerned' (*1 Cor.* 2:14). He says in that same passage that 'the princes of this world' did not know it (verse 8). By 'princes' Paul does not only mean members of royal families; he means the leaders, the great men in every realm and walk of life. The religious leaders of the Jews did not recognize our Lord, nor did the Greek philosophers. 'For had they known it,' says Paul, 'they would not have crucified the Lord of glory.'

Why did they not know him? There is only one answer: their minds and understanding were darkened. He appeared amongst them; they looked into his face, they looked into his eyes, they heard his teaching. They could not explain him, though they admitted that there was a problem. They asked, 'How knoweth this man letters, having never learned?' (*John* 7:15). They could not understand how a carpenter could speak with authority. On top of that, they saw his miracles. They saw all this, and yet they just dismissed him as 'this fellow'. God incarnate stands before them in all the glory and the beauty of his person, and they say, 'Away with him! Crucify him!' What is that but utter darkness?

Do you believe in God? Do you believe in Jesus Christ, the Son of God? Have you asked yourself that question? If you have not, why not? With all the evidence that you have before you, in nature, in creation, in history, in the story of the church, in the lives of the saints, in prophecy, and prophecy fulfilled, why is it that you reject him and refuse him? Thomas Binney has given the answer:

Oh, how can I, whose native sphere
Is dark, whose mind is dim,
Before the ineffable appear
And on my naked spirit bear
The uncreated beam?

I may have told you before that perfectly true story that we find in history, a story that illustrates the blindness of the natural mind even in one of its really great men. The story concerns William Wilberforce, the man who started the movement for the abolition of slavery, and his great friend William Pitt the Younger, prime minister of Great Britain. William Pitt was a brilliant man, but he was not a Christian. William Wilberforce, however, was, and William Wilberforce's greatest desire was that his friend Pitt should become a Christian also. So one Sunday morning here in London he took Pitt to listen to one of his favourite preachers, a man called Robert Cecil. William Wilberforce was ravished, his heart was moved, his intellect enlightened, as that saintly Robert Cecil was expounding the Scriptures and unfolding the riches of God's grace in Christ. It was to be in heaven to William Wilberforce and he was wondering what was happening to his friend.

The service ended and they walked out, and William Pitt turned to William Wilberforce and said, 'I haven't the faintest, the slightest, idea what that man has been talking about.' That is it! That is to have your mind darkened: expert in politics, expert in many other respects, great statesman, but when you come to the realm of the spiritual, the mind 'darkened', no understanding, incapable of following.

And the same is true of the heart: 'Because the carnal [natural] mind is enmity against God: for it is not subject to the law of God, neither indeed can be' (*Rom.* 8:7). Have you ever thought of that? Why do men and women hate God? Why would most people who are not Christians be delighted if it could be established tomorrow morning that there is no God, and that there never has been, and that all this talk of God is rubbish and nonsense? Why desire that? What is the explanation? Man hates God, the God who sends the sun and the rain, fructifies our crops, gives us life and health and strength: man hates him. That is the state of the human heart. Do you believe in God? What is your attitude towards him?

And unfortunately this antagonism is not confined merely to our view of God and the state of our hearts towards him. Listen to Paul saying what we are with respect to one another: 'For we ourselves also', he says, 'were sometimes foolish, disobedient, deceived, serving divers lusts and pleasures, living in malice and envy, hateful and hating one another' (*Titus* 3:3). Am I exaggerating? Is it not the simple truth? By nature we are hateful creatures, and we hate one another.

I say again that I am most grateful to these friends who write biographies and autobiographies. The more we are told about the great men and women of this world, the more I, at any rate, see the truth of the Bible. The dishonesty, the lack of trust, all the scheming and plotting that goes on behind the scenes. It is in you, my friend, by nature; it is in me, it is in all of us. What creatures we are! That is the state of the human heart – there is no question about it.

And the will and the desires – here it is in summary form in Titus: 'Disobedient, deceived, serving divers lusts and pleasures'. Is it not true? Are you not a creature of lust? Have you never lusted in your life? And then consider again the lists given by Paul in Ephesians 4:25–5:5 and Colossians 3:5: lying, anger, stealing, corrupt communication, bitterness, clamour, evil speaking, malice, foolish talking and jesting, inordinate desire, covetousness. Think of your imaginations. Where does it all come from? It is you, my friend: it is in you. All this is in man. It is what he desires. It is but a sheer description of human nature!

Oh, you say, I wish I had not come to listen to all this sort of thing! Do you? You are running away from facts, then. Do not say any more that you reject the gospel because you believe in thinking and honesty and reasoning and facing the facts. These are the facts! They are the facts about you, about every one of us by nature. That is why a gospel is necessary. So the apostle says to these Ephesians who have now been converted and are Christians: 'This I say therefore, and testify in the Lord, that ye henceforth walk not as other Gentiles walk [are still walking]' (*Eph.* 4:17). And that is how they walk, that is how they live. There, then, is man by nature.

So is it not obvious that if I am left in that state and condition, though my sins are forgiven, and though all my guilt has been taken away by the death of Jesus Christ on the cross on Calvary's hill, if I am left like that, well, then, for me to go to heaven would put me in hell, for, 'God is light, and in him is no darkness at all' (*1 John* 1:5). There is no lust there, no passion, no evil desire; there is no drink there, none of the things by which man lives by nature and in which he delights. They are entirely excluded:

Nought that defileth can ever enter in.
Mary Ann Sanderson Deck

And if I am only forgiven and left at that, as I am, with this nature that is mine as a result of sin and the Fall, then, I repeat, it would be terrible for me to be in the presence of God, and holiness and purity. I could not stand it; it would be intolerable.

The New Birth (8:4–5, 12)

So the Christian message does not stop at the mere proclamation of the forgiveness of sins and reconciliation to God. No, no, it goes on to say that this gospel changes men and women. Look at these Samaritans, you see how they were, but in verse 8 I read: 'There was great joy in that city.' They became new people.

What is this? This is the great New Testament message of *regeneration*. Regeneration! And if this is not true, then the works of the devil are not undone, because when man fell he not only became guilty, but also his nature was perverted. His mind, his heart, his will fell, as I have shown you; the whole of him fell. His very body fell, and that is why we are diseased, that is why we die. There would have been no death but for sin. That is the nature that we have all inherited. 'Behold, I was shapen in iniquity; and in sin did my mother conceive me' (*Psa*. 51:5). We are born rebels, we are born hateful and vile – every one of us. That is the simple truth.

But here is a message that tells me that Christ came into the world not only to bear my punishment and to reconcile me to God, but also to fit me for heaven. He came to do something to me that enables me to enjoy God even in this world. What is it? I must be 'born again', this is his message, and this is what Philip preached to these Samaritans, this great message of the rebirth, of regeneration. It is the message that our Lord himself preached to Nicodemus:

Verily, verily, I say unto thee, Except a man be born again, he cannot see the kingdom of God . . . Verily, verily, I say unto thee, Except a man be born of water and of the Spirit, he cannot enter into the kingdom of God. That which is born of the flesh is flesh: and that which is born of the Spirit is spirit (John 3:3, 5–6).

This is it! You must be made anew, you need a new nature, a new heart, a new mind, you must be a new person. And he has come to do this for us. This is the wonderful, amazing, astounding doctrine of regeneration and the rebirth.

This new creation is the act of God. The God who made the world and made man at the beginning, in Christ makes us anew. Get rid for ever of the notion that becoming a Christian simply means being forgiven or trying to be a little bit better than you were before; you cannot be. If you were left where you were you would remain what you are and you would degenerate.

Thank God that, being justified by his grace, we have regeneration and that this is the action of God. He operates in the soul by the Holy Spirit. Do I understand it? Of course not! 'Marvel not', said the Lord Jesus Christ to Nicodemus, 'that I said unto thee, Ye must be born again. The wind bloweth where it listeth, and thou hearest the sound thereof, but canst not tell whence it cometh, and whither it goeth: so is every one that is born of the Spirit' (*John* 3:7–8). No, no, I thank God I do not understand it. It is a miracle. It is the Creator who in the beginning created the universe taking hold of me, making me anew, putting a new principle of life into me, implanting a new disposition into me. We are made 'partakers of the divine nature', says the apostle Peter (2 *Pet.* 1:4).

Did you know that the Son of God took on him our human nature and combined it with himself, in order that he could give that back to us? We are given this absolutely new nature, this new life – 'The Life of God in the Soul of Man', and it is marvellous, it is wonderful. 'Therefore if any man be in Christ, he is a new creature: old things are passed away; behold, all things are become new' (2 *Cor.* 5:17).

The Christian now has a new mind; he begins to understand spiritual truth. 'He that is spiritual judgeth [understands] all things, yet he himself is judged of no man' (*1 Cor.* 2:15). The princes of this world did not know these things. 'But God hath revealed them unto us by his Spirit: for the Spirit searcheth all things, yea, the deep things of God' (*1 Cor.* 2:10). By nature I do not understand this and I would not have been interested in it. But now that I have a new mind I am interested. The gospel message is now the most amazing thing in the universe; there is nothing like it. And the more I get to understand it, the more I revel in it and enjoy it.

And, thank God, he also gives us a new heart. He takes away the stony heart, and gives us a heart of flesh (*Ezek.* 11:19). The old enmity to God has gone, and our supreme desire is to know God, for God is love, and we want to love him and to know him. The greatest trouble for us as Christian people is that we do not love him more, that we do not know him better. We want to, this is our supreme desire; and we want to please God: 'To hear thy dictates, and obey.'

And Christians are given a new will. We have new desires, new hopes that were not there before. We had had no desire for purity, for holiness, for cleanliness, for a knowledge of God and of Christ. But now these are what we desire above all else.

We want to get rid of sin; we want to enjoy holiness. We say, 'Create in me a clean heart, O God; and renew a right spirit within me' (*Psa.* 51:10). Or, with Charles Wesley:

Oh for a heart to praise my God,
A heart from sin set free.

My prayer is not merely that I may no longer do the things that made me miserable, but that I may get rid of that heart that ever made me desire those things: that lust, that passion, those evil desires and imaginations. I want:

A heart that always feels thy blood
So freely shed for me.

And that is what he gives us. We have a new mind, a new heart, a new will, new desires. The Christian is a new person. 'I live', says the apostle Paul, 'yet not I, but Christ liveth in me' (*Gal.* 2:20). He has a Spirit within him, the Holy Spirit, the Spirit that was in Christ himself. He is in the believer, and he works in us.

So you are not left to yourself. God puts this new principle within us. 'Now if any man have not the Spirit of Christ, he is none of his' (*Rom.* 8:9). 'Know ye not', says Paul, 'that ye are the temple of God, and that the Spirit of God dwelleth in you?' (*1 Cor.* 3:16). He is in us, and he works in us. He illumines the mind, he moves the heart, he creates desires and aspirations. 'Work out your own salvation with fear and trembling. For it is God which worketh in you both to will and to do of his good pleasure' (*Phil.* 2:12–13). He will be in you and he works within you, and you are aware of a power within you that was not there before.

Not only that; this blessed Christ is there ever looking upon us and waiting to help us. The author of the epistle to the Hebrews puts it like this:

Forasmuch then as the children are partakers of flesh and blood, he also himself likewise took part of the same . . . Wherefore in all things it behoved him to be made like unto his brethren, that he might be a merciful and faithful high priest in things pertaining to God, to make reconciliation for the sins of the people. For in that he himself hath suffered being tempted, he is able to succour [to help] them that are tempted (Heb. 2:14, 17–18).

He has been in this world, and he was tempted 'in all points . . . like as we are' (*Heb.*4:15), but he never fell. Now he is looking down on you and he sympathizes, and he is waiting and ready and willing to help. And he can do it. He defeated all the powers of evil:

He breaks the power of cancelled sin
He sets the prisoner free.
Charles Wesley

He said in the days of his flesh, 'If the Son therefore shall make you free, ye shall be free indeed' (*John* 8:36). 'Whosoever committeth sin', he said, 'is the servant of sin' (*John* 8:34). It is no use saying that you are not a servant. It is all very well to say, 'I could stop that tomorrow.' Why do you not stop it, then, if you really want to? You cannot. You are a slave. We are all slaves by nature. But the Son of God is there in all the glory of his power. Therefore the Christian sings:

I need thee every hour;
Stay thou near by–

Why?

Temptations lose their power
When thou art nigh.
I need thee, Oh, I need thee;
Every hour I need thee:
Oh, bless me now, my Saviour;
I come to thee.
Annie Sherwood Hawks

He is there! I am not left to myself. I have a new nature; the Spirit is working in me, getting rid of the pollution, sanctifying me, preparing me for the Glory; and even before I get there I have, in

Christ, access to God. 'Therefore', says Paul, 'being justified by faith, we have peace with God through our Lord Jesus Christ: by whom also we have access by faith into this grace wherein we stand' (*Rom.* 5:1–2). In your hour of need you can pray to God in the name of Christ, and you will be heard, and you will be helped. He has become your Father in Christ. He says he has loved you 'with an everlasting love' (*Jer.* 31:3). He knows all about you, the very hairs of your head are all numbered (*Matt.* 10:30); nothing can happen to you apart from him.

That is what Philip preached in Samaria. He preached Christ. And they believed him, and 'there was great joy in that city' as the result. Is there much joy in your heart? The message that Philip preached is God's message for you. I have described your nature to you as you are by your natural birth, and you know it is true, and you will never get rid of that. 'Can the Ethiopian change his skin, or the leopard his spots?' (*Jer.*13.23). Of course not! It is impossible. 'That which is crooked cannot be made straight' (*Eccles.*1.15). But, 'With God nothing shall be impossible' (*Luke* 1:37).

Remember, I am preaching to you the power of the Creator, and in Christ he will create you anew. Not only will he pardon you, he will receive you. He will put power into you, he will make you conqueror, he will deliver you. And he will go on with the process until you finally stand before him perfect, 'not having spot, or wrinkle, or any such thing' (*Eph.* 5:27).

So Philip preached Christ to them. Have you believed this? Have you experienced it? This is something that works, it happens, and a man or woman is not a Christian unless they know the truth of this, and know something of its power. 'I am not ashamed of the gospel of Christ' – why not? – 'for it is the power of God unto salvation to every one that believeth' (*Rom.* 1:16).

5

The Only Hope

Therefore they that were scattered abroad went every where preaching the word. Then Philip went down to the city of Samaria, and preached Christ unto them. . . But when they believed Philip preaching the things concerning the kingdom of God, and the name of Jesus Christ, they were baptized, both men and women (Acts 8:4–5, 12).

Whatever view you may take of history, you must realize that the history of the world cannot be understood truly without taking into consideration the story of the Christian church. Take our world as it is today. One of the most powerful nations in the world is the United States of America, and that came into being because of Christianity. Whatever you may think of the United States now, you must acknowledge that there would never have been such a nation had it not been for the Pilgrim Fathers who first went there because of their belief in this gospel of our Lord and Saviour Jesus Christ.

The Christian message is, therefore, still of the greatest importance, and this passage shows us what exactly that message is. We read here that Philip 'preached Christ' to the Samaritans, and we have seen that this is the essence of this message. But we have also seen that the message goes further. Thank God that it does. The message that Philip and these other people preached included the doctrine called the new birth, regeneration, the teaching that God operates in the souls of men and women, changing them, giving them a new start, giving them a new heart, a new outlook, a new nature, new desires. 'Therefore if any man be in Christ, he is a new creature: old things are passed away; behold, all things are become new' (2 *Cor.* 5:17). This is a part of the message.

Now that is the point at which we have arrived, and I put it like this: the apostle John says that the Son of God was 'manifested' (*1 John* 3:8), that the Son of God came into this world for this grand object: that he might destroy the works of the devil, that he might undo all the harm that the devil has done in this world. And we have been considering the way in which he does this work for us personally. I want to emphasize this – the gospel is primarily personal. It must be. The first thing it does is to put each of us individually right with God and enable us to live in this world. But now I want to emphasize that it is not only personal.

There are many people who taunt the evangelical presentation of the gospel on the grounds that it is always personal. 'You people who are in a world like this,' they say, 'are just worried about your own little souls. That shows how selfish and self-centred you are, how small-minded. As long as you are all right you don't care about anybody else.' Well, our answer is that until individuals are put right, there is not much hope for our world, for the world consists of individuals, after all. In a sense, there is no such thing as humanity: it is human beings who constitute humanity. So you cannot put this country right if you do not start with individuals. The best periods in the history of this country have been the periods when there have been the largest number of Christian people in the nation. But the gospel is not only personal, there is another aspect to it, another element in it, and it is to this that I now particularly want to call your attention.

Now this second aspect of the gospel is most important at the present time. It is always important, of course, but I feel it is now unusually important because, owing to some of these modern discoveries, one of the most urgent problems for us all is the future of this world. This Sunday we are thinking of two world wars.[1] The first world war, well, that was bad enough, but the second was worse, and if there is a third, it will be worse still. World War I produced the aeroplane and the tank, and that made war more horrible than it had ever been before, and we know that the last war took the horror much further. What of the next?

We are living in a time when the whole question of the future existence of this world is very much in the balance: day by day,

[1] This sermon was preached on 12 November 1967, Remembrance Sunday

almost, we are hearing about new developments in the construction of bombs and rockets and other weapons of war. So the question, 'Is there any future at all for the world?' is perhaps more urgent than ever before. Is there any future to history or are we at the end? That is why I call your attention to all this on this particular Sunday, which is observed as Remembrance Sunday. People have been thinking of wars today, and, I trust, also thinking of the world as it is now, and the world as it is going to be.

Now the Christian gospel has a great deal to say about the future of our world. And I want to show you that it really is the only message that tells us anything at all that is worth listening to about the future. So I come back to my fundamental proposition: 'For this purpose the Son of God was manifested [came into this world], that he might destroy the works of the devil' (*1 John* 3:8). And I want to show you that the works of the devil do not stop at what he makes us do as individuals. He has affected the whole world, the whole of humanity and, indeed, the whole universe. But in addition to that, I want to show you how the Son of God is on a programme that will undo completely all the works of the devil.

My first proposition is that the Christian message alone, exclusively alone, gives us any hope with regard to life and this world. Now I must start with this. We are living in an age when people think it is clever to deny the Christian message and to dismiss it as being almost insulting to 'the modern man'. But I would reply by saying that there is nothing else that can help us.

Let me show you what I mean. The apostle Paul reminds the Ephesians of their condition before they became Christian and this is how he puts it:

Wherefore remember, that ye being in time past Gentiles in the flesh, who are called Uncircumcision by that which is called the Circumcision in the flesh made by hands; that at that time – before they became Christians – *ye were without Christ, being aliens from the commonwealth of Israel, and strangers from the covenants of promise, having no hope, and without God in the world* (*Eph.*2:11–12).

And that is the position of the world today: it is entirely without hope.

But I must prove this in detail. People scoff at this Christian message; the majority think that we are fools to be here in church.

But what are they turning to? Well, you may have read about it. A number are turning to what they call humanism. There are not many, I agree. I read in a newspaper a fortnight ago that the humanists had had a meeting in Holborn here in London and they were boasting in that paper that as the result of their having 'their four best speakers in the country' – among them Professor A. J. Ayer – they had had an audience of 800 people. They are not doing too well, are they?

However, I am concerned, rather, with what the humanists have to offer to people. I am not surprised that they do not get more to their meetings, in spite of all their intellectualism, for what has humanism to offer? Forgetting all their negative criticisms of the Christian faith, for which there is a complete answer, let us ask them a question: What do you have to offer? What do you have to give us?

And the answer is: Nothing! Humanists can offer us nothing because the teaching of humanism is that there is nothing beyond man, nothing outside man. Human beings are the biggest beings in the universe and there is nothing outside the human mind and thought and scope – nothing at all. Humanists rule out God, they rule out the supernatural completely. Nothing is true except that which man can understand and comprehend. Man is the measure of everything. So go to them and ask them what their remedy is for the world as it is today, what their remedy is for this world torn by two world wars and piling up its armaments – and what do they have to say? They appeal to men and women to be reasonable and to behave in a rational manner! They have nothing else to offer.

Now I could even examine that. I could ask what humanists mean by rationality – for many of them believe that human beings decide their own morals and their own way of behaving. So, for example, as long as a man wants to do it, and feels it is right for him, there is nothing wrong in him choosing to leave his wife and children to go and commit adultery.

And they are surprised that nations fight, though they themselves fight as individuals. You see, you must start with the individual. It is very easy to denounce war or the behaviour of other people in different parts of the world; it is very much more difficult to live a decent and a clean and a pure life yourself. So it all ends in talk: humanists have nothing to give us.

It is the same with philosophy. When the Son of God came into the world nearly two thousand years ago it was to a world that knew a great deal about philosophy. The great Greek philosophers had all taught before our Lord ever came into this world. But philosophy could not help people; it had not solved their problems. The statistics of those days – and they had statistics then! – showed that the percentage of suicides amongst philosophers was the highest of all. That is bankruptcy. Even at its very best, philosophy did not understand and had nothing to offer.

This book of Acts tells us that these philosophers were divided into 'Stoics and Epicureans'. They were able people – I do not want to detract from their cleverness – but what did the Stoics have to offer to people in a world like this? It was only this: 'All you can do is clench your teeth, brace your shoulders, be a man, stand up to it.' The philosophy of courage, the philosophy of grit.

And that is still what the philosophers have to offer us today. They do not pretend that the world is going to be better, these Stoics. They say that the only thing to do is just to decide to go through with it and not to whimper and cry and run away. Be a man! We heard it, of course, *ad nauseam*, during the war. 'London can take it! Britain can take it!' That is stoicism. But there is no comfort there. You resign yourself to your fate and make the best of a bad job. I agree, it is better than cowardice, but it does not give you any hope.

It was exactly the same with Epicureanism. Live for the moment, they said, enjoy yourself as best you can; 'Gather ye rosebuds while ye may'! And so you leave it at that. Modern philosophies are all variants of those ancient teachings that were already proved bankrupt before the Son of God ever came into this world.

Then politics! Is politics going to put the world right? I need not stay with that now, but I am old enough to remember when people used to think that politics could do everything. I am old enough to remember the days when these politicians, whose biographies are now being written, were really worshipped. People thought that politicians could solve the world's problems. I knew men and women who turned their backs on Christianity and the church because the politicians were going to put the world right. But there is no need to answer that now. One of the great problems in this country may now be that we have so lost faith in politicians that this in itself has become a menace.

But what about Christian pacifism? It is equally useless and hopeless. Why is this? Because it is not Christian, to start with. Some people think that Christianity is a message that we must put an end to war, and that if we could only persuade people to seek to do this, then it could be achieved. 'Pacifism,' they say, 'is the one message that is needed. But that is nothing but humanism using Christian terms. It is not Christianity at all. Our Lord never taught that he was going to banish war. He said the exact opposite. Is it not amazing that people can read the New Testament and still represent him as a pacifist and say that the Christian message is a message to abolish war? Paul said that 'evil men and seducers shall wax worse and worse' (*2 Tim.* 3:13) and it was the Lord himself who said that right until the end there shall be 'wars and rumours of wars' (*Matt.* 24:6). What a true prophet he was! He said that, remember, nearly two thousand years ago. He said that this was a world of trouble, a world of sorrow, a world of sin and a world of shame.

He never said that he was going to deliver the world and make it a better place in that sense – never. Indeed, he said quite plainly of a time just before he would return again: 'When the Son of man cometh, shall he find faith on the earth?' (*Luke* 18:8). He also said, 'And as it was in the days of Noe [the days before the Flood], so shall it be also in the days of the Son of man. They did eat, they drank, they married wives, they were given in marriage, until the day that Noe entered into the ark and the Flood came, and destroyed them all' (*Luke* 17:26–27). He said exactly the same of Sodom and Gomorrah. The people of those towns were thoughtless and heedless, life had never been so wonderful! They were having a very good time in the cities of the plain; they were like London, or New York, or Paris. There is nothing new in all this; they were experts. Sodom and Gomorrah! Today's clever fellows could have taught them nothing. They were experts in all the perversions, in all that the modern man seems to be craving for and wants to make legal. 'And [they] knew not until the flood came, and took them all away' (*Matt.* 24:39). When they awoke, it was too late.

So this is the position, these are the things to which the world is pinning its faith. But all history has demonstrated that there is no hope there. What, then, of the present hour? As I have said, the crisis is more acute today than it has ever been. A book has come out quite recently called *The Myth of the Machine*. The author, Professor Lewis Mumford, is a man who has studied this problem all his life. He is not a Christian, he is a humanist really, but he is terrified of the machine and what the machine will do to humanity. There is no doubt that man has become the victim of his own inventions. Our scientific knowledge and ability have grown and grown in a phenomenal manner but the whole problem of the world at the moment is that there has not been a commensurate growth in morality, in understanding, in knowing how to harness these marvellous discoveries for beneficent purposes. Is man going to destroy himself with his own machines? This is the problem facing the world. And the world has no hope whatsoever to offer. It is completely bankrupt. It is staggering in the midst of the problem, and there is no one who can help us.

There is only one message of hope in the world and that is the message that Philip preached when he went down to that city of Samaria. It is the message that was gossiped by these ordinary people who were scattered abroad from Jerusalem as the result of the persecution. What is it? How does this Christian message deal with the world as it is today? The first answer is that it holds out hope, and this is because it is the only teaching that explains the state of the world and the state of man in it. Now to me this is elementary. If you cannot diagnose a condition, how can you treat it? If the world is all wrong in its explanation of the cause of our troubles, how can it possibly put them right? People are tinkering with symptoms, fiddling away with particular problems, when the whole thing is wrong. That is the tragedy of the world.

But let me show you in detail a little of what I mean. I say that this message alone has an explanation of our troubles and the cause of our ills – but what is it? And the message of the Bible is as plain as anything can be. I will refer to it later from the personal aspect, but I want now to look at it in general. The world is as it is because an evil power is in control of it. I know this sounds fatuous and utterly ridiculous to modern men and women. That does not surprise me. Look at their behaviour, they cannot think straight. That is their trouble, and, most important of all, they are blind spiritually.

Oh, let me again quote the apostle Paul in Ephesians 6: 'For we wrestle not against flesh and blood' – man is not the problem; what then? – 'but against principalities, against powers, against the rulers of the darkness of this world, against spiritual wickedness in high [heavenly] places' (*Eph.* 6:12). There is a power that Paul calls 'the god of this world' (2 *Cor.* 4:4), 'the prince of the power of the air, the spirit that now worketh in the children of disobedience' (*Eph.* 2:2). It is impossible to explain human history without that.

According to the teaching of the Bible, what happened was this: God made a world and he made it perfect, and he made man perfect and put him in this world. So why have things gone wrong? Why is the world as it is? It is entirely due to the fact that a bright angelic being created by God rose in jealousy against God, rebelled against him and persuaded others to follow him. That is the devil. He came into this perfect world that God had made, and tempted man, and succeeded in persuading him to disobey God and to rebel against him; and the result was that man fell. He not only fell into sin, but he also fell from God, he fell from the position in which God had placed him; he became a fallen creature.

Now this is the most serious thing of all. For instance, take this question of wars. Here we are thinking of two world wars. Why are there wars? Let the apostle James answer that question: 'From whence come wars and fightings among you?' he asks (*James* 4:1). That is the question. Oh, you say, there is no difficulty about that. Wars come because a Kaiser arose, or a Mussolini, or a Hitler. In this way you explain the whole issue. Wars are because of politics and politicians.

But then I ask my question: Why did Hitler behave as he did? Why did the Kaiser? Why do the politicians behave as they do? Why should they? They are men and women as we are, why should they all be bad and you and I be so good? Can we avoid all responsibility by saying that it is just these other people, that wars are started by governments and world leaders? Are they fools? Are they worse than everyone else?

Well, if so, why did you elect these leaders? You see, it all comes back to you and to me, does it not? And that is what James says: 'From whence come wars and fightings among you?' Here is the answer that he gives:

Come they not hence, even of your lusts that war in your members? Ye lust, and have not: ye kill, and desire to have, and cannot obtain: ye fight and war, yet ye have not, because ye ask not. Ye ask, and receive not, because ye ask amiss, that ye may consume it upon your lusts. Ye adulterers and adulteresses, know ye not that the friendship of the world is enmity with God? whosoever therefore will be a friend of the world is the enemy of God (James 4:1–4).

What does all that mean? It means that nations are just the individual writ large. With the individual it is always 'I' first, is it not? It is what *I* want that matters, and if another person has what I want, I must have it. My desires, my lusts, my passions! Is that not how the world is living at the present time? That is what individuals are doing, and that is what countries are doing. So it is no use your detaching yourself from society and saying, 'The politicians or the Government are doing this or that.' That is the very thing you are doing in private!

They are only doing on a big scale what you are doing in your own little sphere – lust, greed, passion, desire, evil, anger, hatred, malice, spite, ambition, all the things that I was dealing with earlier, which are in men and women as the result of the Fall and of sin.

Men and women individually are fallen and governed by lust and desire and all these things, and so are nations; hence wars and fights and jealousies, hence capital and labour; hence the rivalries between unions; hence the fact that trade union members do not trust their leaders. Nobody trusts anybody because, they say, 'They are all out for themselves. They are being bought.' But those saying it are ready to be bought themselves. This is the trouble with the whole of society and with the whole world, and it is only in the Bible that you are told that.

This is the only adequate explanation. Men and women as the result of sin and the Fall are under the dominion of sin and of Satan. And not only that but, according to the teaching of the Bible, the whole universe has suffered as the result.

Now this is something that we do not remember as we should. The teaching of the Bible is that God not only made man perfect but he made him the lord of the whole of creation. And it tells us, further, that when man sinned, not only was he punished, but also the whole of creation was punished. You will find all that in the third chapter of the book of Genesis. God 'cursed the ground', and man who had lived happily, easily, just picking fruit and eating it, now had to work and earn his bread by the sweat of his brow, and 'thorns and thistles' came in (verses 18–19). Something has come in, even into brute nature. Animals were not meant to fight and to devour one another; this is not natural, this is unnatural. The whole universe, the whole of creation, has been cursed as a part of man's punishment. There is no other way of understanding your world and your universe.

So man's fall is the cause and the explanation of all our troubles, and, therefore, it follows, of necessity, that it is utterly useless to appeal to man to put things right. Man is governed by something much bigger and deeper than his mind and intellect, he is governed by his lusts, he is governed by his desires and by his passions. Able, knowledgeable, well-trained, cultured men and women are no more immune to the lusts of the flesh than the most ignorant fellow. Your duke and your labourer are drunk together – there is no difference.

So I repeat that it is utterly useless to appeal to men and women to put this world right. It is the one thing they cannot do. They would if they could. They are trying, they have been trying. That is the whole story of civilization. But they cannot do it. The powers that are within them are greater than they are – evil forces, drives, passions, lusts, and the devils – and the devil over it all. Under the dominion of sin and of Satan, they cannot liberate themselves. They have tried in vain throughout the running centuries and to ask them to do so today is to display unutterable ignorance of history and the truth of human nature. To expect them to do so is still greater folly.

But, thank God, I am here to preach the message of God – the Word! Philip 'preached Christ unto them'. Thank God for this blessed name. He preached 'the things concerning the kingdom of God, and the name of Jesus Christ'. Jesus Christ is the only hope for the world, the only one who holds out any hope for us on this Remembrance Day evening.

But it is most important that we should understand how Christ delivers the world. He does not do it by his teaching alone! That is the fallacy. Many people think, 'Oh, yes, you're right, Jesus Christ offers hope, and he does it by his teaching.' They think that as our Lord's teaching is applied gradually by men and women, the world will slowly become a better and better place, until eventually the people will turn their swords into ploughshares, and wars will be banished, and the world will be perfect. The teaching of Jesus! It will act as leaven. It will change the whole world, and we will solve all our problems!

But that is not the truth. That is nothing but to turn the gospel of Jesus Christ into a political or a social programme that you and I must put into practice, and, as I have already shown you, that is the one thing that we cannot do. Christian pacifism – I want to say it again on this Remembrance Day – is a denial of the Christian gospel. It is neither Christian nor truth. It is a delusion. It is folly. If human beings could bring about peace, Christ would never have come into the world. He came into the world because men and women cannot deal with the problem, because they are incapable, because they are lost, because they are completely helpless. Our Lord would never have come into the world but for that. If exhortation and teaching and examples could have saved the world, the law given through Moses would have done it. But it could not and it was known when it was given that it could not. 'What the law could not do, in that it was weak through the flesh . . .' (*Rom.* 8:3). There is the answer.

But what, then? If it is not only by his teaching, how does our Lord give us hope? It is by what he has done, by what he is still doing; and, still more, by what he is yet going to do. Let me summarize this. He is the only hope for the world. Why? Well, first of all, look what he did while he was here on earth. He conquered evil, he conquered the devil. Look at all the great men in the Old Testament, the patriarchs, the saints. Every one of them sinned, every single one of them was defeated by the devil. The devil is 'the god of this world', as we have seen. He gets everybody down, and we all by nature become his slaves. The world has only seen one person who could meet the devil and conquer him: Jesus Christ! Jesus of Nazareth, the Son of God. '[He] was in all points tempted like as we are, yet without sin' (*Heb.* 4:15). The devil could not get him down. Our Lord defeated him, he repulsed him. Read the account of his temptation. He has already conquered our arch-enemy.

But our Lord also did something else while he was here. As we read here in Acts 8, there were poor people in Samaria who were devil-possessed. Devils can possess people. They can take hold of the personality without the person realizing it. And there were many cases of devil-possession when our Lord was in this world. But he could drive out devils. He was the master of devils, and they trembled when they knew he was coming. They knew who he was. They cried out, 'What do we have to do with thee, thou Jesus of Nazareth? art thou come to destroy us?' (*Mark* 1:24). The devils recognized him when men could not. They knew he was their master. He had absolute authority over them. He cast out devils; he healed diseases. That was in the days of his flesh.

But – and this is a message for Remembrance Sunday – he has not only conquered the devil and all his emissaries and agents and forces, he has conquered the devil's final weapon. What is that? Death! Death and the grave. And he conquered them by dying on the cross. The devil was very pleased with himself when he got men and women to condemn Jesus Christ to death, and to nail him on the tree; he thought his arch-enemy was finished. Here he is, he says, dying on a cross; we have got him; we have finished him; even he could not stand against us. There was triumph in hell when Jesus Christ was dying on the cross. But they made the biggest mistake of their lives.

Listen to what Paul says happened on the cross: 'Blotting out the handwriting of ordinances that was against us, which was contrary to us, and took it out of the way, nailing it to his cross; and having spoiled principalities and powers, he made a shew of them openly, triumphing over them in it' (*Col.* 2:14–15). They thought that was the end but it was not. He died. His body was taken down and laid in a tomb, but that was not the end of the story. 'He burst asunder the bands of death, he arose triumphant o'er the grave.' Death could not hold him! He is the Son of God. He has all power. Death, grave, hell – nothing! He burst it all. The resurrection is the pronouncement and proclamation of a final defeat of the devil and all his forces. 'The last enemy' has been conquered.

The humanist cannot tell you anything about death. He has got to die himself and he does not know what will happen. He thinks it is the end. But it is not the end. Nobody can see through death but here is one who can not only see through it, but has also passed through it! 'O death, where is thy sting? O grave, where is thy victory. The sting of death is sin; and the strength of sin is the law. But thanks be to God, which giveth us the victory through our Lord Jesus Christ' (*1 Cor.* 15:55–57). My dear friends, he has done this. It is an accomplished fact.

Where is he now? He is seated at the right hand of God in the glory everlasting. Hope for the world? This is the only hope for the world. Statesmen, philosophers, all are fumbling, baffled, bewildered, with nothing to say to us and no hope to give us. Do you want to know the only hope for the world? Here it is. We are told that after his resurrection, 'Jesus came and spake unto them, saying, All power is given unto me in heaven and in earth' (*Matt.* 28:18). And that is the truth. Having finished his work here on earth, he ascended into heaven, and he sat on the right hand of the Majesty on high. That is his position. God raised him from the dead, says Paul to the Ephesians, 'and set him at his own right hand in the heavenly places, far above all principality and power, and might, and dominion, and every name that is named, not only in this world, but also in that which is to come: and hath put all things under his feet' (*Eph.* 1:20–22). Your great world, and your bombs, and your governments, and your rockets, all are under his feet. All power is in his hands. The universe is his. History is under his control.

What is he doing? He is 'expecting till his enemies be made his footstool' (*Heb.* 10:13). He is acting. He is acting through a meeting like this, you know. He is calling people out of the world, and from the dominion of sin and of Satan – calling us out, setting us apart in his kingdom. He is preparing for something that is coming. He has been doing this for nearly two thousand years. That is why the gospel is preached, that is why I am called to preach – to warn you of these things, to tell you about him and how you can be delivered here and now from the thraldom of this world and its final hopelessness and uselessness; to tell you that you can be delivered out of it now.

But what is he delivering us for? That is what he is doing now, but, oh, what he is going to do! He will come again. This is the 'blessed hope' (*Titus* 2:13). Were it not for this, I would have no hope whatsoever. But here is the hope: all authority is in his hands, the world is his. I do not understand why he permits things to happen, but he does. This is part of his way, perhaps, of convincing us of our sin, seeing what we make of life when he leaves us to ourselves. It is his love, perhaps, to allow us to suffer hell in order that we may awaken to the folly of what we are doing and turn back to him. I do not know. It is possible. 'The goodness of God leadeth thee to repentance' (*Rom.* 2:4).

But what I know is this – that he will come back into this world, and will judge all his enemies, and destroy all evil. He will destroy the devil and all his forces. He has already defeated them, but then he will destroy them finally and all who belong to Satan. Let there be no mistake about this. Whoever follows the devil and the way of the world and rejects Christ and his message, will go to eternal perdition. But then he will purge evil and all the effects of evil entirely out of the universe. He himself talked about 'the regeneration' that will take place in the universe when he, the Son of man, returns into this world (*Matt.* 19:28).

And he is going to do this, my dear friends, this is the great message of the whole of the Bible. It is all summed up, as it were, in the last book, the book of Revelation. This is the kind of proclamation that Revelation makes, here is a prophecy of what is going to happen:

And the four and twenty elders, which sat before God on their seats, fell upon their faces, and worshipped God, saying, We give thee thanks, O Lord God Almighty, which art, and wast, and art to come; because thou hast taken to thee thy great power, and hast reigned. And the nations were angry – of course, we are seeing it now – *and thy wrath is come, and the time of the dead, that they should be judged, and that thou shouldest give reward unto thy servants the prophets, and to the saints, and them that fear thy name, small and great; and shouldest destroy them which destroy the earth. And the temple of God was opened in heaven, and there was seen in his temple the ark of his testament: and there were lightnings, and voices, and thunderings, and an earthquake, and great hail* (Rev. 11:16–19).

There is going to be 'new heavens, and a new earth, wherein dwelleth righteousness' (2 *Pet.* 3:13). Not as the result of political action, not as the result of good resolutions on the part of men and women or parliaments or nations. No, no, the coming again of the Son of God. It is the only hope. And he is coming, and he will destroy all his enemies and all who belong to them, and he will make a new heaven and a new earth, and all who believe in him – they will be in it. We will be changed; our very bodies will be glorified. We will be like him, and we will be reigning with him and judging with him – and we will know all the wonderful and blessed results of all this.

Let me read to you again a marvellous description of what we can be looking forward to.

Therefore are they before the throne of God – men and women like ourselves – *and serve him day and night in his temple: and he that sitteth on the throne shall dwell among them. They shall hunger no more, neither thirst any more; neither shall the sun light on them, nor any heat. For the Lamb which is in the midst of the throne shall feed them, and shall lead them unto living fountains of waters: and God shall wipe away all tears from their eyes* (Rev. 7:15–17).

No more Remembrance Sundays, no more weeping, no more sighing, no more sorrow – it will all have gone, finished once and for ever.

And the whole of creation will benefit from this great regeneration. Read again that glorious prophecy of the prophet Isaiah. This is what is going to happen as certainly as we are here this evening.

The wolf also shall dwell with the lamb, and the leopard shall lie down with the kid; and the calf and the young lion and the fatling together; and a little child shall lead them. And the cow and the bear shall feed; their young ones shall lie down together: and the lion shall eat straw like the ox. And the sucking child shall play on the hole of the asp, and the weaned child shall put his hand on the cockatrice' den. They shall not hurt nor destroy in all my holy mountain: for the earth shall be full of the knowledge of the LORD, *as the waters cover the sea* (Isa. 11:6–9).

Oh, blessed, glorious day! It is coming! 'For we know that the whole of creation', says Paul, 'groaneth and travaileth in pain together until now' (*Rom.* 8:22). The very creation is also going to be delivered 'from the bondage of corruption, into the glorious liberty of the children of God' (verse 21). And again we read in Revelation:

Behold, the tabernacle of God is with men, and he will dwell with them, and they shall be his people, and God himself shall be with them, and be their God. And God shall wipe away all tears from their eyes; and there shall be no more death, neither sorrow, nor crying, neither shall there be any more pain: for the former things are passed away (Rev. 21:3–4).

These 'former things' gone for ever, the devil defeated, consigned to eternal perdition, and the whole universe, not only men and women who believe in him, but the whole cosmos restored, perfected, regenerated, glorified, and there we shall be for ever and for ever with him, the blessed and glorious God. My friends, this is the only hope, and it is a certain hope.

How do I know it is certain? How do I know that this is not all some kind of fairy-tale, some marvellous fantasy? I know it like this. This is a realistic message that tells you the plain unvarnished truth about yourself and about your world, and also about God and his purpose and his plan. The certainty of the future is based upon what has already happened. Look at this book, the Bible, and the fulfilled prophecy. God said away back at the beginning that he would send a deliverer. Centuries passed, people said, 'Where is the promise of his coming?' (2 *Pet.* 3:4). But he came. Read the prophecies concerning the babe of Bethlehem, written eight centuries before it happened – how correct they are in the details! Fulfilled prophecy! That is why I say that the prophecies still to be fulfilled are certain.

Then look at him when he came into this world; look at his mastery over evil and over the devil; look at his conquest of death, and his resurrection. These are facts. The apostle Paul preached 'Jesus, and the resurrection' (*Acts* 17:18). It was not a theory. The apostles said, 'We are his witnesses of these things' (*Acts* 5:32). They had seen him alive, they had seen him dead, they had seen him buried, they had seen him risen. These are facts.

And there is the whole subsequent history of the church and her story, which is only explicable in terms of the power of the risen Christ. There would not be such a thing as the church today were it not that he has kept her going. People like you and I would have wrecked the church centuries ago. But he keeps it going. He sends revivals and renews his people. Why is this? Because he is unchangeable. 'Jesus Christ the same yesterday, and to day, and for ever' (*Heb.* 13:8). The thing is certain.

So I want to leave you with some questions. What does all this mean to you? How do you react to it? Do you believe it? Are you tempted to say, 'But you're as pessimistic as everybody else. I thought I would get a message tonight that would put me right, and put everything right in the world.' Did you? Then you have misunderstood the gospel. There is no such message. Nobody else has it. I do not have it. You are in a world of sin and shame, a world of sorrow, a world of lust and passion and evil; and it will remain like this until he comes again.

But believe on him now and you can be delivered from the power of the world. You can get out from the dominion of sin and Satan. You can be set free even while you are here. And I have told you what you can look forward to beyond this world, when he comes again. I have told you of the glory that is coming. And if you do not believe it, you have nothing to look forward to but a perpetuation of what you have now, only ten times worse; and there will be no relief, no intermission, no hope of its ever ending. It will be eternal destruction from the presence of the Lord.

That is the message. If you believe in Jesus Christ and his great salvation, there is hope for you now, there is hope for you for all eternity. Hope in life, hope in death, hope for ever and for ever. Peace and joy now, immediately, and peace for ever. Everlasting consolation and good hope; the only hope, through Jesus Christ the Son of God, the Saviour and the Lord of all who believe in him. Do you believe in him? The only hope for you individually, the only hope for the cosmos, lies in the Son of God, the Saviour of the world.

6

Repent and Believe

Then Philip went down to the city of Samaria, and preached Christ unto them. And the people with one accord gave heed unto those things which Philip spake, hearing and seeing the miracles which he did. For unclean spirits, crying with loud voice, came out of many that were possessed with them: and many taken with palsies, and that were lame, were healed . . . But when they believed Philip preaching the things concerning the kingdom of God, and the name of Jesus Christ, they were baptized, both men and women (Acts 8:5–7, 12).

The gospel, let me remind you, is a very definite message. It is not vague philosophizing, or a message about people simply trying to do good and to live a better life and urging one another to do so. No, no, it is called 'the word'; it is a distinct word, a well-defined word. The New Testament constantly tells us that all these early preachers preached the same message. You did not have in the early church the situation that you have today in which people all completely deny one another while calling themselves Christians. Paul is never tired of reminding us that the message that he preached was exactly the same message as that preached by all the other apostles. And here it is quite plainly in Acts 8. It is the 'word', and it is, as we realize, a word about the Lord Jesus Christ. Now we have been considering the gospel message that comes as the result of the appearing in this world of the Son of God and all he has done on our behalf.

So that is the first point: without this message there would never have been a church or a single Christian. Now this is obviously a most important matter; we have to start with the message. If there is any difficulty or confusion or uncertainty about the message, obviously nothing can happen at all, and we have tried to deal with that. But it still leaves us with a question: How does one become a Christian? That message is essential; yes, but many people hear this message and do not become Christians. That is what I am considering with you now. What is this peculiar thing that happens that results in people becoming Christian as the result of hearing this message? Now that, fortunately, is also shown us very plainly and clearly in this particular incident in Samaria – as it is in most places in the New Testament.

We can put it like this: the gospel calls for our acceptance and for our obedience. Now this is stated frequently. Peter himself had put it clearly to the members of the Sanhedrin. He had pointed out in his address before the Sanhedrin, recorded in the fifth chapter of Acts, that 'we are his witnesses of these things; and so is also the Holy Ghost, whom God hath given to them that obey him' (verse 32). That is it. The gospel calls for obedience.

In other words, this is not just a message to sit and listen to, and think about, and express various opinions on, and nothing more. If that is the position, you will never be a Christian. It has to be obeyed, it has to be received, it has to be accepted. But the way in which this is generally put in the New Testament is this: if we are to be Christian, then we must obey the commandment of the gospel, which says to us, 'Repent ye, and believe the gospel.'

The call to repentance is the first note in New Testament preaching (*Mark* 1:15). Let me show it to you in general. Look at the pages of the New Testament, look at the Gospels, which mark this new beginning. For four hundred years there had been no prophetic voice amongst the Jews, the children of Israel; they had been conquered by the Romans, and everything was at a very low ebb indeed in every respect. Then suddenly something happened, and it began with a man called John the Baptist. We read, 'Now in the fifteenth year of the reign of Tiberius Caesar, Pontius Pilate being governor of Judaea . . . the word of God came unto John the son of Zacharias in the wilderness' (*Luke* 3:1–2). And John became a great phenomenon: his preaching, his astonishing life, his amazing personality.

And what did John the Baptist preach? He preached 'the baptism of repentance for the remission of sins' (*Luke* 3:3). That was his great message. He called upon people to repent. He was preparing the way, he said, for the great Deliverer, the great Messiah who was going to come. And he warned the people that this was the most momentous event that had ever happened in human history. He said, 'The axe is laid unto the root of the trees: every tree therefore which bringeth not forth good fruit is hewn down, and cast into the fire' (*Luke* 3:9). He said that it was no use the people saying that they were Abraham's children, that would not help them at all. And he said, 'God is able of these stones to raise up children unto Abraham' (*Luke* 3:8). John's message was a great call to repentance in preparation for the coming Messiah.

And then we are told that our Lord suddenly appeared, and began to preach. What did he preach? Now this is what I read at the beginning of Mark's Gospel: 'Now after that John was put in prison, Jesus came into Galilee, preaching the gospel of the kingdom of God, and saying, The time is fulfilled, and the kingdom of God is at hand: repent ye, and believe the gospel' (*Mark* 1:14–15). There it is from his own mouth. And he continued to preach this message constantly.

Take that extraordinary parable on repentance in Matthew 21 that our Lord preached to the Pharisees and scribes. The whole point of it is the need for repentance. He said, in effect, 'You have not repented. The publicans and sinners have repented and have gone into the kingdom, but you, having heard the message, have not repented.' That is what kept them out of the kingdom. The door of entry into the kingdom of God, the way to become a Christian, is by repenting. It is the first step.

So our Lord went on emphasizing this. And then, after his departure and his ascension, there came the great event on the day of Pentecost, when, as he had promised, our Lord sent the Holy Spirit upon the church and the disciples were filled with the Spirit. Then they began to speak, and a crowd gathered, and Peter, filled with the Spirit, stood up and addressed the crowd. What did he preach to them? He showed them how, in their ignorance, they had crucified the Son of God, and we read this:

Now when they heard this, they were pricked in their heart, and said unto Peter and to the rest of the apostles, Men and brethren, what shall we do? Then Peter said unto them, Repent, and be baptized every one of you in the name of Jesus Christ for the remission of sins, and ye shall receive the gift of the Holy Ghost (Acts 2:37–38).

It was the same message: John the Baptist's message, the Lord Jesus Christ's message and now the message of the apostle Peter, the first spokesman of the Christian church. 'Repent, and be baptized . . .'; 'Repent ye, and believe the gospel.'

And you get the same message running right through the New Testament. The apostle Paul, saying farewell to the elders of the church at Ephesus, reminded them of how day and night, both in public and in private, he had not ceased to preach to them – what? – 'Repentance toward God, and faith toward our Lord Jesus Christ' (*Acts* 20:21). Now this is clearly the great message of the Christian church; repentance is essential before anyone can become a Christian. You can hear the gospel, but listening to it does not make you a Christian. You cannot be a Christian without repenting. It is this that is always emphasized first of all.

So that raises for us, acutely, the question of what exactly repentance means. How do I know whether I have repented? Now the very details that are given us here of what happened in this city of Samaria tell us exactly what repentance means. You have only to take the words that are used in the narrative and at once you see the plain, unmistakable meaning of this vital term. We are told, 'Philip went down to the city of Samaria, and preached Christ unto them. And the people with one accord gave heed unto those things which Philip spake, hearing and seeing the miracles which he did.' And again in that twelfth verse: 'But when they believed Philip preaching the things concerning the kingdom of God, and the name of Jesus Christ, they were baptized, both men and women.'

So let us look at this passage. First, the people 'gave heed'. This means they gave earnest heed. They not only heard, they listened. Now this must be examined because it is the vital term. What does it imply? Obviously, it implies, in the first place, a readiness to hear. It is an astounding fact that many people are not Christians because they have refused to hear, and this is because they have been blinded by their prejudices. Like the members of the Sanhedrin, they do not want to hear, they are determined not to hear, and at all costs they will not hear.

It is possible for you to be in a meeting like this and refuse to hear. You are hearing words, you are hearing the sound of my voice, but you can stop yourself hearing, you can stop yourself listening. God knows, many people have done that, and a large number of people are still refusing to hear the gospel. They sometimes take this stance because they feel they know all about it, and think it is a lot of nonsense. They do not want instruction; they do not want any help. You know the kind of thing I mean.

Take the man who says, 'I'm not a Christian.' So you say, 'Why not?' And he pours out a whole lot of clichés: 'Nothing in it. Tommy rot. Played out. Science has disproved it.' Then you begin to ask him about the contents of the Bible, and you find out at once that he does not know anything about it. He has never read the Bible and he has not the slightest idea as to what the Christian message really is. He may think it is a lot of sob-stuff, and that Christian people just spend their time singing hymns and choruses, and complimenting one another.

Or someone else may say, 'I'm already a Christian, I'm already living a good life.' So he has never heard the gospel, and if you really present it to him, he will not listen because he thinks it does not concern him.

Or another way, of course, in which you can fail to hear the gospel is by listening with the one avowed intention of turning it down. So you latch on to a word – anything that will serve to put it down.

In other words, people can listen without giving the gospel any chance at all. They are determined at all costs to have nothing whatsoever to do with it. They are prejudiced. They have already decided – pre-judged – the message. But you see how different these people were in Samaria: 'The people with one accord gave heed unto those things which Philip spake.' My dear friend, have you got an open mind? Are you really ready to listen to this message? Have you ever given it a fair hearing? Is it not wrong from every standpoint to dismiss a message, a teaching, before you have ever listened to it, when you know nothing about it? But that is the tragedy of the times.

Oh, people may attack the church or a preacher or Christian people whom they happen to know, but that is not attacking

Christianity, that is attacking the failure of particular Christians, which is very different. It is quite impossible for anybody to become a Christian without listening to the message. Patently, the first thing we must do is listen to it, and listen to it fairly, listen to it honestly.

Now let us be frank: you do not like a prejudiced person, do you? What do you think of a man who will not listen to what you happen to believe, your hobby or your pet theory? Perhaps you are a politician and you hold particular political views; what would you think if, when you went to address a meeting, the people just began singing the moment you began speaking, and did not allow you to utter a single word? What would you think of them? But perhaps you have been behaving just like that with regard to the gospel. You may not have joined in a public disturbance, but you have shut your ears, or sung to yourself. You can make it impossible for this word to penetrate your mind. That is the opposite of repentance. These people in Samaria, look at them! They *gave earnest heed*, they really did listen. They said, 'What has this man got to say?' and they gave him a chance.

Now I could contrast these people in Samaria with others. Look at those Stoics and Epicureans in Athens when the apostle Paul went there. Some of them said, 'What will this babbler say?' (*Acts* 17:18). They described him as a 'babbler' before they had even heard him. That is prejudice. That is what they did with our Lord. The Pharisees never listened to him! They were so blinded, so prejudiced against him, that they never allowed his word to come to them. Though he was speaking the gracious words of God, and was himself the love of God incarnate, they never allowed themselves to hear him. So he said to them, 'He that hath ears to hear, let him hear' (*Matt.* 11:5) – and that was why he uttered such an injunction.

So that is the first step, but it does not stop at that. Repentance means not only that we are prepared to listen to the message, but also that we are prepared to think again. This is a further step, is it not? The very word 'repent' indicates that. It is from a Latin word that means 'think again', and that is a good definition of what is meant by repentance. The gospel calls upon all of us to reconsider certain questions.

Repent and Believe (8:5–7, 12)

Now we all come to this gospel with our philosophies, with our views of life. Everybody lives according to some theory, everybody has a working philosophy of life. We all have some standard, some set of rules by which we live and operate and which we feel are the best way for us to live. We justify what we do and do not do. Here it is, and it is a complete circle. Then we meet somebody who is a Christian. Maybe we meet accidentally, or we may be working with them, or studying with them. Somehow or another, we come into contact with these people and they tell us that they are Christians.

When this happens to you, here is the vital question: Are you not only prepared to listen, but also to think again? Are you prepared to reconsider the questions that are put to you by the gospel: What is man? What is life? How should one live in this world? What is death? What lies beyond it? These great questions. Up until this point, we have all said, have we not, 'What *I* say is. . .' But now the gospel comes to you and says, 'Wait a moment, I have heard what you have said, are you prepared to reconsider it? Are you prepared to re-examine these questions?' The gospel says, as the great Oliver Cromwell said to the leaders of the Church of Scotland: 'I beg you in the bowels of Christ, think it possible you may be mistaken.' That is it. Having listened, you re-think, re-examine, and look at this message all over again, allow yourself, for a moment, just to consider the possibility that you may be wrong. Listen to this alternative, to this other point of view.

But, of course, that is not the end. Repentance calls us to go a step further and not only reconsider and re-think, but consider the possibility of changing our minds. That is the meaning of the Greek word for repentance – *metanoia* – think in a different way. Here, again, is a step that has to be taken. These parables that our Lord uttered on this whole question of repentance illustrate this perfectly. Take the parable of those two sons whom their father sent into the vineyard. The father said to the first boy, 'Son, go work to day in my vineyard.' But the boy looked at his father and said, 'I will not.' That is it; that is instinctive, is it not? 'I won't. What right has my father to command me? I'm a young man now. I've come of age. I'm going to live my own life in my own way. I've got my own plans for today, why should I go to work in the vineyard?' So he turns to his father brusquely and says, 'I will not.' But, said our Lord, 'Afterward he repented, and went.' What did he do? He reconsidered, he re-examined his words. Though he had spoken with absolute confidence and assurance, he looked at his father's request again. He thought about it again, and he changed his mind; he repented and did the thing he said he would not do (*Matt.* 21:28–29).

Now that is the essence of repentance, and it is always true of it, because all of us by nature are opposed to this gospel. This opposition is universal. The people who crucified the Son of God were representative of the world. We are opposed to God. We do not like the very idea of God. We are trying to get rid of him. Men and women by nature hate God, so they must be ready to change their minds, and they will do so if they are truly repentant.

And, lastly, the final element in repentance is, again, shown perfectly in the parable we have just considered. Having listened, having reconsidered, having changed our minds, we then do what the gospel tells us to do: 'Afterward he repented, and went.' In other words, repentance is not merely intellectual, it involves action, conduct, behaviour; it involves a revolution. Whereas we were going one way, we turn round and we go the other way.

The great illustrations of repentance in the New Testament show it all so plainly, and none more dramatically than the account of the apostle Paul going down to Damascus to massacre the Christians and destroy the church, which ends up with Paul preaching the gospel in Damascus. That is repentance.

Having, then, looked at what repentance is, let us now consider what it is that leads to repentance. What is it that makes a man or woman repent? How did these people in Samaria become Christian? Here they were, they were listening to Philip in the spirit that I have been outlining to you. But what was it that influenced them? And the answer is that they faced the evidence: 'And the people with one accord gave heed unto those things which Philip spake, hearing and seeing the miracles which he did.' Or, as the twelfth verse puts it, 'But when they believed Philip preaching the things concerning the kingdom of God, and the name of Jesus Christ, they were baptized.' It is, again, this great matter of paying attention to the truth which is preached. I repeat, you must listen to the evidence. You have controlled your prejudices, you have said that it is unintelligent, apart from anything else, to damn and blast a thing without knowing what it is. Oh, how often have I known it here in my experience!

Thank God, there are men and women in this congregation tonight who can testify to the truth of what I am saying. They were first brought here by some friends who wanted them to hear the gospel and become Christians, but they did not want to come, they did not want to hear it. They said it was a lot of nonsense and they had already seen through all that before. But the friends put such pressure to bear upon them that at last they gave in and said, 'All right, we'll come.' But they were determined to explode it and pull it to pieces and show what utter rubbish it was. That is the condition in which they came.

But now, thank God, they are Christians. In spite of themselves, they began to listen to the evidence, they began to listen to the argument and they began to listen to the truth that was preached, and once they allowed themselves to hear it, their whole attitude began to change. Christianity was not the rot that they had thought it was, nor was it a series of affecting stories about mothers and babies and children and all the rest of it. No, no, it was argumentation, it was the presentation of a great body of truth. They had never heard of this, they had never thought of it, but now they began to listen to it, and this, as we have seen, is the vital step if anyone is to enter into the kingdom of God. They realized that this gospel message is the exposition of a great plan and purpose of the almighty God for this world of time; they began to realize that this was something that was practical politics, if you like, because it talks about life in the world as it is today. And they began to hear that God is concerned in all this, that it is not only men and women who are trying to put the world right, but that God has a purpose and a plan. And so they began to hear that God had promised this, away back in the Garden of Eden at the very beginning and that there was a revelation of God's plan of salvation even in the Old Testament.

Now Philip preached about that in Samaria. These Samaritans, let me remind you, had the five books of Moses, the first five books of the Bible, and in those books there are all these adumbrations of the gospel, of God's plan of salvation. Philip began to tell them about it and to unfold this great plan of God for world redemption. And then he was able to point out how, in the coming of this person called Jesus of Nazareth, these Old Testament promises and prophecies were being verified and fulfilled. The apostle Paul used to do this every time he entered into a synagogue. He knew that the Jews had their Old Testament Scriptures, so he just presented the argument like this: 'Opening and alleging, that Christ must needs have suffered, and risen again from the dead; and that this Jesus, whom I preach unto you, is Christ' (*Acts* 17:3). Why did Paul say this? Well, the Jews as a nation were rejecting the gospel because they said that this idea that the great Deliverer is one who dies in helplessness on a cross is rubbish. The Deliverer will be a great prince, a great hero. And because Jesus of Nazareth was neither, and because he was just a carpenter who died on a cross, they would have nothing to do with him.

So Paul began to reason with the Jews out of their own Scriptures, and began to show them that the Old Testament had always said that this Deliverer, when he came, would die, that he would be led 'as a lamb to the slaughter' (*Isa.* 53:7), and would not be as they expected at all but almost the exact opposite, with a visage that was marred, and weak, and they would see him dying and buried. Paul showed them that they were prejudiced and did not understand their own Scriptures; and it was only those who began to listen to him who saw the argument, and then it happened to them as it happened to these people in Samaria.

But this is the method of presenting the gospel. Christ is the fulfilment of prophecy. Take the great prophetic details that you find in your Old Testament – one prophet even said that the Messiah would be born in a place called Bethlehem; others said how he was to be born, and how he was going to live, that he would ride into Jerusalem on the foal of an ass, and that he would be crucified. 'My God, my God, why hast thou forsaken me?' says the twenty-second Psalm, and our Lord uttered those words on the cross as he was dying.

So here is the evidence and this is what Philip preached in Samaria. He took what they knew and he showed them the relevance of it all and the fulfilling of it all in the Lord Jesus Christ.

And then he told them the astounding story of the Lord himself, this amazing person – what he did, what he said, how he had been crucified, how he had been buried but how he had risen again and had manifested himself to the chosen witnesses, then had ascended into heaven in the presence of some of them, and had, as he had promised, sent down the Holy Spirit on the day of Pentecost. And Philip said he was a witness of this, and was filled with this Spirit, and they could see that he was. This is the kind of evidence by which they were confronted.

And then Philip preached about the character of the Christian life. He expounded the Sermon on the Mount, and spoke about the righteousness that God demands of men and women. He painted that portrait of true living, and they began to feel that this was essentially right. Have you felt that? Have you realized that if only everybody in this world lived according to the Ten Commandments and the Sermon on the Mount, the pound would not have had to be devalued, amongst other things, because everybody would be honest, and everybody would work an honest day's work for an honest wage, whether master or servant. There would be no war in Vietnam, no divorce, and no crime. If everybody lived as this gospel would have us live, our problems would all be solved and the world would become Paradise. Philip began to show this, and these people began to see it.

And the moment you stop to think of it, what can you say against this gospel? What, for example, have you got to say against our Lord's words, 'Blessed are the poor in spirit . . . Blessed are they that mourn . . . Blessed are the meek . . . Blessed are they that do hunger and thirst after righteousness . . . Blessed are the peacemakers . . .' (*Matt.* 5:3–9)? This is the gospel that you dismiss as an insult to an intelligent man. But you have never heard it. Listen to it, I beseech you. See its essential righteousness and purity and cleanliness and holiness – what can you say against it?

And then listen to what it tells you about yourself. I have often said it and I say it again to the glory of God: if I had no other reason for believing this book to be the Word of God, this is enough for me. It is the only book that tells me the plain unvarnished truth about myself. The newspapers do not, they flatter us. The politicians and everything else around us does the same. Modern man with his insight and understanding – marvellous! Wonderful! How the Christians of the past centuries are despised! But look at the world today, look at the mess, look at the problems, look at the chaos and confusion.

Now the gospel makes you face all that. Sob-stuff? My dear friends, it is the people who are at home looking at the television who are having the sob-stuff. This is reason, this is understanding, this is truth, and it shows men and women their real nature, it makes them see themselves as they really are.

So Philip preached that to the Samaritans; and then, beyond that, he told them about the judgment to come. He told them that God is the maker and the owner and the judge of this world, and that every one of us has got to meet him. The clever fellows with their television programmes and their cynicism and their sneering and their suggestiveness and their innuendoes, they have all got to die and stand before God. And all the ignorant people that clap their hands at their inanities, they, too, have all got to die. Life is much bigger than you have ever thought, and you are responsible for your thoughts and actions. You will have to give an account to God of what you do in this world. You say, 'I don't believe in Christianity. I believe in getting drunk on Saturday night and having my fling and doing what I like.' All right, you may say so, but what do you think you will be saying in a hundred years' time? To start with, where will you be? What do you know about it? Have you faced the fact that you will not be here?

Now these are the issues that this Christian message talks about, this is the truth that Philip propounded to those people in Samaria, and they listened to him. There was something coherent about this, there was something right, there was something noble. The evidence! The evidence of the message.

But it was not only the evidence of the message that challenged the people to repent. Did you notice this further aspect: 'The people gave heed unto those things which Philip spake, hearing and seeing the miracles which he did. For unclean spirits, crying with loud voice, came out of many that were possessed with them: and many taken with palsies, and that were lame, were healed.' This is another very vital part of this whole process of repentance. The message is there, and the message is essential. Yes, but, I say again, you can hear it and it does not touch you. What brings it home? What is it that makes a person a Christian? Oh, it is this power that comes upon them. The power! And these people felt it and saw it. They saw the evidence before their eyes, they saw people out of whom devils had been exorcised, people who were healed.

But not only that, it was their *hearing*. Sometimes God grants miracles. Not always: miracles are rare, exceptional. He grants powers; he can do so at any time, whenever he chooses. But there is a power that God always gives in connection with this Word when it is preached in sincerity and truth – it is the power of conviction. And these people felt it. Yes, you can control yourself up to that point, but then you hear the message and then this power comes upon it. This is what Paul means when he writes to the Thessalonians, 'Our gospel came not unto you in word only, but also in power, and in the Holy Ghost, and in much assurance' (*1 Thess.* 1:5). He is saying that, suddenly, as they listen, people are not merely hearing words, but are also feeling something. A power attends it; their minds are illuminated; their consciences are disturbed. They are aware that God is dealing with them, that something is happening to them. You cannot become a Christian without that.

Now this, again, runs right through the Bible. You find it even in the story of John the Baptist. John, we are told, used to preach on certain occasions to a king called Herod. Herod had arrested John the Baptist and thrown him into prison because John had told him the truth about himself. This man was living with his brother's wife and John, though this man was a king and he was nothing, denounced him, and so the king had thrown him into prison. But that king could not leave him alone. We are told that King Herod sent for John frequently, and he gave commands to his soldiers and prison-keepers to look after him and to treat him kindly. 'He heard him gladly', we are told (*Mark* 6:20). Why? Oh, it is this power of conviction.

And later on in this book of the Acts of the Apostles there is that great dramatic picture of Paul preaching before Felix, the Roman governor, and Drusilla, his wife. And we are told that as Paul 'reasoned of righteousness, temperance, and judgment to come,

Felix trembled' (*Acts* 24:25). Why did he tremble? He was the Roman governor and Paul was a prisoner standing there with chains hanging from his wrists, yet Felix 'trembled'! Oh, it was this power upon the Word, this conviction of the Holy Spirit. Felix knew that what Paul was saying was right. It was true. And it was condemning him. Felix, too, was living in adultery, and Paul was pressing him on the questions of 'righteousness, temperance, and judgment to come', and he trembled. This is power – power of conviction produced by the Holy Spirit.

And I have reminded you of how it happened when Peter was preaching on the day of Pentecost. There he was, expounding the Scriptures, and suddenly in the midst of the sermon the people began to cry out saying, 'Men and brethren, what shall we do?' (*Acts* 2:37). This was conviction, the Holy Spirit's conviction! People disturbed, people made to see themselves, people unhappy, seeking deliverance. Conviction! And here in Samaria, 'The people with one accord gave heed unto those things which Philip spake, hearing' – and that is hearing by the Spirit, convicting hearing – 'and seeing the miracles which he did.' There was the evidence, it was before their eyes.

And the other thing, I have no doubt, was this – they were now seeing quite clearly the contrast between what they had known until this moment and what they were beginning to hear and beginning to see. This can be summed up quite simply like this – they were aware of the contrast between Philip and Simon Magus.

There was a certain man, called Simon, which beforetime in the same city used sorcery, and bewitched the people of Samaria, giving out that himself was some great one: to whom they all gave heed, from the least to the greatest, saying, This man is the great power of God. And to him they had regard, because that of long time he had bewitched them with sorceries.

They had paid great attention to Simon, you see; they had listened to him and he had seemed to be doing wonders. But he had been playing with them and bewitching them. And now the Samaritans were confronted by Philip and they were amazed at the contrast. They had been conscious of a type of power in Simon and they were conscious again of power in Philip but there is greater power in the Holy Spirit. And they were aware of differences in the two men. In Philip they saw not the braggart, not the boaster, not the man who sets himself up, but the humility of the Christian preacher, the man who had come to serve, a man who was not talking about himself but talking about the Lord Jesus Christ. Simon had set himself up as some 'great one', but the Christian does not speak about himself, he is not there to advertise himself or to get personal followers. No, no, he is nothing, he is nobody, he is always talking about this other, this Jesus, this Christ, this Son of God, and about what he has done. They saw the contrast and it moved them and they said, 'This is different.'

I shall never forget as long as I live an illustration of this in my own personal knowledge and experience. It was in connection with the conversion of a woman who was not only a spiritist but a medium, who used to earn her living partly by acting as a medium. I will never forget what that woman told me. She was due to be in Cardiff on a Sunday night acting as a medium and was going to be paid three guineas – this was all of thirty years ago. But she was not well and was unable to go. As she was sitting in her house looking through the window, she saw people going to a certain chapel. And she did not know why, but she suddenly thought, 'I wonder what happens there? Let me go and see.'

So she came into the meeting, and this is what she told me afterwards: 'I was immediately conscious of power. I know about power. I know what it is to be used by powers. I know what power means in an unseen and a spiritual sense. I was conscious of a similar power in that meeting but there was one great difference.'

'What was that?' I asked.

'Oh,' she said, 'I felt that the power in your meeting was a *clean* power.'

That is a spiritist paying tribute to the Holy Spirit. And that woman became a Christian. She was truly converted, absolutely changed. Formerly she had ridiculed Christianity. She had believed thoroughly in spiritism – yes, and had made money out of it and lived the life that so many of them do. But she was really convicted and she repented at that first visit.

The Holy Spirit. There are other spirits – there is the power of evil, the power of evil spirits. This man Simon Magus was filled with those spirits and he was using them, and they can do marvellous things. That explains a lot in this world, as I have shown you. Yes, but there is another power, and what is the difference? It is a *holy* power, a clean power, a healing power, a restoring power, a purifying power – the Samaritans felt it and they saw it. They saw the terrible contrast between what they had been and what he was, what they had known and what they now saw before their very eyes. That is the evidence that these people considered – the message, the messenger, the power that they felt and were aware of.

And so it leads to this – these Samaritans believed the message. In other words, they did not just sit back intellectually and say in a detached way, 'This is interesting. This is new, something we've not heard before and, indeed, there's a lot to be said for it.' Nor did they stop merely at accepting the evidence. It was irrefutable but they did not stop at that. No, no, over and above being convinced in the mind, and seeing the fairness and the rightness, the coherence and the wholeness of the message, and everything else I have mentioned, they saw one other thing, something that is an absolutely essential part of becoming a Christian, and it is this – the relevance of all this to themselves. The gospel message has got to be personal.

Anyone of intelligence looking at this message, and looking at that which the world has, must see the superiority of this gospel. All people are bound to, if they are truly intelligent and really do control their prejudices. There is nothing that can be said against the gospel – nothing at all. But that does not make you a Christian. You can accept the message philosophically, you can accept it intellectually, but that still does not make you a Christian. No: you only become a Christian when you cease to sit, as it were, on the judgment seat and look down upon it. Only when the position is reversed, and you are down there and it is speaking to you, do you become a Christian.

The message comes to me personally. I realize that this is not just something to listen to and to express an opinion about. This is speaking to me. This is telling me the truth about myself. This is telling me the truth about my life, the truth about the fact that I have got to die and I am not ready. It comes home! I realize that all this is true about me and it leaves me undone. And I think of eternity and my eternal destiny, and I know nothing about it, and I am unprepared for it. Then I see that I cannot afford to sit in a detached way and make my clever jokes and remarks – I cannot do this. Who am I? I am here today, and gone tomorrow. This speaks to me and it tells me the truth about myself.

And then in my utter hopelessness and helplessness I hear it telling me that in spite of all that is true of me, God loves me. That is what Philip told them, in effect. He said, 'You did it in ignorance. You did not understand. You did not know. You were blind, ignorant. But I want to tell you that "God so loved the world, that he gave his only begotten Son, that whosoever believeth in him should not perish, but have everlasting life." Listen,' said Philip, 'I am talking about the Son of God, "Who loved me, and gave himself for me"' (*Gal.* 2:20). And he has done that for you.

And so one hears this great message of deliverance. But no one is prepared to listen until they have seen their need of it, until they are convicted, until they see themselves as they truly are and become alarmed and in some shape or form cry out, 'Men and brethren, what shall I do?' Then the blessed answer comes: The Son of God, Jesus of Nazareth, came into the world in order to die for you, in order that your sins might be remitted. He has borne your punishment, he has taken your guilt upon him and received the punishment it deserves. He died for you, in your stead, in your place. 'He died that we might be forgiven' – and you look on and you say:

And can it be, that I should gain
An interest in the Saviour's blood?
Died he for me, who caused his pain;
For me, who him to death pursued?
Amazing love! How can it be
That thou, my God, shouldst die for me?

Charles Wesley

'They believed', and that is what to believe means. They saw it and they jumped at it. They clutched at it, they accepted it, they thanked God for it.

And there was only one further thing to do: 'When they believed Philip preaching the things concerning the kingdom of God, and the name of Jesus Christ, they were baptized, both men and women.' What is this? Well, I will tell you what baptism means: it means a complete submission to this teaching, and, above all, to this blessed Lord. He himself ordained that his people give evidence that they have repented and believed the gospel by submitting to baptism. They just acknowledge and confess their sins. They have stopped defending themselves, they have stopped trying to justify themselves, they acknowledge that they are hell-deserving sinners. They admit it, they have nothing to say in self-defence, they have been all wrong. But they also testify that they believe that the blood of Jesus Christ can cleanse them from all sin and unrighteousness. 'His blood,' they say, with Charles Wesley, 'can make the foulest clean, his blood availed for me.' That is what they are confessing as they submit to baptism – that they believe that, whatever they have been or done, it is all blotted out by the blood of Christ, that Christ has died that they may be forgiven, and that they now can receive the righteousness of Christ, his perfect obedience to his Father, his holy life – and they are 'clothed with righteousness divine'.

They believe that. Then they hand themselves over to this blessed Lord, they take up their cross and begin to follow the Lord Jesus Christ. They have become Christians and now belong to the Christian company, the Christian community, the Christian church, and their greatest desire is to know more and more of this blessed Lord who has loved them and given himself for them.

7

Great Joy

And there was great joy in that city (Acts 8:8).

I have been showing you how people go hopelessly astray in their understanding of the character and nature of the Christian message. But here now, as we look at this eighth verse, I want to show you that they do exactly the same in their view of the results of believing the gospel and becoming a Christian.

Now what is the common idea of what it means to be a Christian? Ask the world, ask yourself, if you are not a Christian, what your idea of Christianity is. Why have you rejected it? Why have you made fun of it? And I am quite sure that if you are honest you will have to admit that people have the notion that Christianity would make them miserable. Miserable Christians, they say; narrow-minded Christians! The popular idea of Christianity is that it robs us of all the pleasures and the enjoyments of life, that it puts us into straitjackets, makes us wear camel-hair shirts, and teaches us – to quote Milton – to 'scorn delights and live laborious days'.

Christians have turned their backs on life, they do not know what life is. Living, as they do, little, cramped, narrow, confined kinds of lives, always striving, struggling to live good lives, and always having to say no, they miss the big things. Christianity, it is said, is nothing but a mass of vetoes and prohibitions and restraints. It is always telling us not to do things and to give up things, and to make sacrifices. So to become a Christian, therefore, means that you cease to be a man or woman and become just a bit of a misery crawling through life.

And, contrariwise, the world would have us believe that it is full of joy and pleasure and happiness. Look at the bright lights and listen to the music and the laughter and the merriment. There is the world, full of great abandon, full of a spirit of enjoyment, in contradistinction to this wretched, miserable, confined kind of life that is lived by Christian people who have retired out of life and given up everything that is big and great and wonderful and full of joy.

Now I think there will be no dispute that that is the common idea with regard to the Christian faith. People often sum it up in a term that they use without knowing anything of its historical origin or its real meaning, the term *Puritanism*. This word conjures up a picture of people trudging wearily along through life, missing everything, living negative, restricted, restrained lives.

Now there is only one answer to all that and here it is: 'There was great joy in that city.' This was the result of becoming Christians. There had been no joy in that city before Philip came there and preached and before they had believed the gospel. As we know, the position before that was that the people were more or less under the tyranny of this sorcerer, Simon, who had bewitched them and had got them to believe his own great estimate of himself. My dear friends, is it not important that we should go back to the record? Christianity something that makes people miserable? The truth is the exact opposite and I want to consider this with you now.

My first proposition is that it is Christianity alone that can really give us joy. I am making this an exclusive claim: it, and it alone, can bring true happiness. Now this is Christianity's claim. I could easily spend my time now in giving you quotations out of the Scriptures to show you that this is the claim throughout the New Testament. But take that striking example that we come across in Acts chapter 16 in the famous story of Paul and Silas being arrested, tried and condemned in a very unjust manner. Having been judged guilty, they were scourged, which means that they were beaten; we are told that their captors 'laid many stripes upon them' (verse 23). The prisoners' backs were lashed with whips that were made of thongs. Their backs would be bleeding and great weals would arise. It was agonizing. We read that 'when they had laid many stripes upon them . . . the jailor . . . thrust them into the inner prison, and made their feet fast in the stocks' (verses 23, 24).

They had not only had to suffer indignity, they had been treated shamefully and cruelly and their poor bodies were wracked with pain. What was their reaction? 'And at midnight Paul and Silas prayed, and sang praises unto God: and the prisoners' – the other prisoners – 'heard them.'

I hope you realize the contrast. Paul and Silas were not the only prisoners in that prison. They were the only Christians, but there were other prisoners there, typical prisoners of the world, in for drunkenness, for theft and robbery, for murder, for a thousand and one crimes. And these prisoners – probably some of them had been there many times before – had never had an experience like this. Suddenly at midnight, zero hour, they heard these two men singing praises to God. Rejoicing! At midnight! In the innermost prison, with their feet fast in the stocks, and their poor backs writhing in agony as the result of this cruel scourging and whipping to which they had been subjected!

Now I want to put this to you as the strongest challenge I am capable of making. Here is the challenge to you if you are not a Christian: Could you do that? It is all very well to have a kind of joyousness and abandon and happiness when all is going well. The test is, what can you do at midnight in those conditions? Are you happy then? Are you full of joy then?

And then notice the jailor after his conversion: 'And when he had brought them into his house, he set meat be them, and rejoiced, believing in God with all his house' (verse 34). A short while before, that jailor had drawn his sword and was on the verge of committing suicide, but now he rejoiced in God 'with all his house'. Now these are but random examples. This, I repeat, is taught throughout the New Testament. It is the Christian message alone that can really give us joy in the world.

Let me prove my negative first. The world cannot give us joy. Unfortunately, no special ability is needed in order to demonstrate this. The world itself makes it abundantly plain and clear – we always hear 'the still sad music of humanity'. The world's pleasure at its best is never perfect, there is always something lacking. As the phrase puts it, there is always a fly in the ointment. The happiness, pleasure, and joy that the world can give does not last. Examine your own experience; even at its best, it does not last.

And then things happen to us in life. Unfortunately, we have to get older, and there are joys and pleasures and happinesses when you are young that do not appeal when you are old: they have gone. And your faculties begin to decay, and you cannot respond to stimuli as you used to, and illness comes. All these shatter joy, the joy of the world. And, of course, the death of loved ones, accidents, losses – oh, a thousand and one things happen to us in this life. And the world, of course, simply has nothing to say to us as it robs us of our joy. As the Bible puts it, 'The heart knoweth his own bitterness' (*Prov.* 14:10). And so, when things go wrong with you, you find yourself alone. Everybody else continues with what they had been doing, and with what you once did. Now you cannot join in, and you are a bit of a nuisance to them and they do not want to see you. You have your own unhappiness, your own sadness, and they do not want to be with people like that, you are spoiling the party. And so you are left severely to yourself.

Now the world, of course, admits this. It does not do so consciously, but by the various ways of escape that it is so constantly offering to us, it admits that it cannot give us real joy. I need not remind you of these escape routes, we are all familiar with them. What is the meaning of the pleasure mania that characterizes this present age? There is only one answer. It is an indication of the profound unhappiness of this generation. The greater the concentration on the organizing of pleasure, the greater the corresponding misery and unhappiness. When people have to pay to be made happy it is a sign that they have no happiness within. The more you have to buy your happiness and your joy and your pleasure, the more you are admitting that you need it and cannot find it. This is escapism. It takes you out of yourself. You look at the films, and they come one after another, and as long as they come, you forget your troubles and think you are happy. Then the films end, and you are left to yourself.

A second form of escape is drink and drugs. This is the whole explanation of why people become slaves to drink and drug taking. I am talking about the fact that people find that it is essential to take drugs to keep going at all. Drug taking has become the great characteristic of this age, and it is a tremendous admission of the inability of the world to give us joy and happiness. People are tired, they are frantic, they are unhappy, so they resort to these expedients to get some kind of relief and release and escape. The world is thereby admitting that it cannot really help us.

That is the state of the world in general. But someone may say to me, 'That's all right, but you're dealing with people who don't think and aren't intelligent and for whom there's no way out but to abandon themselves, but surely philosophy can help us, surely the people who are thinkers can give us joy?' Well, can they?

Now it is about time we asked the world to face facts. There was philosophy in this world before the Son of God ever came into it, but those philosophers could not give people joy or happiness. They could tell people how they ought to live but they could not do it themselves. It is a fact, not stated in the Bible but in secular history, that the proportion of suicides amongst the philosophers of ancient Greece was higher than that of any other group in society. The philosophers!

Indeed, you can put it like this: the more you think about life, the sadder you become. And, therefore, you will never find joy in the teaching of the great philosophers. The best they can offer us is some kind of outlook that will enable us to 'stick it'. We have already briefly considered the two popular philosophies at the time of our Lord – Epicureanism and Stoicism, the two great teachings that Paul encountered when he visited Athens. But neither of these could give people joy. The most they could do was to help people somehow to put up with life and get on with it. I have often quoted certain lines of the poet Dryden which seem to me to sum up very correctly the whole philosophy of Stoicism:

> *Since every man who lives is born to die,*
> *And none can boast sincere felicity,*
> *With equal mind, what happens*
> *Let us bear –*
> *Nor joy nor grieve too much for things beyond our care.*
> *Like pilgrims to the appointed place we tend,*
> *The world's an Inn, and death the journey's end.*

That is the philosophy of the world at its best. You see how it is put: 'Since every man who lives is born to die.' Now that is right, is it not? Most people do not get as far as that. Most people think they are going to live for ever. What utter fools we are! It does not matter whether you are young, or old, or middle-aged, you can die at any moment.

'But,' you say, 'a baby was born a minute ago; there is someone who is beginning to live.' I am equally entitled to say that there you see someone who is beginning to die. The moment you begin to live you are beginning to die. The moment you enter into life you are going out of life. There is a second less, a second less, a second less. It is only a matter of time.

Every man who lives is born to die,
And none can boast sincere felicity.

What Dryden means by that is, of course, that there is no such thing in this world as unmixed happiness. None can boast sincere, unadulterated felicity, happiness and joy. It is not possible; it has never happened.

What do you do, then? Well, says the Stoic, this is what you do:

With equal mind [with a balanced mind], *what happens*
Let us bear . . .

Put up with it.

How do you do that? How do you put up with life? How do you stand up to 'the slings and arrows of outrageous fortune'? Or how do you 'take up arms against a sea of trouble'? How do you manage to keep on your feet and not be knocked down by life and not give way to drink or drugs or something else to escape for the time being? 'With equal mind,' says the Stoic. Cultivate self-control, cultivate balance, cultivate courage, cultivate grit. Do not give in. Above all, keep a very steady rein on your feelings. Here is the whole art of life, says the philosopher. And this view is as typical of philosophy today as it was at the time of our Lord.

If you want to go through this life still standing on your feet, says philosophy, never allow yourself to be too happy, never allow yourself to be too unhappy. Do not rejoice too much, says the philosopher, you do not know what is waiting for you round the corner. Do not let yourself go, do not have your fling, do not abandon yourself, you will soon be weeping. This is philosophy.

And then, on the other hand, philosophy says: Do not be too sad, do not grieve too much. Things are never as bad as they appear to be. Time is a wonderful healer and things will get better, they are not always going to be as bad as this. That is the best that philosophy can give you. Is that joy? Is that happiness? Is that abandon? Is that exultation? Of course not. It is negative resignation.

Let me give you another quotation. The world does fool itself, does it not? The world rejects Christianity because it says that it is so happy and so full of joy, but Walter Savage Landor wrote these words in his poem, 'Dying Speech of an Old Philosopher':

I strove with none, for none was worth my strife.
Nature I loved and, next to Nature, Art:
I warmed both hands before the fire of Life . . .

How marvellous! How wonderful! I was an intellectual! Oh, I was one of the select few! I worshipped nature, I understood art, and I was a connoisseur. I appreciated this and that and I was one of the critics. I spoke delicately. 'I warmed both hands before the fire of life.' What a blaze! What a wonderful thing life is. But listen to how the poem continues:

It sinks, and I am ready to depart.

The fire is going out. I am getting old. The supply of fuel is ending. 'It sinks' – what has he got? Nothing! It comes to an end. That is life, that is philosophy at its best.

There is man with his mind and his reason and here is your so-called 'modern' humanism. Humanism? It starts with human beings and ends with human beings and has nothing to offer you. There is no joy at any moment, no consolation, nothing to help you in the hour of your greatest need. Everything is just left to you. There is nothing outside you, they say. Here you are, you were made like this, so do your best. Humanists urge you, some of them, to try to be moral. Others say that every man is a judge of his own morals and it does not matter what you do.

But all this is not only true of philosophy, it is equally true of all the so-called great world religions. If there is one thing that I cannot understand, it is the way in which Christian people seem to be beginning to say, 'Ah, we can get some help from Hinduism, and we can get some help from Buddhism', and so on. My dear friends, do you know that every one of those religions is profoundly pessimistic? Do you know what Hinduism really teaches you? It is this: the only hope you have ever got of having any kind of real joy is by undergoing a series of reincarnations by means of which you continue to come back into this world, perhaps as a rat next time, and something else the time after that. It teaches you that you go on being reincarnated time and time and time again, until eventually you have purged something out of yourself and you arrive at peace and joy. That is Hinduism.

What is Buddhism? What has this to offer you? Its only hope is that some time, in some future millennia, you will just cease to be an individual person. You will simply go out of existence and be absorbed into some absolute, into some Nirvana. It is profoundly pessimistic.

The countries that adhere to these religions are all profoundly unhappy and pessimistic. And I have not gone into the cruelties associated with the name of Muhammad. Now there – there are your great world religions.

And then there are other forms of belief, of course, seen in the cults. These teach that you should not be miserable. You are only miserable because you do not think straight. You say you are suffering pain in your body, but you should not be, there is no such thing as pain, there is no such thing as disease. You think there is and therefore you have pain, but if you realized there was no disease, you would not have the pain. Autosuggestion! You say to yourself, 'Every day and in every way I am getting better and better.' So you buoy yourself up and to you it is marvellous. *I* am!

Then there are politics and sociology. A favourite idea is the theory that if we can put the world right we will all be happy. This has been the fatal delusion of all people who have put their ultimate faith in politics – that you can legislate joy. Give everybody a free house, give everybody plenty of money and no work, and we will all be perfectly happy. It is always coming. The utopia! But it has never come and it never will.

Look at the world today. These are the ideas it is full of, these are the things to which it turns from Christianity. Ah! I have forgotten one – psychology! This is the belief that claims you can be happy if you undergo analysis, if you get your personality reconstructed. But the question is: Is any of this giving you real joy? Is this giving you real happiness or real peace? And the answer is eternally, No! We know that because all these teachings that are being offered to you encourage you either to fool yourself deliberately, or to drug yourself so that you cannot think, or to try for the time being to change your circumstances in order that you might forget yourself and your troubles. So they are doomed to failure.

And on top of it all, if we are honest with ourselves, there is always the conscience, the sense of condemnation, the remorse that follows our wrong words and actions. And that is why we are unhappy and depressed. We kick ourselves. We say, 'I'll never do that again!' and then we do. And so we go this miserable round. We keep getting temporary relief, knowing afterwards, when conscience begins to attack and remorse comes in, that we were fools, that we were wrong, that we have drugged or abused ourselves in some shape or form, and simply knocked ourselves out for the time being. We have not faced the facts. We have been dishonest. We are cads. We are fools. And down we go again to the depths of depression.

And because we have nothing that can give us any relief, and neither has the world, we have to go back again and go round and round in the same old sorry circle, and the result is profound misery and unhappiness. And the more intelligent we are and the more we think about it, the more unhappy we become. The truly great philosophers have always been agreed in talking about what they term 'the tragic sense of life'. Or, as I have often put it to you, do you think it is an accident that Shakespeare's greatest plays are tragedies? No; it is because life is tragic.

The world is a tragic place. Read human history; it is a history of wars, of fights, quarrels, deaths, murders, unhappiness, misery. Take the human record, the human story, there it is, the tragic sense of life! The very atmosphere of the world in which we live is one that depresses, and that is why humanity has had to busy itself so much and has had to expend so much energy and money in trying to manufacture pleasure, in trying to produce some kind of joy. But, as we have seen, the happiness does not last, it is only temporary, and eventually it leaves us to ourselves and the problem of our own souls. 'The heart knoweth his own bitterness' (*Prov.* 14:10), and we are all left to the bitterness of our own hearts. So there it is. I make my claim that there is nothing in the world today that can give us joy and gladness and happiness apart from this gospel.

How, then, does the gospel do it? Now it is very important to grasp that the gospel's whole approach is entirely different. Thank God for it. This is from God, not from man. We have seen what human beings do, even at their best. We must start with the gospel; this is not human. It is not human theory or philosophy. This is God acting. This is the God who has made the world and made us men and women. He knows us as we do not know ourselves. He knows there is only one way for us to be happy and he has provided it. That is the message that Philip preached to the people in Samaria.

The great characteristic of this joy that the gospel gives is that it is a happiness that is not dependent on external circumstances. The world, as I have told you, in its attempts to give us joy and happiness, always does one of two things: it either tries to manipulate our circumstances or else it drugs us and makes us insensitive to them. But the gospel is entirely different; the gospel puts joy within us. Here is the first great secret. This joy comes up from within and is a part of us. It is not manufactured from outside; it is a condition of being. This very gospel that I preach to you gives you joy, not by changing the circumstances and the surroundings, but by changing *you*. Oh, what a profound point that is! Let me quote once more:

> *The fault, dear Brutus, is not in our stars,*
> *But in ourselves, that we are underlings.*
> William Shakespeare: *Julius Caesar*

It is not other people, it is not what happens to me, and it is not the world, that makes me miserable. It is I myself who am wrong. And the gospel deals with me and not with my circumstances. It puts me into a position in which I am immune to circumstances, and this is why it, and it alone, can succeed. Nothing else approaches the problem in this way. All other attempts at finding happiness go along the two lines I have indicated to you and they must and do end in failure. But here is the gospel method: by putting me right, by putting a spring of joy within me, it stops me being dependent on what happens outside me.

Now look at it here in Acts 8. Look at these people in Samaria. They were unhappy, but now I read, 'There was great joy in that city.' Yet nothing had been changed in Samaria except these people; the other things remained exactly as they had been. There was no change in the circumstances, there was no change in wages, in food or in climate, only in the people. And because the people were changed, though the circumstances remained exactly the same, there was great gladness in that city.

And this is precisely what the gospel offers to do for you and for me. It tells you not to pin your faith in a changed world because you will never get it. It tells you to stop saying, 'If only!' 'If only this happens I shall be happy.' The gospel tells you that probably this will not happen, and even if it did, you would not be happy for long. You think that everything will be perfect for you one day; of course, we have all thought that. We start out in life thinking that everything is going to be different for us. Our fathers have all been fools, they have all been wrong, but we are going to have complete happiness. We will never get it.

Now this, you say, is pessimism. It is! But it is pessimism only in terms of the delusions held by humanity. In fact, it is realism; it tells you the truth. But it tells you, at the same time, that you can receive a joy, and a gladness, and a happiness that will remain irrespective of whatever may be happening to you. You will be unaffected by circumstances because the joy is within you yourself.

How, then, does the gospel give us this joy? Here again we come to what I regard as one of the most important discoveries men and women can ever make in this world, and it is this: joy is always a by-product. The fatal fallacy of the world is to seek joy directly, to chase after it. But if you set out just to find joy and happiness you will never succeed, never. Joy always comes indirectly and if you do not understand this, you will never know true joy. That joy that Christianity gives, that the gospel message gives us, is a joy that always results from believing the truth.

It was as the result of believing Philip's message that the Samaritans became happy and obtained joy. Philip did not get up and say, 'Now you are miserable, but I can tell you how to be happy.' And he did not follow that up with some psychological treatment that worked them up into a great state of excitement and happiness. Nothing of the sort! He preached Christ to them; he preached 'the Word' to them. He told them of what God had done by sending his Son into the world, who this Jesus was, what his death and resurrection meant. He preached Christ – all that we have been considering together. And it was as they saw this and believed it that they found themselves with their very souls flooded with this joy. Joy always comes to us indirectly.

The New Testament never comes to us and says, 'Be happy. Cheer up. Pull yourself together. Come on, let's all be happy together.' There are people who do sometimes try to say that. I want to be honest in this pulpit. There are some gatherings, some forms of religion, which call themselves Christian, that do that and work up people's feelings. If that applied to us, I would have spent most of my time here tonight in making you sing. I would have got more popular tunes, and have put more and more emotion into it, until at last we were all marvellously happy, all drunk, as it were, with singing hymns and choruses. That is so often purely psychological. I cannot see any essential difference between that and feeling happy as the result of taking alcohol.

But that is not the joy that they had in Samaria. That is not the joy of which the New Testament speaks. Instead of merely telling you to be happy and cheer up, the New Testament says this: 'Blessed [happy] are they which do hunger and thirst after righteousness: for they shall be filled' (*Matt.* 5:6). Happy people are not those who have been seeking happiness, they are those who have been seeking righteousness. You see the difference? The world is looking for happiness and joy, but it never finds it. It cannot. By definition it is impossible. You must not seek happiness directly. 'Blessed' – happy, joyous, to be congratulated, to be envied – 'are they which do hunger and thirst after righteousness: for they shall be filled.'

Or here is another way in which the New Testament puts it: 'Rejoice in the Lord alway: and again I say, Rejoice' (*Phil.* 4:4).

Again, you see the difference? It is not merely 'rejoice', but rejoice 'in the Lord'. It is as you look at him, it is as you believe this message concerning him, that you become joyful and happy and get what the New Testament message is offering to us all. No, no, it does not give us a treatise on happiness – that is what the cults do. The cults and the psychologists and so on come to you and say, 'Are you miserable? You need not be. Come with me; do this and you will soon be happy.' And, of course, because of the self-foolery and self-deception of human nature, you can persuade yourself that you are happy. Sometimes you are told to say that there is no such thing as disease and pain, and you try to put that view into practice, but then a loved one dies and you are down in the very depths of misery and despair: you find there is disease after all.

Human beings are strange creatures! You can play tricks with yourself. You can fool yourself. You can persuade yourself that you are happy when you are not. Of course, by taking drugs you can do this very quickly, but it can also be done without drugs. Psychology and the cults really can make you feel happy. But it is trickery; it is false. Your circumstances remain and you are essentially the same, with the added factor that you have been fooling yourself. But the gospel does not do it in that way; it says: 'Rejoice in the Lord alway: and again I say, Rejoice.' You do not look at yourself, you look at him, and, as you look at him and believe in him and submit yourself to him, and as he operates in you, you find yourself like these people in Samaria – 'There was great joy in that city.' If you had asked them to explain it, they could not have done so except to say, 'We believed what this man Philip said to us.'

Let me show you just in a few further headings how the gospel brings this joy. Why is anybody unhappy or miserable? Well, one great cause, always, is the past. The past! What I have done, what I have been; the accusation of conscience; the sense of guilt. We know about this, do we not? You cannot get away from your past. Of course, we like to think that we can, but it is impossible. There is a terrifying word about this in the Old Testament. Some of the children of Israel wanted to stay on the eastern side of the River Jordan and not cross over to the other side. They were allowed to do so and they gave a pledge. And this is what they were told: As long as you keep to your agreement, you will be happy and you will be blessed. But then we read, 'But if ye will not do so, behold, ye have sinned against the LORD: and be sure your sin will find you out' (*Num.* 32:23), and this is, of course, universally true.

Many a man has thought he could find peace of conscience and happiness by running away. He has done something in this country and he is miserable. He says, 'There's only one thing to do – I'll clear out and cross the ocean and go and live in South America. Nobody will know me there, nobody will have ever heard of all this. I'll find happiness and freedom.' And off he goes. But there he is many years later, sitting in his shack far away from where he was brought up. Suddenly it all comes back to him! 'Be sure your sin will find you out.' You cannot get away from it. What I have done I have done, the past is there and I know that I have got to answer for it, and how can I? And I listen to a gospel that tells me that God is holy and righteous and true, that he is the judge of the earth, that he has made human beings and made them responsible, and that I have got to meet him and to face him, and I know I cannot. I try to forget my troubles. I try to forget my guilt. I take alcohol or drugs and plunge into pleasure. I am no longer thinking of my guilt and I think I am happy. Then I am alone and back it comes. It is the morning after the night before and I feel the remorse, the agony, the accusations – and how can I stand before God in the judgment? I cannot! While I know that I am wretched, I cannot be filled with gladness. My guilt is there and I cannot get rid of it.

There is only one way to get rid of that guilt, and that is to look at this Christ, this Jesus of Nazareth, this Son of God; I look at him on the cross and know that my sins have been dealt with. He has borne them in his own body on the tree. He has taken my guilt upon himself.

He has received my punishment. God has smitten him for me. And God is just and righteous, and will not punish the same sin twice over. If he has punished it in Christ, he will not punish it in me. I know, when I look at him, that my sins are blotted out and forgiven. 'The past shall be forgotten.' It is forgotten. 'A present joy be given.' That is how I deal with my past, and it is the only way I can do so.

The world in its cleverness comes to me and tells me, 'It's no use crying over spilt milk.'

'It's all very well,' I say to the world, 'but I can't help crying. I should not have spilt it. I should not have done it. I know I'm wrong and my conscience accuses me.'

I repeat that there is only one way of getting rid of your past, and the misery that thinking of the past produces; it is to know that God in Christ has 'cast all our sins into the depths of the sea' (*Mic.* 7:19). It is as if they had never been; he will never look at our sin again.

And then the present: how can I have joy and happiness and peace in the present? 'It's all very well for you to say to me,' says someone, 'that Jesus Christ the Son of God has died for my sins, and that the past is blotted out, but I am still faced with the same world. There is the world, and the flesh, and the devil, and I am the same person. So am I to go on living this same hopeless life? Am I to go on with this endless round of striving, only to be defeated and to fall down in failure?'

That is a perfectly fair question. How can I be happy in the present, how can I have joy, knowing myself to be what I am by nature, knowing what the world that is round and about me is, that it is against me and that it is enticing me always to evil and to hell? The apostle Peter said, 'Dearly beloved . . . abstain from fleshly lusts, which war against the soul' (*1 Pet.* 2:11) – and they do. The world is organized against us, it is organized against our souls, it is always enticing us away from purity of soul, cleanliness, chastity, holiness – the noblest attributes. It is enticing us away into lusts that 'war against the soul'. How can I be happy in such a world?

And there is only one answer: it is this same gospel. It does not merely tell me that my past sins are forgiven, it gives me new life, it makes me a new person, it gives me a new start, it gives me a new understanding of everything – of life in this world, myself, the whole purpose of life and of being, of world history, the beginning, the end. Not only that, it puts new desires in me, and gives me a new purpose in life, a new form of enjoyment. This idea that the Christian life is a miserable life is the biggest lie of the devil. Of course, what the devil says is this: If you become a Christian you can no longer read, what is it – *Last Exit from Brooklyn* or *to Brooklyn* or whatever it is[1] – you cannot read things like that any more, and, of course, you are going to stop reading everything that really is enjoyable, and you will have to be reading that miserable book, the Bible.

My dear friends, if only I could make you see what a book this is! If you really want enjoyment, here it is. I know something about that other life, but if I may give my witness and my testimony, there is no joy that I have ever known that is comparable to the joy of delving into the treasures of this book. Oh, the marvel and the wonder of it! It amazes me more and more! I am sorry for you who do not understand the Bible. You need the Spirit of God, and, once you have received the gift of the Spirit, you are introduced into the most thrilling life that is conceivable. Drudgery? It is sheer happiness. My great trouble is that I have not enough time to read it.

And prayer! And the fellowship of the saints! And talking about these things! It is because you do not know anything about this that you regard it as drudgery and a task and the Christian life as a miserable existence. To live for God, miserable? Why, it is the greatest privilege and the greatest happiness: 'Only to do thy will, my will shall be.' How wonderful it is to be delivered from the slavery of sin. How wonderful to do what I want to do and no longer have to fall and always do what the devil wants me to do. For I have been given new power – new power to live, new possibilities of victory. Why, in Christ, I am told this: 'Resist the devil, and he will flee from you' (*James* 4:7). Even the devil!

And on top of it all, what is there comparable to the knowledge that as believers in the Lord Jesus Christ, we are born again? In this world we are children of God and we can always go to him knowing that he is ready to receive us. When you are suddenly taken ill, or a loved one is taken ill and the world seems to come to an end:

When all things seem against me
To drive me to despair;
I know one gate is open,
One ear will hear my prayer.
Oswald Allen

[1] *Last Exit to Brooklyn*, a novel, subject of an obscenity trial at the time.

Oh, the privilege of knowing in time, in this world, that you are a child of God and have access into his eternal presence!

What of the future? The answer is still the same, and that is why this joy of the Lord is a lasting joy, a joy that goes on irrespective of circumstances. Is there anything that tends to make us all more miserable than fear of the future? What a terrible power imagination has! Suddenly, when everything is perfect round and about you, and you are having as near as the world can ever give you to unmixed pleasure and happiness, a thought flashes into your mind: What if I shall not be here in a year's time? What if these loved ones shall be taken? And you are in the depth of despair. You are as miserable as your soul can ever be. Imagination! You cannot stop these thoughts. And you go on into the future, and you are afraid you are going to lose this, that and the other, and you are already wretched again.

But if you are in Christ, if you are born again, and if you always look to the Lord, and always 'rejoice in the Lord', you will have no fear of the future. Why? You will not be afraid because you will already have faced the future properly. Christians should not be afraid of anything. They do not expect anything in this world. They know that as long as man continues in sin, it is going to be a world of misery and shame and sin and unhappiness. It will be so until Christ comes again. They know this, so they are never surprised, never taken unawares.

And on top of that, they always know that they are in the hands of God. If you can tell me anything that is more glorious and marvellous than to know that you are in the hands of the Maker and the Controller of the universe, I would like to know what it is. 'We know that all things work together for good to them that love God, to them who are the called according to his purpose' (*Rom.* 8:28). We know that. We do not always understand it, but we know it. And the older I get, the more I understand it! 'God moves in a mysterious way his wonders to perform', and when he appears to be cruel he is being kind. 'For whom the Lord loveth he chasteneth' (*Heb.* 12:6). Discipline is always for our good.

And, indeed, I know, beyond that: 'He that spared not his own Son, but delivered him up for us all, how shall he not with him also freely give us all things?' (*Rom.* 8:32). If you but knew the love of

God to you, if you but knew how he loved you – and here is the measure of it: he has so loved you that he sent his only Son into this world for you. He sent him to the cross to bear your sins, to receive your punishment. He so loved you that he has done that for you! Can he withhold any lesser thing? Of course not. He is pledged to you, he has set his heart upon you, he loves you 'with an everlasting love', and nothing can happen to you apart from God. Here is the basis of a lasting gladness.

And even death and the grave have lost their terror. They are in his hands; they are under his control. I recently had the privilege of expounding from this pulpit Romans 14, verse 9: 'For to this end [for this cause] Christ both died, and rose, and revived, that he might be Lord both of the dead and the living.'[1] He is the Lord of death and the grave: there is nothing to fear. He has conquered all our enemies and he is in the glory. And there, as he told us before he left the world, he is preparing a place for us:

Let not your heart be troubled: ye believe in God, believe also in me. In my Father's house are many mansions: if it were not so, I would have told you. I go to prepare a place for you, and if I go and prepare a place for you, I will come again and receive you unto myself; that where I am, there ye may be also (John 14:1–3).

'Rejoice in the Lord always.' And you can; it does not matter what happens, you can always rejoice in him. You know that you are in him, that you are safe, that he will keep you. Here is the basis of Christian joy.

Fading is the worldling's pleasure,
All its boasted pomp and show;
Solid joys and lasting treasure
None but Zion's children know..
John Newton

Oh, have you heard his call?

Today thy mercy calls us
To wash away our sin,
However great our trespass,
Whatever we have been;

[1] Now published in *Romans: An Exposition of Chapter 14:1–17, Liberty and Conscience* (Edinburgh:Banner of Truth, 2003).

Great Joy (8:8)

However long from mercy
We may have turned away,
Thy blood, O Christ, can cleanse us
And make us white today.

Oswald Allen

Wherever he may guide me,
No want shall turn me back;
My Shepherd is beside me,
And nothing can I lack:
His wisdom ever waketh,
His sight is never dim;
He knows the way he taketh,
And I will walk with him.

Green pastures are before me,
Which yet I have not seen;
Bright skies will soon be o'er me,
Where the dark clouds have been:
My hope I cannot measure,
My path to life is free;
My Saviour has my treasure,
And he will walk with me.

Anna Laetitia Waring

'There was great joy in that city.' Great gladness! Why? Because they had come to a realization of that blessed truth 'concerning him', and therefore concerning themselves and their eternal future.

My dear friend, have you got this gladness? Are you filled with rejoicing? 'Believe on the Lord Jesus Christ, and thou shalt be saved', and in your midnight, with your feet fast in some stocks, and your body perhaps wracked with pain, you will be able to pray and to sing praises unto God. You will rejoice in him in life, in death, and to all eternity.

8

The Holy Spirit

Now when the apostles which were at Jerusalem heard that Samaria had received the word of God, they sent unto them Peter and John: who, when they were come down, prayed for them, that they might receive the Holy Ghost: (for as yet he was fallen upon none of them: only they were baptized in the name of the Lord Jesus). Then laid they their hands on them, and they received the Holy Ghost (Acts 8:14–17).

Verses 14 to 17 of Acts chapter 8 come as a kind of sequence to what we are told in the earlier part of the chapter. We have been given an account of how the gospel first began to spread from Jerusalem down to Samaria, and amongst the Samaritans – a very important turning point in the history of the Christian church. The history of the church shows a number of these great turning points, and in many ways this was the first, because it was when the gospel ceased to be only for Jews and for Jerusalem in particular, and began to spread amongst the Samaritans, then to other countries, and eventually throughout the whole world.

Now the record tells us that the Samaritans became Christians very largely as the result of the preaching of this one man, Philip, who was an evangelist, a deacon in the church. He had preached Christ, he had preached the kingdom of God to them, and they had believed and been baptized. And, as we have just seen, the result of this was that 'there was great joy in that city'. But this was not the end of the story; something further happened, and that is described to us in the verses we are now studying.

The apostles, as we have been told earlier, had remained in Jerusalem during the persecution of the Christians, and when the astounding news reached them that the gospel had been preached and received amongst the people in Samaria, they sent Peter and John down from Jerusalem to see what had happened and to confirm the work. And we are further told that after they arrived, they prayed that these people, who had already believed the gospel and had become Christians, might receive the Holy Spirit. And then, having prayed, 'laid they their hands on them, and they received the Holy Ghost' (verse 17).

Now this is a most important statement. Here is a text that raises the most fundamental of all questions. The ultimate question that we must consider and face is this: Is there anything apart from this world? Is it the only world? Is there a supernatural realm? Is there a world of the spirit that we do not see? Now this, I say is the fundamental question. There are many other questions in connection with this whole matter of the Christian faith, and it is right to consider them, but I feel that a great deal of time is often wasted. You hear discussions and debates, and it seems to me that they are mostly a waste of time because this first, and most basic, question has not been faced. Is there such a thing as a supernatural realm that is greater and above and beyond this world?

And the message of the Bible is to say that there is. The message of the Bible is to say that God is over all, and this God, who has existed from all eternity, created this world and created men and women. Moreover, the Bible teaches that God not only made the world, but also sustains it and orders it, and you therefore cannot understand what has happened in the world except in terms of him. That is the great case of the Bible. Of course, it puts this in countless ways and forms, but our trouble so often is that we miss the wood because of the trees, and get bogged down with different details. This is what the Bible asserts: this visible world of ours is the result of the invisible, and you only understand the visible when you know something about the invisible.

Now I think you will agree with me that it is no use engaging in particular arguments about our Lord's person and miracles and various other subjects if you already deny entirely the whole of the supernatural realm. I repeat that this is the first, great, fundamental question, and it is raised for us in an acute manner by this story of what happened when Peter and John went down to Samaria and, having prayed, laid their hands on these people.

Let us look at this together. Here, you see, is a great assertion of the supernatural. Now this is being questioned today and it is being questioned in two main ways. The first is by what is called humanism, about which we are hearing so much at the present time. Humanists are deliberately mounting an advertising campaign, and the authorities in the papers and on the television and radio are as usual very glad to help them.

So what does humanism tell us? Well, we have already looked at this. It is a teaching that says that there is nothing outside and beyond this present world. It maintains that human beings are the greatest beings and power in the universe. They are at the centre of the universe and there is nothing outside them. Recently we have been told that the whole trouble is that men and women do not realize that they are gods and can control life. They are a bit reluctant, says this great authority, to realize their own innate powers. They are able, we are told, to create and to do anything they like, if only they realized it. And, further, we are told that nothing is to be believed that human reason cannot understand and accept. Nothing is to be believed unless it can be checked and proved and verified by scientific experimentation.

Humanism denies the supernatural realm altogether. There is no God; there never has been. There are no such things as miracles; there is no intervention from the outside in the affairs of this world. And, it is said, the tragedy of the ages has been that men and women have not grasped this and in their fear and ignorance have believed in unseen powers and forces. The sooner they forget all that and take charge of the world that belongs to them, and exercise these tremendous powers that they already have within them, the better it will be.

Now I do not want to spend our time on the teaching of humanism, but I must mention it because it is the reason why so many people reject the whole of the Christian teaching, indeed, the whole of the Bible. Humanists just say that they do not accept its facts, or they try to explain them away in terms of psychology. Let us look briefly at this contention before I show you the answer that is given here in the Bible itself. There are many answers that can be given to this modern teaching, which, of course, ultimately, is not modern at all. If you read the fourteenth Psalm, you find that the first verse is this: 'The fool hath said in his heart, There is no God.' That was a humanist, away back, probably ten centuries before the birth of Jesus Christ! However, you get fashions and vogues and phases, and humanism is now in fashion. So what is the answer?

There are many answers, but one that I feel is almost sufficient in itself is this: Here is a most arrogant teaching that tells us that the greatest minds that the centuries have ever known have all been wrong and have all been deluded fools. Here is a teaching that tells us that all these mighty teachers were wrong, both those who have held positions of importance in the church, and other Christian men and women. I have often given you their names from this pulpit, starting, if you like, with the great apostle Paul and then St Augustine, and coming down the centuries to the Reformers, some of the great statesmen and many others. All these men and women who have believed in God and in Christ and in the supernatural – humanism tells us that they were all fools, in spite of their great ability and the great benefactions that they have given to the world.

But not only that, it is patently wrong to say that nothing is to be believed except that which can be proved by scientific experimentation. Surely the greatest and the most important things in life are not subject to scientific proof! Have you ever been in love? Can you test it by scientific experiment? Can you give reasons why you love one person and not another? Of course not. The highest human experiences (forgetting the gospel for the moment), all our highest and deepest experiences are outside the realm of scientific investigation. We need to say to this modern generation, 'There are more things in heaven and earth, Horatio, than are dreamt of in your philosophies.' Stop for a moment and think, and you will see how utterly inadequate human reason is to explain some of the profoundest experiences in life.

Moreover, humanism is a teaching that gives us no explanation whatsoever for the origin of this world. 'But,' you say, 'evolution explains it.' Evolution does not explain it, because the theory of evolution has to start by supposing that there was something in existence and it does not tell you where that came from, quite apart from the fact that its explanation of what happened to that original whatever-it-was – mere gases or anything else – does not explain *how* it happened. Evolution can put forward theories, but it cannot prove them. So it breaks down at its own evaluation. The theory of evolution is not subject to scientific experimentation. You just cannot do it because you always start with matter. So here you are with the primary questions: Where has the world come from? Where has man come from? And you have nothing but a theory that cannot be subject to experimentation since you cannot go back to the beginning. Nobody was there and nobody knows. So humanists are having to rest on a theory, even though, according to their own presuppositions, you should only believe and accept that which you can prove.

Furthermore, humanism is unable to explain man himself. Take the study of mankind, take anthropology. Its evidence is that right from the beginning primitive people everywhere have always had a belief in a supreme being, a supreme God. The sense of God is universal; people are born with it. It asserts itself so that they have to fight against it; they have to try to prove it is wrong. Why is this? Why this notion, this idea of an ultimate supreme being? Humanism does not begin to explain that.

Then look at civilization. Civilization is the attempt to deal with this world and its problems apart from God. But look, for example, at man's efforts in terms of education, and look at their obvious failure. The world has been grappling with itself and its problems for so long. Humanists turn to us and say, 'Look at your Christianity, it has been preached for two thousand years, why doesn't it put the world right?' But our answer, of course, is that it has never claimed that it would do that. It has not come to do that, except in its own way.

But let me pass the question back to the humanist. What are the achievements of civilization, indeed, of civilization in this twentieth century? Look round about you and you get your answer. There are people trusting to themselves. They have been doing it especially for the last hundred years and look at what they have produced. Do their achievements begin to explain who they are? Is man merely an intellect? No, no, man is complex. The problem of man is this extraordinary contradiction that is in him. There is so much that is noble and good and excellent, but there is so much that is low and vile and cruel and ugly. He advances in the realm of the mind while at the same time retrogressing in the realm of morals.

Look at this present civilization of ours – you see it on the front pages of your popular newspapers – there is some astounding scientific discovery, alongside some account of people who want to go back to the jungle and are imitating primitive dances and howling and shouting as if they were savages. Educated people behave like that and in the other ways that we considered when we were looking at the case of Simon Magus and his influence upon the Samaritans. Now I say that you must explain this astounding contradiction, the high and the low, the advance and the retrogression. And in terms of humanism, in which man is the judge of all things, you have no adequate explanation. So there are some obvious reasons why we do not accept this humanistic teaching.

But above and beyond all those arguments, there is the message of this book that we call the Bible, which, as I want to show you, simply cannot be explained at all if man is the greatest being in the universe. The Bible tells us that God is there and that God is intervening in human affairs, and that it is God's intervention that gives us any hope at all in the world at the present time.

But I must just mention a second attack upon the supernatural, which is from what is called deism. I must mention this because its implications for Christianity are often misunderstood. There are people who say, 'I'm not a humanist, I believe in God, I believe in a Creator', but they tell us that they believe that God created the world and afterwards left it to itself. You know the famous illustration: God is like a watchmaker who makes a watch, winds it up and then puts it down and does not interfere with it any further. Deists agree that God is and that he has made the universe, but they say that having set it on its course, he does not interfere with it at all. They deny the miraculous and they deny the incarnation of the Son of God; they believe that men and women should be religious and that, because God made them, they should try to live to his glory and according to his laws. But there is no intervention on the part of God. God has made human beings and it is now up to them to do everything – to save themselves or to fail to do so.

Now you notice that though there is that one great difference about whether or not there is a God, in practice, the two positions – humanism and deism – virtually come to the same thing, and this is what I am concerned about. Is there a God? Does God intervene in the life of this world? Are we left to ourselves solely and completely? Is there any point in prayer? Is there any hope of salvation, anything that I can look forward to? These are the great questions, and the great case that is made by the Bible is that the answer to them all is, 'Yes'. The Bible puts this before us in two forms. It does so in its teaching, but, still more important, in many ways, it does so in the history that is in the Bible, in the facts that are recorded there and the explanation of those facts.

What, then, is the teaching of the Bible? In its essence, it is the teaching about God; and it tells us that there are three blessed Persons in this Godhead: God the Father, God the Son, and God the Holy Spirit.

First, the Bible tells us that God is the Creator, the almighty Creator of all things that are: 'In the beginning God created the heaven and the earth' (*Gen.* 1:1). He is the Creator and the Sustainer. He ordains and controls the affairs of the world and humanity. Now this, in its essence, is the great truth that is emphasized in the Old Testament, and here, it seems to me, is the argument that is so much ignored at the present time – the great story of the Jews is in itself the complete answer both to humanism and to deism. Read the story of the Old Testament; you can confirm it from your secular history books, because the nation of the Jews is a fact of history, and the history that is recorded in the Old Testament is not only biblical history, it is secular history also. How did the Jews ever come into being? How do you explain the story of that people – everything that happened to them that is recorded in the Old Testament, indeed, everything that has happened to them since then – how do you explain all this? And I suggest to you that there is only one adequate explanation, and that is God.

That was the Jews' own explanation of themselves. They could not explain themselves and their history in any other way because they were a small nation and were often very foolish. They were nothing in comparison with the great dynasties and empires that surrounded them, and they would undoubtedly have been crushed and destroyed time without number had it not been that God had intervened. The Old Testament is a record of the constant interventions of God in a miraculous manner for the deliverance of his people. You must face the fact of the Jews, of the nation of Israel, and all their strange vicissitudes. (I am putting these things very broadly now in order that I may give you a comprehensive argument.)

But, secondly, and much more important than that argument about the Jews, and central to the whole biblical message, is what we find here – the coming of God the Son into this world. In the Old Testament there is constant prophecy about some great one who is to come, and then the New Testament tells us that he has come, it tells us of the appearing on the field of history of Jesus of Nazareth.

Now here is my challenge to all who like to call themselves humanists or deists or anything else – the phenomenon of Jesus Christ. Look at him, he belongs to history. I have often pointed out that you do not begin to understand human history apart from this person. The world that does not believe in him has to acknowledge that he has divided history. Our very date – 1967 – indicates that. He is in control of history. As the hymn puts it:

In the cross of Christ I glory,
Towering o'er the wrecks of time.
John Bowring

And the most momentous things in the history of the human race have been the direct result of the coming of this person into this world.

So look at the person of Christ; look at his teaching; look at his death upon the cross on Calvary's hill; look at his resurrection; look at his ascension. There would never have been a Christian church but for these facts. This is not theory, it does not claim to be. These are the sheer facts of history.

Now this book of Acts – and this is why we are dealing with it – is a book of *acts*, a book of facts, a book of history, and the whole case that is made by these early preachers is, 'We are witnesses of these things (see *Acts* 2:32). Peter could turn to the crowd on the day of Pentecost and say: You know these things, you have seen them (see *Acts* 2:22). Scientific verification? Here it was. The people of Jerusalem had seen these events; they had seen this person. Peter was not telling them a fairytale. He was telling them about someone whom they had seen and heard, someone they knew, whose miracles and death they had witnessed. They were witnesses!

So you must look at these things: God the Son, Jesus of Nazareth. Here is a phenomenon. You cannot explain him in terms of evolution; you cannot explain him in terms of civilization. He breaks all the rules. As Isaiah says in his fifty-third chapter, he is 'as a root out of a dry ground' (*Isa.* 53:2). You cannot explain his origin, you cannot explain what he did or how he behaved and, above all, you cannot explain his resurrection, his conquest of death and the grave. Here are facts that have brought the church into being.

And then, thirdly, the Bible tells us about the other great Person, God the Holy Spirit. We are told that he 'moved upon the face of the waters' (*Gen.* 1:2) – he was brooding over the face of the deep at the original creation. We read about him coming on men and women in the Old Testament and giving them abilities. But especially we learn about him from our Lord's teaching. Our Lord always refers to him as 'he', not 'it', not as an influence. Above all, I commend to you a study of our Lord's prophecies concerning the coming of the Holy Spirit. When he was about to leave the people, our Lord said to them, 'Let not your heart be troubled: ye believe in God, believe also in me' (*John* 14:1). He went on to say, 'I will not leave you comfortless: I will come to you' (*John* 14:18). He was not going to leave them to themselves. He said: I am going, but I am going to send you another teacher, another comforter, another person, who will be with you, and who will guide you and lead you into all truth, and bring back to your remembrance the things I have been teaching you. Do not be distressed at my departure. I will send him, and when he comes that is what he will do for you.

So there is the essential teaching of the Bible: 'God in three Persons, blessed Trinity', operating on this world, dealing with it, moulding its history, bringing to pass their own great and eternal purposes and plan of salvation. But, obviously, in view of my text,

I have now to concentrate in particular upon the activity of the Holy Spirit, and, of course, it is in the realm of his activity that we see most clearly the evidence of the supernatural realm, and have the greatest proof of the activity of God in human affairs, and the only hope of salvation.

What, then, is the work of the Holy Spirit? It can be divided into two main categories, and we see both demonstrated to perfection in this story of what happened amongst the Samaritans. There is, first of all, what we may call the *general* work of the Spirit. His first general work is that of enlightening us. According to biblical teaching, because of sin, because of the Fall, our minds are fallen, and we are all in darkness. Why do men and women not believe that they have souls? They do not understand because they are dark and blind. Why do they say that this is the only world? Because they cannot see the other. Why do they not believe in God? The Bible has given the answer in the Old Testament – it is because unbelievers are fools (*Psa.* 14:1). As the result of sin, they have become dulled in their understanding, in their minds, in their reasoning, in every aspect of their beings.

And there is ample evidence of this. I shall not go over it now because I have already dealt with it, in a sense, but this is how the apostle Paul sums it up: 'But the natural man receiveth not the things of the Spirit of God: for they are foolishness unto him: neither can he know them, because they are spiritually discerned' (*1 Cor.* 2:14). People in sin are like people who are entirely lacking (to use a random illustration) in a sense of music and an appreciation of music. You may play them, for example, a symphony by Beethoven or by Brahms and they will tell you to turn off 'that beastly noise'. Why? Because, you see, they have no appreciation. They do not understand music and so cannot follow it and do not want it. Similarly, the 'natural man' lacks a spiritual faculty, and so says that the realm of the Spirit is all nonsense and foolishness. Such people are deluding themselves about the highest things of all.

What, then, does the Spirit do? First, as I said, the Spirit enlightens us. The apostle says, 'But we speak the wisdom of God in a mystery, even the hidden wisdom . . . which none of the princes of this world knew: for had they known it, they would not have crucified the Lord of glory' (*1 Cor.* 2:7–8). Paul says, 'Eye hath not seen, nor ear heard, neither have entered into the heart of man, the things which God hath prepared for them that love him' (*1 Cor.* 2:9). Men and women, with all their scientific observation, say, 'We cannot see God. Go up in a spacecraft – you will not see the Father, Son, and Holy Spirit. Therefore they are not there.' Paul answered them before they ever thought of their argument – 'Eye cannot see . . .' He speaks of God 'dwelling in the light which no man can approach unto' (*1 Tim.* 6:16). You can go higher and higher into space but you will never arrive at the realm in which God dwells. God is Spirit! You are dealing with a realm that is entirely beyond the reach of human beings at the very acme of their achievements. But the Spirit enlightens – 'But God', says Paul, 'hath revealed them unto us by his Spirit: for the Spirit searcheth all things, yea, the deep things of God' (*1 Cor.* 2:10).

Have you never thought of this? Take someone who for most of his life has been a humanist or a deist, or anything you like, and suddenly becomes a Christian. Look at a man like the apostle Paul himself. There he was, opposed to Jesus Christ, telling us, 'I verily thought with myself, that I ought to do many things contrary to the name of Jesus of Nazareth' (*Acts* 26:9). He hated him, he reviled him, he said, in effect, 'This man is a blasphemer. He says he is equal to God. He claims to be the Son of God! It's monstrous. I must stop it.' And Paul was absolutely sincere and genuine. And yet you think of him, do you not, as the great apostle Paul, preaching Jesus Christ and the gospel. What brought about the change? Oh, it was the enlightenment that the Spirit alone can give!

Secondly, the Spirit not only gives us the ability to understand, he *convicts* us. You know, apart from the Holy Spirit, I do not understand myself. I do not understand the whole of life. What is it that suddenly comes to men and women and disturbs them? They have been perfectly happy living a certain kind of life but suddenly they begin to feel uncomfortable. Something nags at them. Their conscience begins to be disturbed within them. They are troubled and do not know what to do. They try to shake off this unease but they cannot – what is it? This is the convicting power of the Holy Spirit.

Now do not misunderstand me. I know that my reasoning and argument will never convince you of anything, but, thank God, I stand in this pulpit and give you these arguments because I know that the Holy Spirit can convict you, and you know it. You wish he would not, but he does, and he will not leave you alone. And, let me tell you, if he has started with you, he will keep on with you. Be careful how you resist the Spirit. This is part of his ordinary work; that is what he did with the Samaritans. What made the Samaritans believe the gospel? Here was a stranger, Philip; they knew nothing about him. He was just an ordinary man. Why did they listen to him? Oh, it was the Spirit in the man, and he was convicting and he was converting. And he changes and regenerates. He gives us a new nature and a new life. This is his regular way of working.

Then, thirdly, the Spirit goes on doing what we call a *sanctifying* work. Having brought us to realize that we have souls and that we are guilty before God, and that we are lost, the Spirit reveals to us the truth about the Lord Jesus Christ as the Son of God, as one who has taken our sins upon himself and has borne our punishment so that in him we can be forgiven. I believe that and I find peace. I know God, and the Spirit comes within me and works within me, showing me sin and evil that I have never dreamt of or imagined, giving me power and understanding. He brings about a gradual work of sanctification and deliverance from the power and the pollution of sin. That is the regular work of the Spirit.

And the Spirit had been doing all that work in these Samaritans before Peter and John ever came down amongst them. It was because of that work of the Spirit that they believed the gospel and were baptized, both men and women. Now they were attending upon the ministry and the preaching of Philip, and were growing from day to day and were rejoicing in this great salvation. But still this is only the ordinary work of the Spirit, his general work.

But the Spirit also has a *special* work, and it is, perhaps, in this special work that we see most distinctly, not only the reality and the existence of the supernatural realm, and of God in three Persons, but also the mighty action of this triune God in the world and in human affairs. What is this special work of the Spirit, this final answer to all humanism and deism, and all that denies the supernatural and the influence of the supernatural in this world of time? There is, of course, no time to tell you all there is to say about this. I shall only pick out some two or three aspects that are of vital importance.

First, there are the Scriptures themselves. I believe some people are observing this day as 'Bible Sunday'; we do not do that because every Sunday is Bible Sunday. These people mean, of course, that they want you to contribute to the distribution of the Scriptures through the various Bible Societies. Bible Sunday; yes, but what is the Bible? What are these Scriptures? How do you explain them? Can this book be explained in naturalistic terms or solely in terms of innate human abilities and power and reason and understanding?

Well, I suggest that the first honest thing to do is to ask the biblical writers themselves, and they are honest enough to tell you that that is not the explanation. They all tell you that what they have written is what they have received, what has been given to them. They say it in the Old Testament; they say it in the New Testament. Some almost complain about it. There is a prophet called Jeremiah, and poor Jeremiah, because he kept on delivering the message that God gave him, he was always getting into trouble. So he came to a solemn decision that he would speak no more in the name of God. He did not want to be unpopular. He did not want to be maltreated. He did not want to be unhappy. He was not going to say any more. But he had to say more, and what he had to say was not what he had thought out or wanted to say, but what God gave him to say (see *Jer.* 20:8–9).

No, the explanation that these men offer is simply that they had been given a revelation. They were able men, some of them, but some were quite ordinary; some of the apostles were most ordinary men. Indeed, the authorities in Jerusalem, as we have seen, had already dismissed them as 'unlearned and ignorant men' (*Acts* 4:13) – fishermen. They said, in effect, 'What do fishermen know about these things? Who are they?' And this is a question that you have to answer. How was it that a fisherman like Peter could expound Scriptures as he did – as we see in the second chapter of Acts? How could he preach as he did? How could he get three thousand converts as he did? There is only one explanation: it was not Peter, but the power of the Spirit upon him.

And it is the same with all the biblical writings. Revelation! These men did not concoct these ideas. They say, 'The burden of the Lord', or, 'The message of the Lord' came to them. They will tell you how they were taken up by the Spirit. A kind of divine *afflatus* came upon them. They got into a state, if you like, of semi-ecstasy. Suddenly they were receiving messages that they had never thought of at all, and a compulsion to deliver them, and an assurance that they would be guided as they spoke these words and wrote them down. Inspiration! And this is the only adequate explanation of the Scriptures: revelation of the material and inspiration that enabled it to be proclaimed and recorded.

Now this is what the Bible itself says; these are the very statements that are made by the writers. The apostle Paul, for instance, was a brilliant man yet never for a moment did he say, 'This is my understanding.' He said: I was a fool, a blasphemer. I was a persecutor and a denier. But God mastered me, and gave me this dispensation, this knowledge, to deliver to you. So he writes to Timothy and says: 'All scripture is given by inspiration of God' – it is God-breathed – 'and is profitable for doctrine, for reproof, for correction, for instruction in righteousness: that the man of God may be perfect, thoroughly furnished unto all good works' (2 *Tim.* 3:16–17). Peter, obviously, must say the same thing, and he does. Writing in his second epistle, he says, 'Knowing this first, that no prophecy of the scripture is of any private interpretation. For the prophecy came not in old time by the will of man: but holy men of God spake as they were moved' – borne along, carried along – 'by the Holy Ghost' (2 *Pet.* 1:20–21).

So you cannot explain these Scriptures in general apart from revelation and inspiration, which is the work, always, of the Holy Spirit. But let me give you one particular proof of this. This is what we call *prophecy*. To me, the argument of prophecy is sufficient in and of itself, not only to prove the being of God but also the whole of the supernatural realm. I am thinking of the prophecies in the Old Testament, the writings of the great prophets, and other various forms of prophecy. What do I find there? I find most astounding things; I find predictions in detail of events that subsequently came to pass after a long period of time. I find that prophets in the Old Testament said, 'This and this is going to happen.' And those predictions did take place, even in the time of Old Testament history.

But still more important is this: these great prophets wrote hundreds of years before the birth of Jesus Christ, and yet they tell you about his coming. Micah, for instance, wrote that he would be born in a place called Bethlehem. Nobody else knew that, but Micah said it 800 years before it happened. Other Old Testament writers give all sorts of details about his coming, about his life and about his death – all stated plainly and clearly. And you have to explain that; you have to explain how men writing long before the time could tell you precise details that were later proved true. Peter, again, makes this point. Writing to Christian people who had been disturbed by the humanists of their age, who were trying to say that Jesus Christ was only a man and not God, he says:

We have not followed cunningly devised fables, when we made known unto you the power and coming of our Lord Jesus Christ, but were eyewitnesses of his majesty. For he received from God the Father honour and glory, when there came such a voice to him from the excellent glory, This is my beloved Son, in whom I am well pleased (2 Pet. 1:16–17).

Peter says, in effect, 'Now look here. John, James and I were with him on the Mount of Transfiguration. We saw him changed. We were with him. We were with him going up and we saw what happened to him there. He was transfigured, transformed. He was shining with a glory such as we had never seen. We saw it, and we heard the voice from heaven.'

But then Peter continues: 'We have also a more sure word of prophecy; whereunto ye do well that ye take heed, as unto a light that shineth in a dark place, until the day dawn, and the day star arise in your hearts' (verse 19). He is saying: If you do not believe my testimony, go back to the prophets. Take the word of prophecy. Look at what is said. Look at what the prophets predicted in detail. See how it has happened in Jesus Christ. There is your evidence, there is your assurance – all the detailed prophecies concerning the coming of the Son of God

And, indeed, in addition, as Peter was so careful to point out in his sermon on the day of Pentecost, there is the prophecy of Joel. Here was a tremendous event that happened on the day of Pentecost and people said, 'What's this?' Some of them said, 'These men are full of new wine' (*Acts* 2:13). Look at them. Their faces are shining, they are filled with joy, they are in an ecstasy – they are obviously drunk!

But Peter said: They cannot be drunk. They have not had time to get drunk. It is only the third hour of the day. No, no, this is not drunkenness.

And Peter continued: 'This is that which was spoken' – predicted and prophesied – 'by the prophet Joel' (*Acts* 2:16). Centuries earlier Joel had said that after the coming of the Son of God, the Deliverer, the Messiah, God would pour out his blessing upon all flesh. He was doing it; he had done it. This was it! So here, you see, is another tremendous fulfilment and verification of prophecy. How do you explain that? How does a man, so many centuries before the time, prophesy these detailed, historical events in this extraordinary manner?

And then there are the prophecies of our Lord himself. I have already reminded you of how he told the disciples, before he left them, that he was going to send the Spirit upon them. In the first chapter of this book of Acts you see him with his followers and he tells them to stay where they are in Jerusalem. They are not to start preaching, but to wait. And he says, 'But ye shall receive power, after that the Holy Ghost is come upon you' (verse 8). Ten days later he came upon them. Our Lord had predicted it; it came to pass. And that is not the only thing he predicted. Jesus Christ prophesied the destruction of the city of Jerusalem. They did not believe him, but it happened. He was crucified, let us say, in AD 33. Jerusalem, as he described in detail, was destroyed in AD 70.

Our Lord said another thing, and if you want a little bit of contemporary history, listen to this. He said that Jerusalem should be trodden down of the Gentiles for a period of time but that time would come to an end. Do not misunderstand me; I am not saying that the Arabs may not reconquer Jerusalem, but I am asking you to face this fact: what has happened this very year is rather strange, is it not?[1]

[1] This refers to the Six-Day War between Israel and neighbouring Arab states in June 1967. As a result of the war Israel gained control of an area over three times its pre-1967 size, including the West Bank and all of Jerusalem.

Is it not time that we began to think? How easy it is to say that there is nothing beyond man. But how can anybody predict and prophesy things like this? Not only that, as I was pointing out to you earlier, there is nothing that explains the state of the world as it is today apart from this book. Do not forget that it was Jesus Christ who said that there would be 'wars and rumours of wars' (*Matt*. 24:6). In spite of the arrogance and the pride and the civilization of man, our Lord forecast that man would continue in sin and there would be calamities. And we are getting them. It is a fulfilment of his own word. These are facts.

But there are other facts. Look what happened about our Lord's own baptism. There he was at the age of thirty, an extraordinary man, and yet he spent his time working as a carpenter. At the age of thirty he went to John the Baptist and asked him to baptize him. John was unhappy about this but he did it. And as our Lord was coming out of the water, the Holy Spirit descended upon him in the form of a dove, and filled him with power. Though he was the Son of God, he had laid aside all his divine powers. He had taken on him human nature and was determined to live in this world as a man. Therefore even he could have done nothing if he had not received that baptism of the Spirit, for he said after it, as he stood up to preach in the synagogue in Nazareth:

The Spirit of the Lord is upon me, because he hath anointed me to preach the gospel to the poor; he hath sent me to heal the brokenhearted, to preach deliverance to the captives, and recovering of sight to the blind, to set at liberty them that are bruised, to preach the acceptable year of the Lord.

Then Luke continues:

And he closed the book, and he gave it again to the minister, and sat down . . . And he began to say unto them, This day is this scripture fulfilled in your ears (Luke 4:18–21).

The Spirit came upon him and gave him the power and the ability to preach and to work his miracles. He had done none of this for thirty years. Read of his activity for three crowded years; it is all the result of this endowment of the power of the Spirit.

And then come on again to the day of Pentecost. Pentecost is a fact! We would not be here now but for the day of Pentecost. The apostles had been utterly cast down by the crucifixion and the death of our Lord. Certainly he had helped them after the resurrection by preaching to them, but still they did not have power. They could not witness; they did not have assurance; they had no authority. But on the day of Pentecost our Lord sent the Spirit upon them and they were able to speak with authority and power and to do all that we read about in the opening chapters of Acts.

In the fourth chapter of this book of Acts we read of how, in answer to their prayer, 'The place was shaken where they were assembled together' (verse 31). These are facts. And look at what happened to the Samaritans. We are dealing with history here. The Samaritans had believed the preaching of Philip, they had been baptized, they were Christians, the Spirit of God was in them. But, as I read here, 'For as yet he [the Holy Spirit] was fallen upon none of them: only they were baptized in the name of the Lord Jesus.' But, 'Then laid they [Peter and John] their hands on them, and they received the Holy Ghost' (*Acts* 8:16–17). This is a fact. A fact of history, a fact of experience. And it is something that the Spirit has been continuing to do throughout the running centuries.

We have recently been celebrating the 450th anniversary of the commencement of the Protestant Reformation in 1517. How do you explain that? Why did it happen then? Why did it happen through this man Martin Luther? There were many monks, many abler monks, why this man? How was he enabled? Where did the power, the courage, the insight and the understanding come from? Ask Luther himself and he will always tell you that it was not he, it was God, God the Holy Spirit, acting in him and through him. And this is the story also of all the great revivals of history.

You know, my friends, that the church is in a bad condition at the present time, but this is not the first time that the church has been weak and ineffective and cast down. It has been like this many a time before. How has the church kept going? Is it because of men like myself? Not at all! We would have ruined it centuries ago. There is only one explanation – God sending revival. When people have been despairing, at the end of their tether and on the verge of giving up, suddenly there is a sound of a mighty rushing wind and he comes upon them; the descent of the Spirit. As he came upon these men in Samaria who were already Christians, he comes upon the church. It is our only hope. If we are to rely upon men and women and their organized campaigns, good though they may be, we are finished. But when God sends the Spirit! It will be the world under conviction and crying out, 'Men and brethren, what shall we do?' Revivals! The coming of the Spirit of God!

Can you explain the origin of a revival? Can your humanism, your psychology, explain it? They try to, of course. You are familiar with the book, *The Battle for the Mind*.[1] I answered it on this very point and I have never received a reply. You cannot explain the day of Pentecost in terms of psychology. You cannot explain any revival in terms of human activity. I can prove that to you. I have known many men who, not understanding the doctrine of Scripture, have tried to organize a revival; I have seen them doing it! They said that a revival came in the past through people praying all night and making open confession of sins. So a man called Finney said, 'Every time you do that, you can get a revival. You can get it whenever you like.' Well, I have known large numbers of men who have tried that with great thoroughness, but they have never obtained a revival. Never! It cannot be done. A revival always comes unexpectedly, suddenly, in spite of man, and there is only one explanation, it is the activity of God, the Holy Spirit.

Revivals are evidences of the supernatural realm and of the being of the triune God. And the result of this great activity is always, as it was on the day of Pentecost and as it was amongst these Samaritans – clarity of understanding, assurance of salvation and joy in the Lord, exceptional power of speech, understanding, gifts of miracles and healings, tongues maybe – all that was prophesied by Joel: 'Your sons and your daughters shall prophesy, your old men shall dream dreams: your young men shall see visions; and also upon the servants and upon the handmaidens in those days will I pour out my spirit' (*Joel* 2:28–29). Not on your great philosophers only but 'on the servants and the handmaidens' this power shall come. And the history of the church is but a verification of this prophecy of Joel that we see repeated right through this book of Acts.

[1] William Sargant, *The Battle for the Mind: A Physiology of Conversion and Brainwashing*. Dr Lloyd-Jones' reply was *Conversions: Psychological and Spiritual* (IVP, 1959), reprinted in Knowing the Times (Edinburgh: Banner of Truth, 1989).

So, then, I leave you with my question: Are you aware of all this? Are you aware that there is another realm, a supernatural realm? Are you aware that *God is*, and in three Persons? Or do you adopt the view that says that you, and you alone, count, that everything is in your hands, that it is for you to make a perfect world, it is for you to put an end to war, to reconcile separated husbands and wives, to put an end to theft and robbery and chicanery and dishonesty – it is all left to *you* with your teaching and your education and your appeals? Thank God, that is not true, otherwise the world would be utterly and completely hopeless.

Even men who are not Christians are beginning to say strange things today. In the paper a few weeks back I read an interview with an industrial authority and he said, 'The need today is for changed people.' Of course it is! Men and women in sin do not respond to your appeals, they do not want to. You can say, 'But this is unreasonable.' They reply, 'You can say it's unreasonable but I'm fighting for my life.' That is why there is going to be trouble on the railways tomorrow. The labour minister says, 'It's daft', and yet they are doing it. What is the matter?

Now I am only taking one case; they are all 'daft'. What is the use of education and culture? This is the twentieth century, the century of knowledge, the century of man, the century of humanism. But that is the problem, human nature; can you change it? Of course not. It is impossible. The need is for people to be changed, and to be given power. And there is only one way in which that can ever happen, and that is the descent of the Holy Spirit. He can change people; he can give a new birth, a new heart, a new nature, a new life, a new understanding. He has done so. The most glorious periods in the history of this country have always been the periods that have followed reformation and revival. Great advances in science, in art, in literature, in politics, in music, have all followed revivals as men and women who have been changed by the power of the Spirit have then proceeded to deal with their environment.

What happened to these people in Samaria can happen to you, and, if it does not happen to you, you are left to yourself. You cannot deal with yourself; you cannot deal with your world. You have to die and you have to face God in the judgment and you cannot do it. What can you do? Quite right: until you ask that question you are damned. But the moment you ask the question, like those men in Acts listening to Peter who said, 'Men and brethren, what can we do?', the answer comes back: 'Repent, and be baptized every one of you in the name of Jesus Christ for the remission of sins, and ye shall receive the gift of the Holy Ghost. For the promise is unto you, and to your children, and to all that are afar off' (*Acts* 2:37–39).

My friend, the supernatural is around you, and you can enter into it by faith in Christ. Eventually we shall all enter into it, but it will either be to glory, with God the Father, the Son, and the Holy Spirit, or else it will be to eternal spiritual darkness. May God give us grace to listen to the message of this eighth chapter of the book of the Acts of the Apostles, and cry out to him for salvation, and for this fulness of the Holy Spirit.

9

True and False Belief

Then Simon himself believed also: and when he was baptized, he continued with Philip, and wondered, beholding the miracles and signs which were done . . . And when Simon saw that through laying on of the apostles' hands the Holy Ghost was given, he offered them money, saying, Give me also this power, that on whomsoever I lay hands, he may receive the Holy Ghost. But Peter said unto him, Thy money perish with thee, because thou hast thought that the gift of God may be purchased with money. Thou hast neither part nor lot in this matter: for thy heart is not right in the sight of God. Repent therefore of this thy wickedness, and pray God, if perhaps the thought of thine heart may be forgiven thee. For I perceive that thou art in the gall of bitterness, and in the bond of iniquity. Then answered Simon, and said, Pray ye the Lord for me, that none of these things which ye have spoken come upon me (Acts 8:13,18–24).

This is a most extraordinary case, and we are going to look at it together. We have been dealing with the earlier part of the history that is recorded in this chapter, the story of how the gospel first began to spread from the city of Jerusalem. Our Lord had prophesied that it would spread first in Judaea itself, then in Samaria, and then to the uttermost ends of the earth. And we have been seeing how Philip the evangelist took the gospel to Samaria, with marvellous results, and also, incidentally, we have been introduced to this man Simon.

Now this is what we are told about Simon:

There was a certain man, called Simon, which beforetime in the same city used sorcery, and bewitched the people of Samaria, giving out that himself was some great one: to whom they all gave heed, from the least to the greatest, saying, This man is the great power of God. And to him they had regard, because that of long time he had bewitched them with sorceries. But when they believed Philip preaching the things concerning the kingdom of God, and the name of Jesus Christ, they were baptized, both men and women.

And then the record goes on to tell us:

Simon himself believed also: and when he was baptized, he continued with Philip, and wondered, beholding the miracles and signs which were done (Acts 8:9–13).

And then we have seen how the apostles in Jerusalem heard that, as the result of Philip's preaching in the power of the Holy Spirit, a number of these people in Samaria had believed the gospel. Now that was very surprising news to these apostles, who were Jews. They believed the report, however, and sent two of the company, Peter and John, down to Samaria. And, you remember, we were told how, when the apostles had prayed for the people there, they laid their hands upon them, and as the result of that, the Holy Spirit fell upon them. And then we have the extraordinary statement that Simon offered Peter and John money so that he, too, might have the same power.

Now why do I call attention to this? Well, I have many reasons. One is that it is a part of the history, and it is not for me to choose what I expound to you from the Scriptures. As I have been explaining Sunday after Sunday, I am directing attention to these early chapters of the book of the Acts of the Apostles because it is thus alone that we can come to know what Christianity really is, and what the Christian church is meant to be. I have to say, again, that, unfortunately, this is something which has become difficult to know in the modern world where there are so many different voices, so many misrepresentations of the Christian faith. The only hope for any individual or for the world is this Christian message and there is therefore no greater tragedy than confusion with respect to it. That is why we are dealing with it, and here we have the authentic account. If you really want to know what Christianity is, here it is. And the point I have been emphasizing all along is that it is history.

Let us once and for ever get rid of the notion that the Christian faith is just a teaching. It is not. What Christians believe is the result of something that happened in this world of time. It is sheer history and this puts it into a different category from all other teaching. So we must always be true to the history. And as the incident with Simon happened in connection with the spread of the gospel, I must call your attention to it, whether or not I want to. It is not a happy thing to call attention to a case like this, but I want to try to show you how important it is that I do so.

What do we find here? Now there are a number of points that should strike us at once as we come across a story like this. For example, there is the amazing honesty of the Scriptures. They conceal nothing. They are not some carefully concocted account, but an honest report; these are the events that literally and actually took place. I would say once more that if I had no other reason for believing the Scripture to be the Word of God, this honesty would in itself be sufficient for me. The Bible not only paints the good things in its characters and people and institutions, it also tells us the bad aspects. It shows the weaknesses of some of its noblest characters; it shows saints falling into sin. And why does it do this? It is for our benefit. It is open, it is honest, it is a book that you can trust. It is not some special pleading.

And that leads me to add that the purpose of the Scriptures is not to boost Christianity. Now that is where this faith of ours differs from all the cults and so many other teachings. The literature attached to those is always out to boost them. It is like the label on a quack medicine bottle that makes extravagant claims but never tells you anything about the remedy. All is 'in here', everything seems to be perfect. But the Scriptures are not like that at all; they are not, I repeat, a case of special pleading. The Scriptures have only one grand objective, and that is to bring us to a knowledge of the truth. They are not just out to win adherents to the Christian church. Incidentally, of course, that follows, but that is not the primary object.

Now men and women, in their methods and movements and in their institutions, are so different. They are anxious to get adherents, they want to get followers, and they are not always scrupulous as to their methods. The members of the different political parties bring out all the excellencies of what they have done, but they say nothing about the other side. Then when they deal with opposing parties, they only show the defects and say nothing about the good points. Now that is how human beings behave. But the Scriptures, on the other hand, are concerned to present the truth to us that we may know exactly what it is. And, you notice, they do that in two main ways – positively and negatively.

Now so far, in considering the eighth chapter of Acts, we have been looking at the positive presentation of the gospel and of the truth. We have been told what Philip said, and what the others who had been scattered abroad in the persecution said. They preached the Word, they preached Jesus Christ and the things pertaining to the kingdom of God, and we have seen the response. All that is positive. And there, as I have been trying to show you, we have seen what the gospel is, how people believe it and what happens to them as the result of believing it. And we have seen, therefore, a general picture as to what the Christian church is and what its message is.

But that is not the only way of discovering the truth about the church. The Scriptures also present the truth to us in a negative manner, and that is what we have here in this case of Simon the sorcerer. Having been given a positive presentation of the truth, we now see it in contrast with the false, the spurious, that which simulates the truth, that which is merely some kind of temporary appearance.

Now the Scriptures, in their honesty, give us this in order that they may warn us against the false, and in order that we may be more certain of the truth. And so, as we look at the case of this man Simon, we shall not only be seeing what the false is, but, by the contrast that he presents, we shall also see still more clearly what the true is, because, on the surface, this man Simon is in exactly the same position as the others who believed in Samaria – and yet he was not in the same position at all. And as we see why he was not, and how he was not, we shall see still more clearly the true Christian position.

Now why do you think the Scriptures take all this trouble? Why was Luke, who wrote the book of Acts, led and inspired by the Spirit to record the case of this particular man, Simon the sorcerer? And the answer, obviously, is that it is a part of the love of God to us. He is anxious to safeguard our interests.

Or let me put it to you like this: our eternal salvation depends upon our relationship to this message. That is why we preach it. We do not preach it as a human expedient or as something that is going to make us feel a little bit happier for the moment. No, no, we preach it because it not only affects our life in this world, but also our death. I go further, it affects our eternal destiny.

And it is because the Scriptures teach that, and hold that view, that they take the trouble to put a case like Simon before us. As my eternal destiny depends upon my right relationship to this truth, there is nothing in the universe today that is so important as my actually being in that right relationship. I may think I am but I may not be. So the gospel, some of these books, have been written for us in order that we may in no sense deceive or mislead ourselves.

Now I am certain that this is why we have this particular bit of history. How much easier it would have been for the author to slide over this incident and just give us a marvellous picture of the results of Philip's preaching, ending on the note, 'There was great joy in that city.' And then he could have just told us how the apostles came and laid hands on the people with the result that they were filled with the Spirit, and there was still greater joy, and they were thrilled and in an ecstasy – how marvellous! But in fact this discordant note is suddenly thrown in.

Why? Ah, I repeat that there is only one real explanation: it is the love of God that is concerned that we should never be deluded or misled. It is in order that our souls' eternal salvation might be made secure. I see it as a glorious example of God's concern about our souls that he troubles not only to give us the truth positively, but also to give it to us negatively in order that we may examine ourselves by it.

So, then, what is the lesson here? Well, I have tried to divide it like this. The first point that obviously strikes us here is that it is clearly possible for us to think that we are Christians without being Christians at all. It is possible for us to delude ourselves and to imagine that we are Christians when we are not. This is perfectly clear, is it not, in the case of Simon the sorcerer? Others believed the gospel, and, we are told, 'Simon himself believed also: and when he was baptized, he continued with Philip, and wondered, beholding the miracles and signs which were done' (verse 13).

Now I can imagine someone saying, 'What an extraordinary thing to present before us! I would have thought that your great object would be just to do everything you could to persuade people to become Christians.' It is: and yet this is necessary, because this kind of thing can happen. Here is a man who thought he was a Christian, but he was not.

And Simon is not the only one; there are other examples of this self-deception in other parts of the Scriptures. Listen to this from the end of the second chapter of the Gospel according to St John:

Now when he [our Lord] was in Jerusalem at the Passover, in the feast day, many believed in his name, when they saw the miracles which he did. But Jesus did not commit himself unto them, because he knew all men, and needed not that any should testify of man: for he knew what was in man (John 1:23–25).

Now this is what astonishes people so often, and I will tell you why I am dealing with it. We all know many people who are outside the Christian church because they talk about 'hypocrisy'. They are not interested, they say, because Christians are 'a pack of hypocrites'. But I want to try to show you that the church herself is as concerned about hypocrites as you are. The church never pretends that she is perfect.

Here she is telling us that it is possible for people to think they are Christians when they are not, and to come into the church when they really should not be there. This, again, always attracts me in the Gospels. The Lord Jesus Christ, at times, seems to go out of his way to hinder people from coming to him; he discourages them.

Why does he do that? There is only one answer: he has come into the world to save the world. Yes, but when he sees people coming to him in the wrong way or for the wrong reason, he discourages them for their sakes. So we must get rid of this notion that the church is just here as an institution that wants to flourish, as big business and other businesses flourish, with increasing numbers of customers. The man on the street says, 'Those parsons are fighting for their jobs. They're losing people at the present time, so there they are, weeping and cajoling, doing everything they can to win people. They don't care what they do as long as they can get them.'

But I am trying to show you that the truth is the exact opposite. The Bible is not interested primarily in numbers; it is very interested in truth and in reality, and it is this book itself that shows the false, the hypocritical, the spurious, and warns us against it. Our Lord, there in Jerusalem, saw these people coming to him and they were smiling and wanted to join the company. But he would not have them because he knew that they were coming for the wrong reasons. They thought they had understood his message but he realized that they had not.

But that is not the only example that I can give you. Take the parable of the sower in Mark 4. What is the point of that parable? Is it not just to warn us of this very danger? Here is our Lord himself saying that he was not misled by appearances. He says, in effect, 'There are people who seem to accept this truth of mine but they have not really done so. There is a temporary appearance of believing the truth but it is not real, it does not last, it is of no value.' So he puts it quite plainly there in the parable of the sower and in his own exposition of it.

And our Lord gives the same teaching in the three parables that are recorded in Matthew 25. The first one is the parable of the ten virgins, five of whom were wise and five foolish. That is a parable of profession, a parable of people inside the church, all of them thinking they are Christians. But our Lord's whole object is to show that half of them are not Christians at all but are like the foolish virgins. And the same point is made in the parable of the talents and in the parable of the sheep and goats, which is the third parable in that tremendously important chapter.

In all these instances our Lord is showing us that we must be clear about these things. There is nothing more terrible than for people to think that they are Christians when they are not. There is nothing more terrifying than for people to go through a lifetime thinking that they are Christians and that they are safe, and then to find at the end that they have been misleading themselves altogether. You remember the terrifying way in which our Lord puts that at the end of the Sermon on the Mount? These are his very words:

Not every one that saith unto me, Lord, Lord, shall enter into the kingdom of heaven; but he that doeth the will of my Father which is in heaven. Many will say to me in that day, Lord, Lord, have we not prophesied in thy name? and in thy name have cast out devils? and in thy name done many wonderful works? And then will I profess unto them, I never knew you: depart from me, ye that work iniquity (Matt. 7:21–23).

And it is because of this that the Scriptures give us warning stories such as this of Simon the sorcerer. Here is a man who was fully satisfied that he was a Christian, and yet the record shows us that he was never a Christian at all.

So the second point that we must look at raises a question: How does this come to pass? Now I need not weary you in describing the various ways in which it can happen. One of these ways does not happen as much today as it once did. This is that sometimes people think they are Christians when they are not because they have been brought up in a Christian atmosphere. There is this fatal idea that because you are a child of Christian parents you are automatically a Christian. Oh, the history of the church shows this so frequently! The children of Christian parents, in a sense, are in a very dangerous position because they assume they are Christians and everybody else also assumes that they are. They, of all people, need to test and examine themselves in the light of this particular teaching. My dear friend, if you are the sort of person who says to me, 'I was brought up to be a Christian; I've always been a Christian', then I have to say to you that nobody is born a Christian. The whole message here is that to be a Christian you must be born again.

How easy it is to assume that you are a Christian because of your upbringing, your family or custom, or loyalty to parents; indeed, I have known some strange reasons for people falling into this very error of Simon Magus. I remember one man who persuaded himself that he was a Christian for one reason only, and that was that he wanted to marry a particular girl. I am not saying he was dishonest, I say he was misleading himself. What he was really after was to get this girl, and so he, like Simon, said he believed. He accepted everything. But the man was never truly a Christian, as subsequent facts made perfectly clear.

And another very common cause of this tragic mistake, of course, is that certain people always tend to be carried along with the crowd, what is called today 'getting on to the bandwagon'. If there is a religious campaign, or a religious revival, you always find that certain people are carried along. Everybody is believing, so they believe also. Now, again, I am not saying they are dishonest. I could easily demonstrate that there are two main types of hypocrisy – conscious hypocrisy and unconscious hypocrisy – and I am dealing with unconscious hypocrisy. I believe that Simon Magus belongs to that category. He had no idea that his 'belief' was false, and neither have these people who are 'carried along' by the stream, as it were. Everybody seems to be believing, so they believe. They do not quite know why, but they do what others do, and think that they are Christians.

Then, of course, there is another reason, the responsibility and blame for which – let me admit it quite frankly and honestly – is often to be laid at the door of an evangelist who presses for immediate decisions, and gives the impression that if you do not respond at once you will never have a chance again. Nothing else causes such a proliferation of people like Simon the sorcerer. Such pressure should never be brought to bear upon anybody. The more you study this case and see the contrast between Simon and the others, the more you will see this.

No, what makes people Christians is not that they decide for Christ but that they are 'born again'; it is that the Spirit of God lays hold on them. And if the Spirit of God lays hold on them it is bound to become apparent – whether at once, or in ten years' time, I do not care. But that is what is important. It is not the registration on earth but the registration in heaven that matters. And so there is so often this confusion. I could give you many stories, as a pastor, of how this confusion has been brought to pass. People come to me and they say, 'You know, I want you to tell me, am I a Christian or am I not?' – they do not know. Someone will say, 'I took a decision, I signed a card, and I did this, that and the other, but, you know, I doubt whether I'm a Christian.' What a wonderful thing that is; that is the Spirit of God dealing with that person. I always like to be asked that, because here are people who have examined themselves and have not merely gone on with the wrong assumption. It is the Scripture that teaches one to ask questions. I do not rely upon what I say or upon what you do; we must rely upon what the Spirit of God does.

There, then, are four reasons why it is possible for people to think they are Christians when they are not. But the ultimate explanation of it all is this – and this is what comes out so terrifyingly in this case of Simon – it is the deceitfulness of the natural, unregenerate human heart. Jeremiah says, 'The heart is deceitful above all things, and desperately wicked: who can know it? (*Jer.* 17:9). Our hearts are so deceitful that we ourselves do not know that we are being deceived. And the deceit is so subtle. If the heart thinks it can get peace and quiet and rest, if it thinks it can silence its conscience by doing something, it will do it. I repeat that the trouble with all of us by nature is that we not only fool other people, we fool ourselves. That is the greatest folly of all, is it not, that you have fooled yourself? It is because you have forgotten God, who cannot be fooled, who knows the heart and who tries it, and who alone sees us exactly as we are. But the natural, unregenerate heart – oh, how deceitful it is! A man thinks he can be in the church and out of it at the same time; he thinks he can have his fill of pleasure in the world and go to heaven because he believes in Christ. He will believe in anything as long as he gets his own will and his own way. Have you realized that your heart is deceitful? Are you still trusting yourself? If you are, you are not a Christian.

But, in addition, there is the devil, the adversary of our souls. The apostle Paul tells us that the devil sometimes transforms himself into 'an angel of light' (*2 Cor.* 11:14). The devil is quite prepared to tell a man or woman to believe in Christ and to persuade them that they have done so, if in that way he can ensure the loss of their souls. The devil will encourage people to say they believe if he knows that that will silence their consciences. If it will stop them thinking and reasoning and investigating and making sure of where they are, then the devil will make them say, 'All I must do is say I believe on the Lord Jesus. Then I'm all right.' So they say, 'This is wonderful. Now I've said that I can go on and enjoy myself; it's all right – the blood of Christ.'

Oh, how often have we all done this! How often have Jeremiah's words come true: 'They have healed also the hurt of the daughter of my people slightly [lightly], saying, Peace, peace; when there is no peace' (*Jer.* 6:14). I remember a man coming to me who had committed a terrible sin; he came to tell me about it quite honestly, but before I had time to say anything to him, he said, 'Of course, I know it's all right, the blood of Jesus covers it.' He was too healthy; the man had not felt the enormity of the sin. That is how the devil uses Scripture. 'The devils also believe,' says James, 'and tremble' (*James* 2:19), and the devil as an angel of light will get people to take 'decisions' if he thinks that this will stand between them and regeneration and rebirth, and the agony of soul that will lead them to cry out to God to deal with them and to give them new life.

The Scriptures are very realistic, are they not? This is a very unhappy picture, but it is here, my friend, this is what can happen in the church at any time and it tends to happen at all times, especially where the gospel is preached in sincerity and in truth, and we must be aware of this.

Let me show you what it is possible for a false believer to do and say. This is shown here all too plainly and it is terrifying. 'Then Simon himself believed also.' What does that mean? It means that he said that he believed that Jesus of Nazareth was the Son of God – that is what Philip, you remember, had been preaching. He had preached Christ. He had preached the name of Jesus Christ and the kingdom of God. We have seen that the very essence of this message concerned this Jesus, the only begotten Son of God. It was a message about his virgin birth, about his miracles, about his atoning death, about his burial, about his resurrection, his ascension and the descent of the Holy Spirit. And Philip would never have accepted a man who did not say that he believed all of these facts – these historical facts.

These words 'Simon himself believed' mean, further, that he must have assented to the way of salvation. Philip had expounded it and had explained how the Son of God had come into the world in order to be a sin-bearer. He had explained that the only way whereby even God can forgive us is that sin be punished, and he had shown that God had laid on his own Son the iniquity of us all, that he had smitten him and stricken him, and that it is because of that that we are pardoned and forgiven and saved and reconciled to God. And Simon had expressed his opinion on this and had believed.

Now it is astounding, is it not, that it is possible for a man to assent to all this and still not be a Christian? What explains this? Well, this is what we call 'intellectual belief', intellectual assent to the truth. Here is a message, and a man of intelligence who takes the trouble to look at it must be impressed by the evidence, and plenty of evidence was provided for these people by Philip and by what had happened to the others. And Simon said, 'I believe this.' This is terrifying but it is true; it is taught in the Scriptures themselves. It is possible for someone to give an intellectual assent to the propositions of the Scripture and not be a Christian.

Now I am saying this in order that you may see again the honesty of the Scriptures and the honesty of the truly Christian position. Christianity is not concerned about our assent, but it is very concerned about our true deliverance from sin, our true reconciliation to God. So it warns us that there is the awful danger of a mere intellectual assent, and it tells us that this, in and of itself, does not make us Christians.

And, similarly, it is possible for us to be aware of feelings within ourselves, and many are deceived by feelings. Many people have been moved to tears by the description of the Lord Jesus Christ on the cross on Calvary's hill. The preacher can sometimes be responsible for this. A preacher can use affecting stories and illustrations and make people weep, and they think that because they weep at these descriptions of the death of the Son of God, they are truly Christian. They say, 'I was moved by it and I cried.' But, oh, how treacherous are feelings!

There is an old story that used to be told in this connection – it is such a good one that I repeat it. It was about a lady who had gone to a theatre in London one night, leaving her coachman sitting outside the theatre. She was in the theatre for three hours and during this time a snowstorm sprang up. The play was a most affecting drama about a man suffering who had done no wrong. The lady was moved to tears and her heart melted. Oh, she was broken, as it were, by the drama.

When she came out of the theatre, there was the poor coachman, out in the snow, practically frozen on his seat. With not a word of sympathy, not a word of sorrow, not a word of apology, not a word of concern, she just stepped into her coach and was driven home.

You see, you can be moved emotionally but if there is no content to it, it is of no value. That is the position we can find ourselves in, unfortunately, because of our sinful state, the deceitfulness of our hearts and the wiles of Satan.

But notice something even further: 'Simon himself believed also: and when he was baptized . . .' What a prolific cause baptism is of people imagining they are Christians when they are not. There are many who think that they are Christians because they were baptized or christened when they were children. They think that that is a guarantee, that that makes them Christians. Of course, the Roman Catholic Church teaches that explicitly, as do other forms of Catholicism. But there are many who hold on to the idea that baptism makes us Christians.

'Ah, no, wait a minute,' says someone. 'Of course, I can see this nonsense about infant baptism, but surely if a man is an adult, a believer, and confesses faith, then baptism really does do it, he can be certain.'

But this man Simon was an adult, he had made a confession of faith and he was baptized as an adult on confession of faith – and still he was not a Christian. No form of baptism makes a person a Christian; it does not matter what the amount of water, nor the person's age. These are the things with which the devil deludes us. Here was a man believing, baptized, and still he was not a Christian.

Not only that, Simon joined the church. We read, 'When he was baptized, he continued with Philip.' His profession of belief was not a flash in the pan, apparently. It was not a case of deciding one night and never being seen again. No, no, he went the next day and the next – 'he continued with Philip'. You can join the church and still not be a Christian. Even Philip the evangelist, Philip filled with the Spirit, could not detect the man. He accepted him, he baptized him, he received him into the church.

Oh, my dear friends, you may think it is monstrous for me to be saying things like this at a time like this when the Christian church is so small and almost despicable, but I say it for this reason: What matters in the church is not the numbers but the purity, the character. 'One with God is a majority.' It is through a faithful remnant that really is redeemed, regenerated, truly 'in Christ' that

God has always done his mighty deeds. There is no need for me to cajole or to wheedle people into the church, I would be denying my own gospel that is before me if I attempted to do so. No, no, it is for me to show you the danger, the counterfeit. It is my task to warn you against being misled, to help you realize that what makes people Christians is not that they have their names on a church roll, but something profounder, more eternal than that. No, no, you can join the church and still not be a Christian.

And, as I say, you can be interested and amazed even, as this man Simon was: 'He continued with Philip, and wondered, beholding the miracles and signs which were done.'

Now this is remarkable, is it not? Simon to all appearances had become as much of a Christian as all the others. There was a change in his life. He would never have been admitted into the church if he had gone on practising his sorcery. Philip would never have accepted into the church a sorcerer who continued with his chicanery. No, no, the man had given all that up, he had turned his back on it and here he was regularly in the church, amazed and astonished at the marvellous things that Philip did. No man seemed to be more appreciative than Simon the sorcerer.

And yet, you see, the whole point of the story is to tell us that the man had never been a Christian at all. How does this show itself? 'How can we, then, decide?' asks someone. 'How can we ever know whether it is true or whether it is false?'

Perfectly right. It is the most important question you can ever ask, and the answer is given here quite simply and plainly. The false always eventually betrays itself. Listen to how it is put here. Here is Simon and he turns to Peter and John, offers them money, and says, 'Give me also this power, that on whomsoever I lay hands, he may receive the Holy Ghost.' And then Peter turns to him, and these are the words he uses: 'I perceive that thou art in the gall of bitterness, and in the bond of iniquity.' 'I perceive.' 'I see it.' How did he see it? It was because unbelief, this false, this spurious unbelief, always gives itself away, and then it becomes evident, it becomes obvious. But how does it do so?

Well, this again is taught us in many places in the Scripture, and here is a perfect illustration. It is generally something that happens rather suddenly and unexpectedly, and it is in this sudden situation that the poor man who is in a false position betrays himself. Now our Lord said this, it seems to me, in a word that is recorded in Matthew 12: 'But I say unto you, That every idle word that men shall speak, they shall give account thereof in the day of judgment. For by thy words thou shalt be justified, and by thy words thou shalt be condemned' (*Matt.* 12:36–37). By an 'idle word' our Lord means a word that you speak without considering; and it is 'out of the abundance of the heart' that a man speaks (*Matt.* 12:34). It is in what people suddenly say in an emergency that they betray themselves.

Now look at it put perfectly here in Acts chapter 8. Here was a man who to all appearances was a perfectly good Christian. But then the two apostles came down from Jerusalem, laid their hands on the Samaritans and they received the baptism of the Spirit. It was obvious that they had done so – Simon could see it – and immediately he blurted out, 'I will give you money, let me have this power, too.' And at once he betrayed his false and shallow position; it was by this idle word, this unpremeditated word. If you had questioned Simon on his creed, he would have given you the right answers, but in what he said in an emergency, in a sudden moment – ah, there you see the state and condition of his heart! This was the real man now speaking. Suddenly it came out. And that, it seems to me, is true always in this terrible connection. It is our reaction to various unexpected things that happen to us that really shows where we stand.

Let me open this out a little bit more for you. What are the signs? Well, poor Simon, by speaking like this, showed quite plainly that he was still essentially the same man. And that is always the trouble with the false appearance of Christianity; people in themselves remain the same. They add on certain things – they believe and are baptized, they join the church, they look on with admiration and wonder – but their natures are not changed. They are still the same people that they were before and then they betray it! Suddenly they show that they are still worldly-minded, they are still profane.

Though Simon said he had believed the gospel, and though he had given up his sorcery, that which made him practise sorcery was still in him and he wanted to do the same thing in a different way – not by sorcery but this way, which he thought was similar. He had had a power, this was a power, and now he still wanted power. The man was unchanged, though he was prepared to manifest the power somewhat differently.

So we must test ourselves, not so much by what we say as by the general tenor of our lives, by the way in which we practise even Christianity. I have often put it like this: I have seen people thinking that they were Christians when it was perfectly clear to me that they had never been Christians at all. Why not? Because their Christianity was always something that they seemed to be carrying with them in a bag. They picked it up on Sunday morning and they were Christians during Sunday, but then they put it down on Sunday night. Meet them during the week and you would never imagine that they were Christians at all. They said the right things but that was not Christianity. Christianity is through-and-through. Christianity is total. Christianity is in the heart. It is not some addition; it is not something you take on.

And, indeed, there is something more terrifying than that: it is possible for a man to be a preacher of this gospel and not to be a Christian. He can say the right things, he can be orthodox, he can defend the faith, but the man himself may be wrong. There is such a thing as ambition in the church – concern about offices, position, dignities, names and titles. The history of the church demonstrates all this, and it is a part of my business as a Christian preacher to remind you of it. I am not asking you to become a mere part of Christendom, I am not asking you to belong to a great institution, I am concerned about your souls, and this is what matters – not appearances but your relationship to the truth, your knowledge of the Son of God.

All sorts of motives bring people into this false position. For instance, look at the one we have here most prominently – an interest in phenomena, an interest in excitement. Simon saw that the two apostles had this mysterious power; they had only to pray, and lay their hands on people, and the Holy Spirit fell upon them. This appealed to Simon; he liked it and wanted it.

I have known many similar people. There are people who want other people's experiences. They hear somebody saying, 'Until a certain point I was very miserable, but then I became a Christian and my unhappiness went. I've been happy ever since. "Now I am happy all the day."' That, these people say, is the very experience they want. A man is in trouble. He has had a disappointment. His heart has been broken or he has fallen into some sin. So he says, 'If only I could get this man's or that woman's experience.' And he asks how he can get it.

'Believe on the Lord Jesus Christ,' is the reply.

He says, 'I do believe on the Lord Jesus Christ.' But all he wants is the experience.

Do not misunderstand me. We should all desire to have forgiveness of sins and to be delivered from our besetting sins, but that is very different from coveting somebody else's experience. No, no, what matters fundamentally is not experience, it is your relationship to him, your understanding, your knowledge of the truth. Experiences can be treacherous. That, again, is where the cults come in. They counterfeit experiences and lead people astray.

Or it may be the desire, as it was in Simon's case, to get people's powers and gifts. There are people who are out for power. They admire it and do not care how they get it as long as they have it. I have known people come to me and say that they feel called to the Christian ministry, but at times I have been able to detect that their real interest was not in the truth to be preached but in the preaching, in the position of a preacher, a minister. What a treacherous thing the human heart is, coveting experiences, coveting power! And here we see that self-interest still governed Simon. He saw an opportunity for self-importance, for self-aggrandizement, a chance to get people to admire him.

Oh, what a terrible thing sin is! These are some of the ways in which it betrays itself. The man speaks, he blurts out a remark, and in his instinctive words he tells you the whole truth about himself so that you perceive that he has never been a Christian at all.

Another way in which you can test yourself is this: Are you careless or careful in these matters? Look at the parable of the foolish virgins. Here were ten virgins, five wise, five foolish. What was the matter with the foolish virgins? It was that they wanted to be in the kingdom of God, they wanted to go to heaven, yes, but they also wanted to sleep, they wanted to get to the kingdom of heaven in their own way. They were not careful to provide the oil;

they were careless and care-free. And the result was that at a critical moment they found themselves with the door shut in their faces, locked out. That was the whole reason why our Lord gave the parable of the ten virgins. Of course they wanted to be in; of course they thought they were in; they hammered at the door and they said, 'Let us in, we belong.'

But the reply was, 'You do not belong! You thought you did but by your carelessness you gave ample evidence that you had never really belonged at all.'

So a good way of deciding is this: look not merely at what you claim to believe – we must, of course, believe the right things; you cannot be a Christian without believing an irreducible minimum – but test yourself by asking: 'What part does Christianity play in my life? Does it control me? Is it the biggest thing in my life, or is it something that I add on?' Now in the true Christian it is always central; it is always the controlling factor. The Christian does not do the minimum, but is anxious to do the maximum. That is always his concern, even though he fails, whereas the people who are deceiving themselves deliberately always do the minimum.

And then, as our Lord points out so clearly in the parable of the sower in Mark chapter 4, people who think they are Christians when they are not soon show it by allowing the cares of this world, and the various other worries and desires that crop up in life, to 'choke the word'. You see, the seeds all 'sprang up'. But in only one case was there real life. There was an appearance of life in the others but it was not real. And how do you tell the difference? Well, said our Lord, 'The cares of this world, and the deceitfulness of riches, and the lusts of other things entering in, choke the word.' And this is another way in which lack of true faith always betrays itself. It does not matter what I say, finally, it is what I do. What are my priorities? What are the things that control me? What are the things that master me? What are the things that count most and come first with me?

And then another test that our Lord gives is the way in which I react to persecution. Would you like to know whether or not you are a Christian? Here is a very good test. How do you react when people who know you tend to make fun of you because you are a Christian? You say, 'I'm a Christian.' Do you sometimes try to hide that in order that you may have the good opinion of others, in order that others may praise you, or may not laugh at you? Is your Christian faith something that you tend to conceal? You want it, of course – yes, but in your way. And when persecution arises, says our Lord, it withers and shrivels up (*Mark* 4:6, 17). These are the ways in which we can test the reality of our faith.

And the final way in which this man Simon gave proof that he had never been a Christian at all was in his response to Peter's rebuke. Peter rebuked him, and said, 'Pray God, if perhaps the thought of thine heart may be forgiven thee' (verse 22). And that phrase: 'the thought of thine heart' brings out all I have been trying to say. This is what Simon had planned in his mind, this is how he had thought. But his response to that was this: 'Then answered Simon, and said, Pray ye to the Lord for me, that none of these things which ye have spoken come upon me.'

'What's wrong with that?' you say.

Oh, what is wrong with it is that even then he was concerned about the wrong thing. What was animating him was fear of punishment; he did not see the enormity of what he had done, he did not hate this deceitful heart that was in him. He did not ask, 'Oh, how can I be delivered from it?' Not at all. 'Pray for me, that I may escape this punishment.' And that has ever been one of the chief characteristics of this false kind of profession. It is a concern not to go to hell, not a positive desire to go to heaven. The real interest is in this world but we want to avoid the consequences. There is no 'hunger and thirst after righteousness', there is no longing for God and for a knowledge of God. No, no, it is a negative fear and a desire to be saved from the consequences of sin, or the consequences of a life lived according to nature.

There, then, are the lessons that are revealed to us so clearly in this case of Simon the sorcerer. Are you a Christian? Are you sure that you are a Christian? Do not just say to me, 'I believe.' Simon believed. Do not say, 'I've been baptized.' He was. Do not say, 'I belong to the church.' He did. Do not say, 'I rather admire these things.' So did he. Here is the fundamental question: What is the state of your heart? What do you really desire? Do you really know that you have a soul within you that will go on for ever? Are you concerned about that soul? What is your real interest in the Lord

Jesus Christ? You say you believe in him – but do you? Can you give a reason for the hope that is in you? These are the questions, and they are very solemn questions.

We are in this world, in this life, only once – never again. Our eternal destiny is determined in this world and in this life, and it is all dependent upon our relationship to this blessed person. He is not just a cover for sin, he is not just someone who excuses you as you go on with sin. No, no! He preached one to whom he referred as 'Holy Father' (*John* 17:11), the one who had said, 'Ye shall be holy; for I am holy' (*Lev.* 11:44). Is it your desire to be holy, to belong to God, to be delivered from this life of sin and wretchedness and shame, and truly to become a child of God, and an heir of everlasting and eternal bliss? In Simon the sorcerer you see the pretence, the sham, the temporary, the false, that which does not count with God, who sees all things, for 'all things are naked and opened unto the eyes of him with whom we have to do' (*Heb.* 4:13). What is the real desire of your heart? That is the thing that proclaims what you are.

How I thank God that I can say, as I close, that whatever may be your position, if you see that it is wrong, that it is false, do what Peter told Simon to do – repent! Go to God acknowledging it and ask him to make your belief real, to make it true. He will not refuse you. Even to a man like Simon the sorcerer the apostles still say: Pray to God. Repent. Cast yourself upon his mercy. It is not too late.

Blessed be the name of God for so great, so wonderful a salvation that, though we try to fool God, and fool ourselves at the same time, even that does not cast us out finally, if only we repent, if only we acknowledge it and confess it, and ask God to deliver us and to give us a clean heart, a new heart, a pure heart, a heart that is right with him instead of being wrong with him. Thank God that is still the message of the gospel! May God open our eyes and give us all a certainty that we are true believers, born again, born of the Spirit of God, and therefore children of God, heirs of God and joint-heirs with Christ.

10

The Gall of Bitterness and the Bond of Iniquity

And when Simon saw that through the laying on of the apostles' hands the Holy Ghost was given, he offered them money, saying, Give me also this power, that on whomsoever I lay hands, he may receive the Holy Ghost. But Peter said unto him, Thy money perish with thee, because thou hast thought that the gift of God may be purchased with money. Thou hast neither part nor lot in this matter: for thy heart is not right in the sight of God. Repent therefore of this thy wickedness, and pray God, if perhaps the thought of thine heart may be forgiven thee. For I perceive that thou art in the gall of bitterness, and in the bond of iniquity. Then answered Simon, and said, Pray ye to the Lord for me, that none of these things which ye have spoken come upon me (Acts 8:18–24).

As we have seen, this record that we are now considering again makes it perfectly plain and clear that Simon the sorcerer had never been a Christian at all. We have been dealing with this terrifying fact, that it is possible for us to appear to be Christians without really being Christians. We can apparently believe the gospel, we can submit to baptism, we can be received into the church, even, by an official evangelist and still not be Christians at all. And it is to this terrifying reality that we must return.

But now I want to put it to you in this form. Here we are just before Christmas[1] when the thoughts of the church, and of the world, in a sense, turn to the fact of the birth of Jesus of Nazareth, the babe of Bethlehem. Now there is a very great problem here for many people, and it is this that I want to consider with you in the

[1] This sermon was preached on 17 December 1967.

light of what we are told here about this man Simon. There are many people who are genuinely bewildered by the fact that we go on asserting that the Christian faith is based upon history, that it is an historical faith and religion – that is, to them, a great stumbling block. They say that they realize that humanity is not in a good state. They can see the problems. They read their papers, and they know about the crime wave. They see people giving themselves to pleasure and to folly, and they are aware of the whole state of the world, its wars, its problems, its tensions and its difficulties. They know that there is something wrong and they believe that something should be done to put it right. Moreover, they are willing to do that.

These people say that they are ready to believe in religion because men and women need something beyond themselves; they need instruction. Their view of religion is that it is an exalted teaching that tells people what they should and should not do. But this is perfectly right, they say. We all need to be told. We must all be prohibited from doing some things and encouraged to do others. All this, they think, is excellent. Men and women need ethical instruction and should be exhorted to respond to it.

But what these people cannot understand about the Christian position is that we are not content with that, we do not stop at that, but will insist upon saying that certain other things are absolutely essential. For instance, we say that the babe born in Bethlehem was none other than the eternal Son of God, that this was not a natural birth, that this child never had a human father, that his very birth was a miracle. Further, we maintain that at that given point in time something happened that had never happened before and has never happened since, that the second Person of the blessed Holy Trinity left heaven and came on earth in the form of a babe, and was born as a child. A miracle! The miracle of the incarnation and of the virgin birth.

'Now,' say people of the world, 'you Christians insist upon that. And then you go on to insist that when this child grew up he worked miracles – supernatural manifestations. Furthermore, you add that we must believe that our only hope of deliverance and forgiveness and salvation lies in the fact that this selfsame Son of God deliberately went to the cross on Calvary's hill. And you say that we must believe that what was happening there was that God was laying on him our sins, and our guilt, and our iniquity, giving him the punishment that we deserve, and that that is the only way of salvation. You maintain,' these people say, 'that his death was not the death of a martyr, nor the death of a pacifist, nor the death of an honest, good man whom the world could not understand, but that it was a sacrificial and an atoning death, and that it is only as the result of that death, the breaking of his body, and the shedding of his blood, that there is any hope of salvation for any one of us.'

'And then,' they say, 'you go on to ask us to believe that after he died on the cross and was buried in a grave, he literally came out of that grave and rose from the dead – another miracle, something that had never happened before. You say that he is the first-begotten from the dead, the first to rise from the dead. You ask us,' they say, 'to believe that, and to believe he ascended into heaven visibly, and that on the day of Pentecost he sent down the Holy Spirit upon the Christian church. Now,' they say, 'this is the difficulty. You see, we like that teaching that you have in your Bible – we like the teaching of Jesus; we like the Sermon on the Mount; we think the world needs it.' And many of them go on to say that they are quite convinced that if only the statesmen of the world adopted the Sermon on the Mount, if only they put it into practice themselves, and got others to do the same, then the world would be a very much better place. But the problem is all the other teaching.

Now there will be a lot of that kind of thing said during these next eight or nine days. The world is prepared to take this teaching, this ethical instruction, this preaching of peace and of love, and of understanding, and of brotherhood – all this is highly acceptable. It knows it needs it. But the world says, 'Why all the rest of it?' This is the problem that confronts so many. They say that we make it impossible, especially for modern scientific men and women, who do not believe in the supernatural and the miraculous, to believe our message, because we will add on to this most excellent, simple, ethical, moral teaching this supernatural and miraculous element.

Now I am sure that there are many listening to me at this moment who are in this very difficulty and are asking that question: Why all this? Why do you insist upon the deity of this person? Why do you insist upon the miracles? Why do you insist upon his atoning death? Why do you insist upon the doctrine that he has already conquered death and the grave in this miraculous manner and has sent his Spirit upon the church?

So this is the question that I want to consider with you, and I want to consider it in the light of the story of this man Simon the sorcerer who lived in Samaria so long ago, because it seems to me that here is the answer that we need.

Now there is one simple answer, but before I actually deal with it, let me point out this in passing: those who are in the position that I have just outlined are betraying the fact that they have never seen the difference between the Old Testament and the New, that they have never seen the difference, that is, between the law and the gospel – this great distinction that is everywhere in the New Testament. This is how John puts it in the first chapter of his Gospel: 'For the law was given by Moses, but grace and truth came by Jesus Christ' (*John* 1:17). That is what they do not understand.

In other words, the simple answer is this: under the old dispensation the law was given. The children of Israel were given that law, but the whole point of the Old Testament is to show us that the law could not save them. When our Lord came and preached and died and rose again and the apostles began to preach, the Jews were opposed to the message of the gospel because they said that it was against the law. They believed that by keeping the law you could put yourself right with God, that by living a good life, by not doing certain things and by doing others, you could satisfy God. And they did not like this teaching of a Saviour who had come in the way our Lord came, and so they rejected him.

But Paul's reply to them is this: 'By the law is the knowledge of sin' (*Rom.* 3:20). The law can tell you what to do and what not to do, but what the law cannot do is enable you to carry out its commands. It is all very well for me to know what to do, but the question is, how can I do it? Here is the difficulty, here is the rub. As the apostle puts it again in the seventh chapter of the epistle to the Romans, 'I delight in the law of God after the inward man: but I see another law in my members . . .' (*Rom.* 7:22–23).

So under the old dispensation the people were given a law, but they could not keep it. Paul sums it up in these words: 'Therefore by the deeds of the law there shall no flesh be justified in his sight' (*Rom.* 3:20). The law cannot save.

There, then, is the answer to the question, 'Why all this?', put in a sort of theological form. But let me put it to you in a much more human form, in a more dramatic and pictorial manner, as we look at the case of Simon the sorcerer. Why is it essential to believe this miraculous gospel? Why must I believe everything that the New Testament asserts about the Lord Jesus Christ? Or, if you prefer me to put it negatively: Why is it that people object to this supernatural salvation, whereas they are ready to accept an ethical and a moral teaching?

Well, here are some of the answers that I discover in the case of this man Simon. Anybody who objects to this miraculous, supernatural salvation does so primarily because he has never realized the true nature of sin. There is always this difficulty. People do not like the salvation that is offered because they are not aware of their need; they are not aware of the actual condition in which they and the whole world are to be found. Now I can demonstrate this to you from the case of Simon. Here is a picture of a man in sin.

'What is this sin,' says somebody, 'that you keep on talking about?'

Well, what we are shown here so plainly is that sin is not superficial. The problem of man is not on the surface of his life but is very deep down. And it is not simple, it is very profound. And not only that. The trouble with humanity – this thing that the Bible calls sin – is not merely negative, it is not merely the absence of certain qualities, but is a very positive condition. Sin is very active, it is something that manifests itself. So we must start here. If the Bible is right in saying that nothing less than the coming of the Son of God into the world can save humanity, then the problem of human sin must be profound. The trouble with humanity is not just that it is a bit ignorant, that it needs further knowledge, further instruction, further encouragement or further help. No, the Bible says the problem is too deep for that.

Listen to the way in which the apostle Peter puts this truth about sin in speaking to Simon the sorcerer. 'For I perceive', he says, 'that thou art in the gall of bitterness, and in the bond of iniquity.' That is the trouble with you, he says. 'Thou hast neither part nor lot in this matter.' You think you have believed, you think you have become a Christian, but you have nothing to do with it at all. Why? Because you are still 'in the gall of bitterness', you are still 'in the bond of iniquity'.

Now that is Peter's description of sin, and I want to show you what a perfectly accurate description it is. Sin, I repeat, is not merely something negative. But that is the popular psychological teaching today; psychology never likes sin. It says, 'Of course, what Christians call sin is not a positive force as the Bible makes out, it is merely the absence of certain qualities. You must not say that a man is a bad man, all you should say is that he is not a good man.' But the Bible says that sin is vicious, it is 'the gall of bitterness'. As gall is bitter to the taste, so is sin. Sin is essentially bitter, it is offensive, it is vicious, it is something abhorrent.

Now this is the great statement of the Bible with regard to sin throughout both the Old and the New Testaments. There are many descriptions of it. Paul refers to it as 'enmity against God' (*Rom.* 8:7), and is this not perfectly true? Have you not noticed how people who are not Christians are invariably bitter about God? They cannot speak of God without sarcasm, without sneering, without being offensive. They talk about 'your God'! Now that is the gall of bitterness, the very attitude that Peter says is so true of this man Simon. Human beings by nature are haters of God.

'But,' you say, 'I've known many people who aren't Christians but they don't hate God. They don't believe in him but they are not bitter or sarcastic.'

But be sure before you speak! I have known many nice respectable people who have told me in discussion that they believe in God. But the moment I have pointed out to them what the Bible tells us about God, they show their bitterness and their hatred. It is all very well to have a nice and easy surface and to be good and benevolent and kindly and friendly, but scratch the surface and you will always find bitterness. People have their own idea of God; they make their own God. He is not the God of the Bible. They say, 'God is love', and they do not like to talk about a God who is righteous and gives a moral law. They speak with violence and ridicule of 'this God' who, they say, sits on Mount Sinai breathing out slaughter and threatening and damnation. They do not believe in such a God. There the bitterness comes out. As long as God fits in with their ideas and their little definitions they say they believe in him; but the moment they realize who and what God is, the bitterness begins to manifest itself.

This vicious, bitter, gall-like character of sin manifests itself in many different ways, and that is where the subtlety of the devil comes in. I remember very well once having to deal with a person who was beginning to understand the Christian faith and I was given an opportunity to make it clear to her in this way. This lady mentioned two people whom both she and I knew, and she praised them for their kindness and their readiness always to help and their generosity. When I said, 'But they are not Christians,' she was not at all pleased.

'Oh, no, no,' she said, 'you mustn't say that.' And she was very annoyed that I should say that such people, who were always out to do good and were so generous and always helpful and considerate, were not Christians.

I was able to point out, of course, that you can be very good and nice without being a Christian at all, and that the way to test such people is to tell them that they need to be 'born again', and to ask them whether they are relying on the blood of Christ shed on the cross and on that alone. I said that the moment you confront them with that, out comes the bitterness. And it did in that particular case. The two persons whom she had been idealizing because of their benevolence became bitter opponents of this very woman as soon as she became a Christian. That is 'the gall of bitterness'. Ah, we can all put on an appearance of niceness and friendliness. The man or woman of the world can appear to be very much nicer than the Christian; that is because of their sham and pretence. I say once more, scratch the surface and you will soon find bitterness. This is characteristic of the whole of the life of the world. Look at the politicians, look at the excitement – who is trusting whom? Who is trying to knife whom in the back?

That is the gall of bitterness that is ever the characteristic of sin. And the whole conversation of the world as it talks about friendship and brotherhood is a sham. It is nothing but a mere covering, a veneer over the foulness, the bitterness, the viciousness of sin.

Look at what sin does to people's characters. Consider that description in the third chapter of Paul's epistle to the Romans. Here it is: 'There is none righteous, no, not one: there is none that understandeth, there is none that seeketh after God. They are all gone out of the way, they are together become unprofitable . . .' Listen! 'Their throat is an open sepulchre' (*Rom.* 3:10–13).

'But,' you say again, 'that's just not true of everybody. I know very nice people.'

But you listen to what the 'nice people' say of others in private and in secret. No, 'Their throat is an open sepulchre.' Listen to the terrible things that they think and say about one another: '. . . With their tongues they have used deceit; the poison of asps is under their lips' (verse 13). They are serpents. And if you do not realize this, you do not know yourself at all. We are all serpents by nature. What treacherous creatures we are by nature, every single one of us. It is the gall of bitterness that is in us all.

Or take the striking way in which the apostle Paul puts it in writing to Titus: 'We ourselves also were sometimes foolish, disobedient, deceived, serving divers lusts and pleasures, living in malice and envy, hateful, and hating one another' (*Titus* 3:3). And that is nothing but an accurate description of the life of this world. If you say you do not believe that, then you just do not know human nature, or else you are utterly dishonest. The newspapers, the biographies, all prove the truth of this biblical description of human nature. The world is full of treachery and that is because we are sinful creatures governed by sin. That is the state of the human heart; that is the state of the imagination.

And then go on to consider the kinds of things that sin makes people do. Look at it in the case of this man Simon. You see his thoughts; and then he acts, and you see the vile character of his action. Again, this is but a simple illustration of what is so true. Look at the way of the world, look at the way in which it is living, look at the way in which it is behaving. The Bible is full of examples of this kind of thing. Poor David the king falls into sin, you remember. He commits adultery and then murders the woman's husband in order that he might have her. Finally he comes to see that it is all due to that wicked heart of his. 'Create in me a clean heart, O God; and renew a right spirit within me,' he says (*Psa.* 51:10). It is this terrible nature of ours that can make us behave in such ways.

Look at the problems of the world today. Look at the agony; look at the troubles. What can you say about it except that it is vicious, that it is vile? Look at the problems in industry; look at the lack of trust. Why do people not trust one another? Then look at the breakdown of the sanctities. What is the cause? There is only one answer. It is this 'gall of bitterness'. It is this foul, vicious thing that the Bible calls sin.

And, in any case, by its very nature sin is always bitter. In the world there is no such thing as a pure pleasure. There is nothing pure. Something is always lacking. Look at the life of the poor sinner, the man or woman who lives for the world – it always ends in bitterness. 'The way of transgressors', says the Bible, 'is hard' (*Prov.* 13:15). And it always is hard; it always leads to bitterness. There is a perfect illustration in the Old Testament. There was a man whose name was Esau, twin brother of another man called Jacob. Esau is called a 'profane' man; he was not very interested in religious things, in birthrights and things like that. He was a hunter and he enjoyed his food and his drink. Well, he came home one day very, very hungry and when he saw his brother eating some soup, he said, 'Look here, give me that soup.'

'All right,' said clever Jacob, 'I will give it to you if you give me the birthright.' What was the birthright to a man like Esau! 'All right,' he said, and so he sold his birthright (*Gen.* 25:27–34).

What was the consequence? The Bible says that 'he found no place of repentance' (*Heb.* 12:17), which means that he remained in 'the gall of bitterness'. He spent the rest of his life in bitterness, regretting it. And this is always something that sin leads to. 'The way of the transgressor *is* hard.' If you break God's laws, you will always find that you reap bitterness and unhappiness and trouble. The Bible is full of illustrations of this. Peter denied his Lord, and later he went out and 'wept bitterly' (*Luke* 22:62). Judas Iscariot betrayed his Lord, and the remorse and the reaction were so terrible, so bitter, that he committed suicide (*Matt.* 27:5). This is the characteristic of sin.

Bur here in Acts 8 Peter says that sin is not only the gall of bitterness, it is at the same time 'the bond of iniquity'. This is a dramatic way of saying that sin is a form of serfdom, of slavery. And it is because the world does not realize this that it does not see the need of a supernatural Saviour. The world says: 'Give me a law, give me teaching, give me education, give me moral lectures, give me an idealistic philosophy and I will rise to it.' Well, the world has been saying that sort of thing for many, many long centuries. Plato had written his *Republic*, in which he describes the perfect state, before Jesus Christ, the babe of Bethlehem, was ever born. The world has been full of moral teaching and of idealism and philosophy throughout the running centuries – why, then, is it in such terrible trouble? Why cannot politics put the world right? Why cannot education put the world right? Why cannot culture, literature, music, art – why cannot they put the world right? And there is only one answer, it is 'the bond of iniquity'. Every one of us born into this world is born in the bondage of iniquity. We have got evil natures and we cannot change them.

Is not this the experience of all of us? We have the knowledge and the instruction, we know certain things are wrong and yet we deliberately do them. It is so futile to think that you can change people by teaching. Look at the measures that the police are having to resort to – breathalysers, and so on. Why do we have to turn to them? Simply because men and women cannot manage themselves. You can say to people, 'Don't drive if you have taken any drink. See how dangerous it is. Look at the statistics.' And people recognize the statistics, but does that keep them from drinking? No, they cannot help themselves, they are in the bond of iniquity.

And I say again that this bond is slavery; it is serfdom. Every one of us is a serf by nature; every one of us knows what it is to fall into sins that we hate. We make our resolutions, and the world in its folly will be making New Year resolutions in a few weeks. But we will not keep them; nobody can. All the effort of civilization and all the endeavour of men and women to improve the lot of the individual and of humanity is a constant and complete failure, as great a failure today as it has ever been. It is impossible for men and women to deliver themselves. And this is what comes out in the case of Simon the sorcerer. This is why a miraculous, supernatural salvation is an absolute necessity.

But consider, in the second place, what sin is to God. I have simply shown you so far what sin is to human beings, and the moment you really analyse men and women you see that that is the simple truth. But look at sin in the sight of God. Peter again brought this out quite clearly when he turned to Simon and said, 'Repent therefore of this thy wickedness, and pray God, if perhaps the thought of thine heart may be forgiven thee.' 'Perhaps'! But, you notice, Peter said something else to Simon. When Simon offered him money to buy this gift, Peter said to him, 'Thy money perish with thee . . .' 'Perish'!

Oh, my dear friend, if you have never understood the reason for the coming of the Son of God into this world, if you have never understood why he had to die on that cross, then you see it now in this one word 'perish'. This is the whole message of the Bible. This word tells us what sin is in the sight of God. 'God so loved the world, that he gave his only begotten Son' – Why did he do it? Why did he send his Son into the world? Why did he send him to the cross? Why did he send him to the grave? Here is the answer – 'that whosoever believeth in him should not perish, but have everlasting life' (*John* 3:16).

What does this mean? It means that God hates sin. If sin is seen to be foul and vicious, even to those who face it honestly in themselves and in others, what is it in the sight of God? 'Thou', says the prophet Habakkuk, addressing God, 'art of purer eyes than to behold evil, and canst not look on iniquity' (*Hab.*1:13). And the apostle John writes, 'God is light, and in him is no darkness at all' (*1 John* 1:5). Sin is abhorrent to his holy nature. He is the eternal opposite of it, as he has told us quite plainly and clearly. Our Lord Jesus Christ, addressing some Pharisees, put it like this: 'Ye are they which justify yourselves before men; but God knoweth your hearts: for that which is highly esteemed among men is abomination in the sight of God' (*Luke* 16:15).

Of course, it is difficult for us to understand this because we are human, because we are sinful, and because our judgments are warped. Can you conceive what sin means to God who is utter holiness, righteousness, truth, justice – all that is pure and light?

Well, he has told you: he hates it with an eternal hatred and it cannot live in his presence. And he has told us quite plainly and quite clearly that he will punish it. Before Adam had ever sinned, God told him that. He told him that when he was but in a state of probation. And all that he has ever told us since then, through prophets and kings and seers, through John the Baptist, through his own Son, through all the teaching of the apostles, is but the same thing – he says, 'The soul that sinneth, it shall die' (*Ezek.* 18:4).

You do not like that. Who does like it by nature? But it is not what you like that matters, it is what is true, and the great message of the law of God is that sin comes under the condemnation of God and his holy law. Paul writing to the Romans says, 'I am not ashamed of the gospel of Christ'; he is very proud of it, in fact. He is ready, he says, to come and preach in Rome. He will preach to the emperor, he will preach to the slaves, he will preach to anybody. 'I am not ashamed of the gospel of Christ' – why not? – 'for it is the power of God', he says, 'unto salvation to every one that believeth; to the Jew first, and also to the Greek' (*Rom.* 1:16). But, he says, and this is the reason why he rejoices in it: 'For the wrath of God is revealed from heaven against all ungodliness and unrighteousness of men, who hold [down] the truth in unrighteousness' (*Rom.* 1:18).

The wrath has been revealed. God has revealed it in the law, and this is what the world does not know. People say, 'Give us teaching; give us help; give us education; tell us how we ought to live.'

But before you do any of these things, consider this: What about the things you have already done? What about the nature that is in you? What about your relationship to God? And the answer is given in that third chapter of Romans: The whole world has become guilty before God. 'There is none righteous, no, not one' (*Rom.* 3:10). The wrath of God is upon men and women in sin. Furthermore, the wrath of God not only manifests itself in this world, but it is also the teaching that if a man dies in sin he will go on to spend his eternity under the wrath of God, outside the life of God, outside the blessing of God. If a man dies in sin, says the Bible, he will spend eternity without end in a state of miserable, useless remorse, realizing, too late, what a fool he has been.

Now *I* am not saying this, it is the Lord Jesus Christ who said it in his picture of Dives and Lazarus. Here is this wealthy man, Dives. He has a marvellous time in this world – of course, money can buy so much. But at last he dies, and there he is in hell, in torment, and he says, 'Oh, can't I get out of this?' And the answer given to him is this: 'Between us and you there is a great gulf fixed' (*Luke* 16:19–31).

My dear friend, had you realized that? You who object to the coming of the Son of God as the babe of Bethlehem, you who say, 'I don't want your miracles, I just want help and teaching. I don't want to believe that I have got to be saved in this miraculous manner.' There is your problem – you are guilty before God. If you die in your guilt you will go to hell, and hell means a place of torment, a place of useless remorse, a place where you are in agony and suffering, realizing what a fool you are. And you can never get out of it. That is your problem. Now then, you see, this is what is meant by 'the gall of bitterness' and 'the bond of iniquity'.

That is the first great reason why people do not accept this gospel as it is. They have never seen the nature of sin, they have never seen what sin has done to them, what sin is going to do to them, what the consequences of sin are if they die in it. They have never seen all that, otherwise they would be alarmed and would look for a Saviour.

But let me turn to the other side. The failure of these people on the positive side is equally great. Men and women reject this supernatural salvation because they have never understood the true nature of the Christian life. What is it? Well, I can show it you in terms of this picture. If you want to know what it is, just take this man Simon the sorcerer and contrast him with Philip the evangelist, or with any other Christian. People will keep on thinking that to be a Christian is only slightly different from being a non-Christian. They think that when men and women become Christians they are improved a little bit. And that is the whole fallacy. To become a Christian is to become entirely new. The difference between Christianity and the world is an absolute difference.

This is what the Bible keeps on telling us. 'Therefore if any man be in Christ, he is a new creature [a new creation]: old things are passed away; behold, all things are become new' (*2 Cor.* 5:17). The Bible talks, not about improvement, but about rebirth, about being 'born again', having a new heart, a new nature, a new life, a new everything. Now do you not notice how this comes out in this story in Acts 8? We read: 'Peter said unto him [Simon], Thy money perish with thee, because thou hast thought that the gift of God may be purchased with money. Thou hast neither part nor lot in this matter: for thy heart is not right in the sight of God.' Now in the Bible the word 'heart' does not merely stand for the emotions, it stands for the centre of the personality. And it is there, in the centre of the personality, that we go wrong. You do not become a Christian simply by adding on a belief and by stopping this or adding that. You can do all that and still not be a Christian. What makes a man or woman a Christian? It is that they become new people, that they have new hearts.

Peter is saying to Simon: Your heart is not right, that is your trouble. Philip thought that you were a Christian and I accepted his word. You seemed to be one, you had believed, you had been baptized, you had joined the church, ah, but your heart is not right, I can see it now. You have not been changed at the centre of your personality, therefore you are not a Christian at all. Now this is the essence of Christianity. Our Lord shows this in the parable of the sower. The only one of the four specimens that is truly Christian is the one that 'in an honest and good heart' receives the word (*Luke* 8:15). You do not merely take on the message with your head or with your will or with your emotions – the whole person is involved. Now this leads, as we see, to an entire change. It leads to an entire change in a person's outlook and understanding. Look at this poor man Simon – Peter said: 'Thy money perish with thee, because thou hast thought that the gift of God may be purchased with money. Thou hast neither part nor lot in this matter: for thy heart is not right in the sight of God.' Now there is the difference between the world and the Christian.

The man or woman who belongs to the world, of course, thinks that money can do everything. The difference between the non-Christian and the Christian is not in particulars but in their whole attitude and outlook. The world puts its faith in what it can do. Why do people get on? It is because they have brains, because they have a good family record, and influence in the right quarters and because they have money: money opens doors, money in someone's palm will get you almost anywhere. This is what the world relies on and it is all typified by this man Simon. The world believes that nothing is impossible to such people. And that is the ultimate fallacy.

Any man who thinks that he can have the gift of God as the result of something that he offers is just saying that he is not a Christian. A man who comes along and says, 'Here's my good life, give me the gift', is proving that he is not a Christian. A man who says, 'Here's my great understanding, here's my great philosophy, I therefore ask . . .' is not a Christian. A man who says, 'I believe in the uplift of the human race. I'm an idealist, I'm prepared to make sacrifices in order to make the world a better place and I believe in organization. I don't like this supernatural gospel, I don't believe in the birth of the Son of God, I don't like this talk about blood, I don't believe in resurrection, but I believe in reforming, uplifting the human race' – what is he? He is just not a Christian. The whole characteristic of the world is self-reliance: its abilities, its wealth, its influence, its moralities, its religions, its societies, its everything, and here it is; but the moment a man or woman becomes a Christian, they say:

> *Nothing in my hand I bring;*
> *Simply to thy cross I cling.*
>
> Augustus Toplady

'For by grace are ye saved through faith; and that not of yourselves: it is the gift of God' (*Eph.* 2:8). This poor man Simon had joined the church but he had never understood that the essential nature of the Christian life is that we admit that we are paupers, with nothing at all, that we come to God in utter helplessness, nakedness and poverty.

Secondly, of course, there is a different spirit, and here again is something that comes out very strikingly in the case of Simon the sorcerer. Did you notice it? He offers money and says, 'Now here, I'm offering a price, give me this gift. I want to be able to lay hands on people that they may have this gift of the Holy Spirit. You apostles are able to do it, how much do you want? How much does it cost to do this?' You see the implication? He still wants to be important. He wants to go at one bound beyond Philip the evangelist. He knew nothing about Christianity until Philip came down and preached to them, and it was as the result of accepting Philip's message that he was baptized and received into the church. And we are told that he listened to Philip and admired him, '[He] wondered, beholding the miracles and signs which were done.' But Philip did not have the power of laying his hands upon people and getting them baptized with the Holy Spirit. And here was a man, newly converted, apparently, who thought that by offering money he could at once go right over the head of Philip – his conceit, his self-confidence! That is the man of the world – always out for himself, always filled with self-confidence and self-reliance. How different from the apostles, how different from the mighty apostle Paul, who says of himself, 'For I am the least of the apostles, that am not meet [am not worthy] to be called an apostle' (*1 Cor.* 15:9).

My friend, can you not see that this is Christianity? It is not people of the world improved, but people changed completely and made humble and lowly and meek, confessing that they have nothing, that they are nothing. Each says, 'I am what I am by the grace of God', and their desires are changed. But the only thing that this poor fellow Simon wants is forgiveness. 'Pray ye to the Lord for me,' he says, 'that none of these things which ye have spoken come upon me.' That is the man of the world: he does not want to go to hell, he wants to go to heaven, but he is still only concerned about saving his own skin. That is not true Christianity. Christians do not desire forgiveness – they rejoice in the fact that they have it – but their greatest desire is not merely to escape hell, it is also to be holy, to be clean, to be pure. It is to know God; it is to be like him. They want to get rid of the evil heart that was in them, they abominate it, they hate it. And so with David, they cry out, 'Create in me a clean heart, O God; and renew a right spirit within me' (*Psa.* 51:10). And Christians, because they realize what God in his infinite grace has done for them, have a consuming passion to live to the glory of God, to be worthy of this amazing love that God has shed upon them:

Love so amazing, so divine, they say, *demands my soul, my life, my all.* And it is because people do not realize that that is the essence of the Christian position that they do not see the necessity of all that I have put before you. They think that they can apply teaching, they think that they can offer money, that they can do this or that. But the moment you see the glory of standing before God, you realize that nothing will do but an absolute change, a complete renewal, a being 'born again'. And the only way that that becomes possible is that the Son of God should have come into the world taking human nature unto himself, linking it to himself. He is the head of a new humanity and he will make us partakers of his own nature, so that we can become children of God, with a principle of holiness and of life within us.

There, then, is the case of the Scripture. Have you seen it? Have you seen that this is what you need and that without it you can do nothing?

'Very well,' you say, 'what can I do, then? I've been wrong. I, like Simon, have been trusting to things that I have. I can see now that salvation is the gift of God. What can I do? I've ridiculed the blood of Christ. I've laughed at the incarnation. I've made fun of the babe of Bethlehem.'

A man I knew who became a Christian at the age of seventy-seven told me, after he was converted, about something that he had remembered. It had come back to him – and, he said, it had nearly broken his heart. He said to me, 'I should not have taken communion last night.'

'Why not?' I asked.

He replied, 'Thirty years ago I was having an argument about Jesus Christ in a public house and I said Jesus Christ was a bastard.'

And that is what many are still saying about him. Have you said it about him? Have you ridiculed and poured scorn upon the miraculous, the supernatural, the unique deity of the Son of God and all the glories of his salvation? And do you now see it, and are you afraid, and are you asking what you can do?

Thank God, the answer is here for you: Repent. Turn. Peter says, 'Repent therefore of this thy wickedness, and pray God, if perhaps the thought of thine heart may be forgiven thee.'

Repent, my friend, and that means this – acknowledge your folly, the enormity of your sin, the arrogance of your intellectualism, the madness of trusting to yourself and your gifts, or anything, in the sight of God. Humble yourself, acknowledge it, confess it. Stop defending yourself, fall at his feet and just pray to him.

You say, 'How can I pray? I realize now that I have no right to pray.'

Very well; look to this Christ. Here is the message for you: he died for you. He has borne your punishment. He has taken your guilt upon himself. In him you are accepted of God. You cannot pray as you are, but pray in the name of Jesus Christ and God will receive you. There it is.

'Is it possible?' asks someone.

Of course it is! Look at the encouragement that you have even here. Fancy Peter saying to this man who was in 'the gall of bitterness', and 'the bond of iniquity', 'Repent . . . and pray'! And it is my privilege to say the same words to you. Ask God – he is the God of love and mercy and compassion. If you have rejected him and scoffed at his miraculous salvation until this very moment, still I say to you, 'Go to him because "Christ died for the ungodly."' He said himself, 'They that are whole have no need of the physician, but they that are sick. I came not to call the righteous, but sinners to repentance' (*Mark* 2:17). 'The Son of man is come to seek and to save that which was lost' (*Luke* 19:10).

Listen to the apostle Paul. He says, '[I] was before a blasphemer, and a persecutor, and injurious: but I obtained mercy' (*1 Tim.*1:13). I was against him, I blasphemed his name, and yet he loved me, and gave himself for me.

This is the glory of this gospel. It is a gospel for sinners, for vile, gall-like sinners, 'in the bond of iniquity'. It is the message that God has indeed so loved the world that he has given his only begotten Son, that whosoever – whatever he has been, whatever he has done – believes in him should not perish but have everlasting life. Do you have it? Do you have a new heart? Have you come to the end of trusting in yourself? And are you rejoicing today in the fact that the Son of God literally was born as a baby, literally died for your sins and was buried, literally rose again in the body, and is now seated at the right hand of God making intercession for you?

Do you thank God for this miraculous, supernatural salvation? If you do, you are a Christian; if you do not, and if you die like that, you will perish, and your money and your brains and your righteousness and everything you have will perish with you. But, oh, do not perish! Repent, pray to him, cast yourself upon his mercy; and he has given you the assurance that he will in no wise cast you out. Learn the lesson from Simon the sorcerer. Repent, believe, and be saved.

11

In the Villages

And they, when they had testified and preached the word of the Lord, returned to Jerusalem, and preached the gospel in many villages of the Samaritans (Acts 8:25).

Verse 25 comes at the end of the account that has been given of the way the gospel of Jesus Christ began to spread out of Jerusalem throughout Judaea and eventually to this country of the Samaritans. We have been engaged in considering this bit of interesting history for some time, and we have found astonishing things, including the story of Simon the sorcerer. And then comes this twenty-fifth verse that we are looking at now.

Now this verse is a statement that, on the surface, appears to be just a kind of epilogue to this bit of history. There does not appear to be anything special about it, nothing of any particular interest or significance. It just looks as if Luke, the author of this book, is, as a good historian, rounding up the story. He has told us of how these two apostles were sent to Samaria by the other apostles up in Jerusalem and, having told us what they did there, he says, 'Then, after that, they went back to Jerusalem.' That is what one feels when one first reads this verse in a more or less cursory manner. Yet I want to show you that if we do so we shall miss something that is of very great interest and of very true and real significance, especially on a night like this – Christmas Eve.[1] For this is a typical Christian statement that reminds us of some of the most glorious aspects of our Christian faith. This comes out, it seems to me, in what we are told about the action of these apostles.

[1] This sermon was preached on 24 December 1967.

In the Villages (8:25)

Peter and John were two of the leading apostles, and yet, having finished the work they had gone down to do in this city of Samaria, they did not immediately rush back to Jerusalem, their headquarters. No, instead, they 'preached the gospel in many villages of the Samaritans'. This is an astonishing statement. What they did is so unlike the world's thinking and actions, so unlike everything that the world expects, that it conveys to us a most important message. The world, of course, always expects great things to happen in so-called great people, and it always expects great things to happen in great cities. The world is not interested in villages or in ordinary people. Look at its history – it is the record of great people, great events, that always take place in great cities.

But that is not what we have here; indeed, we have the exact opposite. Here are these two men, Peter and John, who, instead of rushing straight back to Jerusalem, preached the gospel in the villages of Samaria. Now why did they do this? In replying to that question, I want to direct your attention to two things: one is the preaching of the message, and the other, which I particularly want to emphasize, is where they preached – 'in the villages of the Samaritans'.

But though I want to concentrate on the second point, let me emphasize the first as well, because this, of course, is what made Peter and John go to the villages. What they did was preach the gospel. That is why these two men did not ignore these villages and rush straight back to Jerusalem as quickly as they could. It was because of the gospel, because of the good news. We are told, 'When they had testified and preached the word of the Lord [in the city where Philip had been preaching] . . . they preached the gospel in many villages . . .' These men were heralds of good news, they had been revolutionized by believing this gospel, by their association with the Lord Jesus Christ, and they were so moved by this gospel, and so thrilled by it, that they wanted the whole world to know it.

And this is, of course, the particular message of Christmas; it is the most amazing thing that has ever happened, that God 'hath visited and redeemed his people' (*Luke* 1:68). It is not surprising that the effect of this gospel has always been to make people sing. The angels sang, 'Glory to God in the highest, and on earth peace, good will toward men' (*Luke* 2:14). It is a gospel that fills people with joy and thanksgiving, and it immediately creates within them this desire to tell everybody else about it. It is the very character and nature of the message that urged these two apostles to do this very thing.

Now if your idea of the gospel is not that it is joyful news, then you have the wrong idea. What is Christianity, this gospel that Peter and John preached? It is good news. If you adopt this modern idea that is being given such publicity, this theory that Christmas is about human relationships, then you will have no gospel. Christmas is not just a message that we should try to be friendly and help one another, love one another and look for love. If it were, we should all be utterly and completely hopeless. But thank God, it is not that at all! It is a message that God has done something, that God has come in. Good news! This gospel that the apostles preached was so wonderful and amazing to them that they could not contain themselves, they could not refrain from speaking.

But now I want to concentrate on this second point: 'They preached the gospel in many villages of the Samaritans.' It is astonishing that they should have preached in the villages. The world, I repeat, can understand their going to the city, but not to the villages, yet this is so characteristic of our Christian message and faith. It is the exact opposite of everything the world knows, everything the world expects. You so often hear people saying today that modern men and women cannot believe this, that and the other, and so we must preach a gospel that they do understand. But if they could understand the gospel, it would no longer be the gospel. The gospel is of God and not of man.

So let me bring out just this one great principle that is shown here so plainly and so clearly, this astonishing reversal of everything that people think and expect. Look at it for a moment as you see it in our blessed Lord himself. Here he is, the Deliverer, the Saviour of the world. How do you think he will come? How did the world think he would come? How does the world still think of these things? Well, I need not waste your time with that. If you had put this question to the world, it would say, beyond any doubt, that there would be some astonishing spectacle, that the heavens would be rent and suddenly he would appear. There would be some great phenomenon, startling in its immensity.

But, of course, you know that he did not come like that. He came unobserved, in an unexpected way: 'Because there was no room for him in the inn'. He was not born in Jerusalem, the capital city, but in a little place, the little town of Bethlehem. Everything about him is always the reverse of what the world with its big ideas expects. And he came as a helpless babe. He did not suddenly appear as a full-grown man, some great phenomenon suddenly bursting forth upon the world. No, no! At first sight it seems to be just another birth of another baby; he was as helpless as every other babe and they laid him in a manger.

Furthermore – and this is so striking – he was born into poverty; the records bring this out. He was not born the son of a king or of some great or wealthy potentate: Mary and Joseph were so poor that they could not afford to sacrifice a lamb but had to bring two turtle doves when they came to present him at the temple. And, again, he was not born in a palace but in a stable.

So do you not see that this idea that the gospel is to be acceptable to modern people is the final denial of the gospel? People say, 'But the modern man can no longer accept this.' Of course not, he has never been able to accept it. The gospel deliberately is the opposite of everything that men and women expect. There is a Welsh hymn that puts this perfectly. I am not going to quote it because you would not understand it, but it states that when he came into the world, he was found not amidst the great, and the noble, or the wonderful, and the mighty, but in a stable, and he went out of the world between two thieves. This is the gospel.

And then look at him as he grew up, how did he spend his time? What was he? He worked as a carpenter, he worked with his hands. He was not trained as a Pharisee, and to the Jews this was monstrous. No man could possibly teach or help or be a redeemer unless he was a trained Pharisee. So they looked at him and they said, 'How knoweth this man letters, having never learned?' (*John* 7:15). But these are the facts. He was a carpenter, an artisan, until he was thirty years of age. What an amazing, what an astonishing, thing.

And even when he set out on his public ministry, when he took up the task of being the Saviour of the world, he did it in a way that the world regards as being almost ridiculous. He did not set up a school of philosophy where the great questions could be handled, the concepts and the contrasts examined, the authorities quoted – never anything of the sort. He was not a great philosopher. Neither was he a great soldier. He did not gather an army together and conquer the Roman Empire that had recently conquered and captured his country, Palestine. Nor did he go to Jerusalem and try to set himself up as a king. There were many people who were urging him to do all these things, but he would not do them.

What was he? He was just a preacher, a simple, humble preacher talking to people about the things of God. And the world could not understand it. His own brethren could not understand it, even his own followers at times could not understand it. But this is how he came. And on it goes; you are familiar with the facts. I am just trying to put them to you from this angle in order that you may see the marvel and the wonder of it all.

So we go on to the point at which eventually he was arrested. He did not resist or fight or use swords. He was arrested in apparent weakness, condemned to death without speaking a word, and eventually was crucified on a tree, and died in an exceptionally short time. He died so quickly that the soldiers could not believe the evidence of their own eyes. Crucifixion is a very slow mode of death yet he suddenly died. In everything from his birth to his death he was the reverse of all that the world in its wisdom has always expected. And here, now, in this chapter, we see this same principle, this same surprising element that comes out in everything concerning him.

But, then, look at another point: look at the people amongst whom he worked, the people amongst whom he still works. When these two great apostles preached to these ordinary village people they were only doing what their Lord and Master had done before them and what he had taught them to do. This is but typical of his action. Have you ever considered this? Look at his own mother – Mary. Who was she? She was a nobody. Of course, if you trace her genealogy, you go back to the great ones, but she herself was not great, she was just a simple virgin. It was God's decision that when his Son came into the world he should not be born of a great queen or some great personage, but of a 'lowly Hebrew maid'.

And on the record goes. The birth into this world of the Son of God was the most staggering, amazing, astounding thing that has ever happened. Who were the first people to be told about it? You know the answer, do you not? It was not the Sanhedrin in Jerusalem, it was not the Pharisees, the scribes, the doctors of the law, the Sadducees, none of your great philosophers of Greece, nor your emperor in Rome. To whom was the announcement made? Shepherds watching their flocks by night!

Now in those days the occupation of a shepherd was one of the lowliest of all; it was not even a respectable occupation. It is by now. Some of the best men I have ever known have been shepherds. But in those ancient times that was not the case, and yet the announcement made by the angel from glory was to the shepherds watching their flocks by night. Oh, what a gospel! And how mad they are who call themselves Christian and yet think in worldly terms, and say that modern people must understand it. I say again that if you start with that postulate you are denying the whole of the gospel. This is the reverse of everything ever known. The shepherds!

Then the time came when our Lord started out on his public ministry and needed helpers and assistants, men he could send out with this great message that he had come into the world to deliver. This was the most important task ever given to human beings – so who did he choose as his disciples? Well, obviously he would go now and canvas the academies and the porches in Greece and pick out the budding philosophers or those who had already established themselves. Or he would send a message to Rome and get some of the great senators or orators. Or he would go to Jerusalem and pick out the leading Pharisees and the greatest authorities on the law. Nothing of the sort! He picked out fishermen, washing their nets, working with their father in the boats. 'Follow me,' he said. He looked at a man who was a tax collector – another despised task – a tax collector called Matthew sitting at the receipt of customs. 'Follow me,' he said. These were the men he chose! Not the great, the mighty, not the learned. No, no, these men. You remember how the Sanhedrin described these apostles later on when they arrested them. They referred to them as 'unlearned and ignorant men' (*Acts* 4:13). But these were the men to whom he entrusted his message. Would you ever think of getting a message across to this great world, with all its learning and sophistication and culture, through men such as these? It is madness. Ah, it is, it is the 'madness' of God! These are the people amongst whom he always worked.

Now let me give you another example, a very striking one that our Lord himself pinpoints for us. Look at the well-known story about John the Baptist in prison. John was getting a bit troubled as to the identity of Jesus of Nazareth. At first, John had looked at him and had said to his followers, 'Behold the Lamb of God, which taketh away the sin of the world' (*John* 1:29); but here he was now, in prison, and to be in prison then was terrible. John was undoubtedly ill and in trouble. So he sent two of his messengers to Christ asking, 'Art thou he that should come, or do we look for another?' You remember the answer?

Jesus answered and said unto them, Go and shew John again those things which ye do hear and see: The blind receive their sight, and the lame walk, the lepers are cleansed, and the deaf hear, the dead are raised up – and then the climax – *and the poor have the gospel preached to them* (Matt. 11:3–5).

Have you ever been struck by those last words? This is one of the most amazing things of all and our Lord himself picked it out – 'the poor have the gospel preached to them'. Why did he single this out? He did so because this is what separates and distinguishes this gospel from every other teaching ever known to the human race; it always has done and still does. Greek philosophy had nothing to give to the poor – nothing at all. You cannot understand Greek philosophy unless you have had some training. Put a philosopher to address the common people and he would have had nothing to say to them, he could not have come down to their level. You had to have this desired learning or culture to be able to appreciate what he was saying. Indeed, the Pharisees had nothing to give to the poor, either. But here is one who has: 'The common people heard him gladly' (*Mark* 12:37). He was the first one who could ever speak to the common people and he did.

So Peter and John here in Samaria were only repeating what their blessed Lord and Master had done before them. Bypass villages? Certainly not! These were the people amongst whom our Lord worked.

And later on the apostle Paul, realizing the tremendous significance of this, puts it in his own way:

For ye see your calling, brethren, how that not many wise men after the flesh, not many mighty, not many noble, are called: But God hath chosen the foolish things of the world to confound the wise; and God hath chosen the weak things of the world to confound the things which are mighty; and base things of the world, and things which are despised, hath God chosen, yea, and things which are not, to bring to nought things that are: that no flesh should glory in his presence (1 Cor. 1:26–29).

What a reversal of everything that the world has ever thought! Where are the great people? Where are the great teachers? Where are the people who really understand life and can teach us? In the colleges – Oxford, Cambridge, London. Oh, the sophistication, the learning – these are the people! But it is the exact opposite here. He entrusted his message to fishermen; he spent his time in preaching to the poor.

And let us remind ourselves of this now. My dear friends, it is the gospel – and the gospel alone – that has ever given any hope to the poor. We are living in an age that is not only godless but is also ignorant of history. The poor, the so-called working classes in this country, may no longer be 'the poor', but they are regarded as such in general. They are no longer interested in this gospel; they are interested in politics. They have turned away from the gospel; they do not attend places of worship. But what they are ignorant of is that every advantage that they enjoy today has come to them as the result of this gospel. Let us remind them of this – that the first endeavours at any kind of poor law relief in this country were made by the Christian church. It was not the state that began it, nor was it Parliament. It is the church that has always cared for the poor, the church that has always taught the ignorant and started schools. It did it in the early days of the Christian faith and it has continued to do so ever since.

And not only in this country – look, too, at other countries. Who is it that has taken knowledge and medicine and instruction and information to the 'backward' races of this world, as they have been called? Every time the answer is that it was Christians. I have never heard of a missionary society started by humanists or by communists or any such people. No, no, it is the Christian church that has always brought the message to the villages, to the despised, to the poor and outcast. Peter and John were here in practice enunciating one of the greatest and most glorious principles of all in connection with our Christian faith.

But then I come on to another factor that is more specific still in terms of this twenty-fifth verse. Look at the places in which our Lord has always worked. When the apostles 'preached the gospel in many villages of the Samaritans', they were but imitating our blessed Lord and Master. Have you ever looked at it from this standpoint? Have you ever considered where he spent his time, the places that were associated with him? The second chapter of Matthew's Gospel brings out this point particularly clearly. Where was he brought up? He was brought up in a place called Nazareth – another village. I was tempted to preach tonight on this one theme of Christ and villages. Villages! Jesus of Nazareth – that is how he was known. What sort of a place was Nazareth? Nathaniel spoke the proverb – 'Can there any good thing come out of Nazareth?' (*John* 1:46). That is the place where he was brought up. Not in Jerusalem, but in Nazareth.

Then where did our Lord spend most of his time? He spent it in Galilee. If you read the Gospels for yourselves, you will find that this troubled many people. They could not understand why he spent most of his time up in Galilee. It was the northern part of the country; it was, indeed, called 'Galilee of the Gentiles'. It was on the borders where their land joined the land of these pagan Gentile nations. Indeed, his own brethren remonstrated with him, saying, in effect, 'Why on earth don't you go up to Jerusalem? A man who wants to make his teaching known does not spend his time here in Galilee, he goes up to the centre of things; that's where the big events take place, in Jerusalem' (*John* 7:3–5). We read on another occasion that some people tried to take him by force to make him a king, but he brushed them off, and 'went up into a mountain himself alone' (*John* 6:15). This was his habit, this is where he spent his time – in Galilee of the Gentiles.

And, you see, what was true of Jesus himself has ever since been true of his followers and his method of working through them. On their way back to Jerusalem, Peter and John were being directed by him through the Spirit, and they had caught his own spirit, as I am going to show you. And so they did not bypass the villages; they stopped there and preached the gospel. And this is one of the most astounding things, I think, that has ever happened in history. How did Christianity first come to Europe? At this time, and later, Europe was the important place. Rome, after all, was the great centre of the world. She had conquered most other countries and Rome – the seat of the imperial government – is in Italy, and Italy is in Europe.

But how exactly did the gospel first come into Europe? What a perfect illustration it is of this text of ours. We are told the story in the sixteenth chapter of Acts. Paul has come to a dead end at Troas; he has had certain ideas about his next destination – he wants to go to Asia and to Bithynia but he is not allowed to (*Acts* 16:7). So he finds himself down at Troas, a seaport, and he is unable to go any further. He goes to bed bewildered, not understanding what God is doing with him. In the night he has a vision – 'There stood a man of Macedonia'. We are told that this man of Macedonia says, 'Come over into Macedonia, and help us' (*Acts* 16:9). And Paul recognizes this as the call of God to him to cross the sea and take the gospel into this great, supreme continent of Europe.

Now, then, here is the continent of philosophy, of Roman law and of government, all the experts, the great people. How are they to be evangelized? Well, you would have said at once, would you not, that the obvious course would be to go straight to Rome? After all, Rome is the centre. Or, if you do not go to Rome, you should at any rate start in Athens, which is the intellectual centre and the seat of the philosophers. But it does not happen like that. Paul goes to a place called Philippi, and, as if to underline this very principle that we are considering together, the apostle does not even preach the gospel in the city of Philippi. Let me read this to you. If you do not see the whole glory of the gospel here, you are blind.

Therefore loosing from Troas, we came with a straight course to Samothracia, and the next day to Neapolis; and from thence to Philippi, which is the chief city of that part of Macedonia, and a colony: and we were in that city abiding certain days. And on the Sabbath we went out of the city by a river side, where prayer was wont to be made; and we sat down . . .'(Acts 16:11–13).

You see the meaning of that, do you not: outside the city wall, just a little place by the side of a river. That is where the gospel is first preached in Europe.

And then, to add to the significance, look at the character of the congregation. You would have anticipated, would you not, that the first thing to do would be to have a preliminary advertising campaign, and especially to send invitations to all the great philosophers, and statesmen – all the people who really determine thought and the whole course of history and what happens in the world. Get them all together and address them. But this is what we are told: They *spake unto the women which resorted thither* (*Acts* 16:13).

You know the story of men's attitude to women, do you not? Women were despised by all the nations. Men alone counted; women were nothing. But the gospel was first preached in Europe to women in a little prayer meeting on a Sunday afternoon outside the city wall. Oh, what a gospel! Can you not see it? Villages! Unknown places! Outside cities! And this has been true in the long history of the Christian church and the spread of the gospel ever since.

Have you ever read the history of the great revivals in the church? Well, if you have, you have read a great deal about villages. Revivals do not start in great cities. They generally start in some place that nobody has ever heard of. I could give you endless examples. They do not start in cathedrals, they do not start in cities, and they do not start with notable people. The story generally is about some unknown person or group of people in some little village or hamlet right off the map and there the fire of God suddenly descends. Daniel Rowland lived in a little village – it is still a little village; Howel Harris in Trevecca, nothing but a hamlet. In Northern Ireland in 1859, just two men, labourers, living in a place that was scarcely even a hamlet – that was where that great revival began. And so it has gone on, in villages!

And then one other thing I want to notice is this: see how our Lord surprises us by what he does to us. Of course, the world thinks of the gospel as something that is going to teach us. They think of Jesus Christ as a teacher who has come to tell us to love one another and to be kind and gentle to one another, to introduce brotherhood and friendship. And so we address the trade unions and the employers and we tell them to try to understand the teaching of Jesus and to put it into operation and to catch the Christmas spirit. Thank God, we do not hear much about that sort of nonsense these days, but we used to hear it such a lot. There is less of that sort of talk these days because by now even the world is beginning to see what utter rubbish and nonsense it is. It has nothing to do with Christianity. Our Lord did not come to teach or to instruct; he did not come to give us an example; he did not come that we might catch something of his spirit. No, no! Why did he come? What did he come to do? He came to change us completely.

Now I want to demonstrate this to you. Here in chapter 8 of Acts, I am told that Peter and John, instead of rushing back to Jerusalem, 'preached the gospel in many villages of the Samaritans'. Do you want to know the exact significance of that? Well, listen to what we read in Luke chapter 9:

And it came to pass, when the time was come that he [the Lord Jesus Christ] should be received up, he stedfastly set his face to go to Jerusalem, and sent messengers before his face: and they went, and entered into a village of the Samaritans, to make ready for him. And they did not receive him, because his face was as though he would go to Jerusalem. And when his disciples James and John saw this, they said, Lord, wilt thou that we command fire to come down from heaven, and consume them, even as Elias did? But he turned, and rebuked them, and said, Ye know not what manner of spirit ye are of. For the Son of man is not come to destroy men's lives, but to save them. And they went to another village (Luke 9:51–56).

Do you understand? John was with James, not Peter, on that occasion, and because the Samaritans would not receive them, they wanted the whole village to be destroyed in a great fire from heaven. That is how John as a natural man, before the day of Pentecost, regarded the Samaritans. But here, in Acts 8, we are told that the same John wanted to evangelize the Samaritans and tell them the story of the gospel.

The same can be said of Peter. You remember how he is depicted in the pages of the four Gospels, but look at him here, he was equally ready with John to preach to the villages in Samaria. What had happened to these men? Well, they had been absolutely and completely changed. Before, they had been typical men of the world and their attitude was: 'These Samaritans will not receive us; crush them, get rid of them, blot them out, destroy them.' But now it is: 'Evangelize them, have a concern for them.' You see the humility of these men? The great men of the world, of course, do not spend time in unimportant villages; they can only function in great cities. If there are some underlings, then send them to the villages. But here were two of the leading apostles and they had time to preach to the villages. It was because they had been so changed, because they had become like their Master, and were now characterized by humility. We are told, 'The common people heard him gladly', and they would hear these apostles gladly.

And now, too, the apostles had a new conception altogether of the purpose of our Lord's coming. They had thought of him as a teacher, as a possible national deliverer, and so they had demanded: 'Get rid of the Samaritans!' But now they understood his words on that occasion: 'Ye know not what manner of spirit ye are of. For the Son of man is not come to destroy men's lives, but to save them' (*Luke* 9:56). And they understood this because they had been baptized with the Holy Spirit. They were not the same men. They were revolutionized, completely changed, and now the love of God was shed abroad in their hearts so that they were filled with a heart of love for these people.

That is Christianity. The Son of God did not come into this world merely to give us an example. Thank God, he did not! I cannot emulate the example of great men, leave alone the Son of God. His example condemns me more than anything I know. He did not come merely to teach me and tell me to pull myself together and to lift myself up and conquer my temptations. Oh, thank God, he did not do that, otherwise I am damned. No, no, 'The Son of man is come to seek and to save that which was lost' (*Luke* 19:10), and Peter and John had now got this message. They were able to tell these Samaritans that they could be saved, that they could be changed and could become new men and women, filled with this same glory.

This is it, my friend; it is a message that is the exact opposite of what the world always expects. The world is prepared to listen to 'Jesus the teacher', the exemplar and so on, but it does not understand the cross, it does not like it. It says that the most shameful thing that has ever happened is the cross on Calvary. No, no, says this message, 'The glory of the cross.' We sing:

When I survey the wondrous cross . . .

Why? Well, because it is there that our Lord saves us by dying for our sins, by paying the penalty for us and setting us free: 'God was in Christ, reconciling the world unto himself' (2 *Cor.* 5:19).

So you see that in every conceivable respect this gospel is the exact opposite of what the man of the world expects. Villages! Ordinary people! Ignoramuses! Yes!

Then let me end by putting a question: Why is the gospel like this? What is the explanation of the fact that it is precisely as I have been putting it to you? Why is this gospel in every respect the reverse of human wisdom? And the answers are quite simple. The first, and, indeed, the comprehensive, answer is to show that it is all of God, and God is eternally different from us. That is our only hope. He said through Isaiah, 'For my thoughts are not your thoughts, neither are your ways my ways, saith the LORD, for as the heavens are higher than the earth, so are my ways higher than your ways, and my thoughts than your thoughts' (*Isa.* 55:8–9). Are you still foolish enough to try to *understand* this gospel? Are you saying, 'Because I am a twentieth-century scientist I can't any longer believe in the miraculous and the supernatural?' Poor blind fool! This is all of God, and it is the exact opposite of what you or anyone else has ever thought. That is why God does it like this.

And, of course, it can be worked out like this: God's purpose is to humble our pride. That is our main trouble – pride of intellect, pride of understanding. Nothing amazes me more than to hear ministers of the gospel, as they presume to call themselves, saying, 'Of course, people cannot take this today' – as if it is people today who decide what is right! People *today*? People, by nature, have never accepted this gospel. The Son of God was rejected when he came into this world because they could not understand him, and this idea that the gospel is something that the natural man is to understand with his learning and his knowledge, is, I repeat, a complete denial of the whole of the gospel. The gospel is as it is in order to humble us, 'To bring to nought things that are: that no flesh should glory in his presence' (*1 Cor.* 1:28–29).

Because it comes in this particular way, the gospel tells you that you are a helpless and a hopeless and a damned sinner, that you are completely lost, and that you can do nothing whatsoever about your own salvation. Do not talk about your good deeds – they are 'filthy rags' in the sight of God. Do not talk about your knowledge and learning – it is ignorance when you bring it to God. You have nothing to contribute, nothing to give at all. You can only become a Christian in one way, and that is as a pauper, as a poor person, as a villager, if you like, as someone who does not know anything, one of these 'clodhoppers' in a village who has never been to London and does not know about London life. That is the condition. 'Except ye be converted, and become as little children, ye shall not enter into the kingdom of heaven' (*Matt*. 18:3). There is only one way to enter into this kingdom and that is that you say believingly –

Nothing in my hand I bring;
Simply to thy cross I cling;
Naked, come to thee for dress;
Helpless, look to thee for grace;
Foul, I to the fountain fly;
Wash me, Saviour, or I die.

Augustus Toplady

That is why the gospel comes like this. At all points it ridicules us and all our cleverness and learning and moralities – it shows that this is all utterly useless; it demolishes it all. The gospel presumes nothing in us except our need.

And then, of course, this fact that the apostles preached in the villages of the Samaritans tells us that in the sight of God it is the soul that matters. God is not interested in your wealth or poverty. He is not interested in your great brain or your lack of intelligence. He is not interested in your learning and sophistication, or in your illiteracy. God sees the soul, and the villager has a soul like the city-dweller. It is the soul that matters, not the things to which the world attaches such significance. It is this blessed Son of God who says, 'What shall it profit a man, if he shall gain the whole world, and lose his own soul?' (*Mark* 8:36). He was as interested in villagers as in townspeople. Why? Because they are all 'souls'. So Peter and John do not rush back to Jerusalem but preach the gospel to the villages of the Samaritans.

And, lastly, and blessed be the name of God for this, the gospel comes in this way in order to show that there is hope for all of us, and that there is equal hope for all of us. Have you been listening to these clever men who try to reduce this glorious gospel to the measure of their understanding of this sophisticated age? Can you understand them? Oh, they have read Russian literature – that is the great thing. You can quote Russian literature! But can you follow them? Do you get any message from them? Do they offer you any hope? Listen to your great philosophers on the television, do they help you? They are very clever, are they not? They bandy about these wonderful terms. Are you any the wiser? Of course not.

Thank God for a gospel that holds out a hope for any of us, for all of us, and an equal hope for all of us. The greatest philosopher that the world has ever known, is as helpless before God as the veriest child or ignoramus. He has no advantage – indeed, what the apostle seems to suggest at the end of 1 Corinthians 1 is that the philosopher is at a disadvantage precisely because of his pride of intellect, his pride in his own understanding and sophistication. Because the gospel is altogether of God, there is hope for all. You are not saved by your understanding; you are saved simply by believing on the Lord Jesus Christ.

That is the message: 'Believe on the Lord Jesus Christ and thou shalt be saved' (*Acts* 16:31). It does not ask you to have understanding; it does not ask you to understand miracles; it does not ask you to understand the virgin birth; it does not ask you to 'understand' the atonement or anything else. All it asks is that you see your need, that you see your guilt, your desperate plight before God, and that you hear someone calling to you and saying, 'Come unto me, all ye that labour and are heavy laden, and I will give you rest' (*Matt.* 11:28). 'Look unto me, and be ye saved, all the ends of the earth' (*Isa.* 45:22). It is just that – it is to believe that Jesus of Nazareth is the Son of God, that he came to die for your sins, to reconcile you to God, and to give you new life and an everlasting hope of glory. Thank God this is a gospel that can be preached in villages as well as anywhere else; it is a gospel that holds out hope to the most ignorant person of the universe tonight, to the blackest, vilest sinner, the most desperate offender, to such a person it holds out exactly the same hope as it does to the most moral, respectable religious people in the world. It is 'the power of God unto salvation to every one that believeth; to the Jew first, and also to the Greek' (*Rom.* 1:16). It is a gospel for 'whosoever believeth': 'For God so loved the world, that he gave his only begotten Son, that whosoever believeth in him should not perish, but have everlasting life' (*John* 3:16). Thank God for the Saviour of the villager; thank God for a gospel that can be preached in the villages of this life and give an eternal hope to whosoever believes in him.

Have you believed in him? Are you one of these villagers? Or did you come into this service at the full height of your modern sophistication? Have you become as a little child, and do you ascribe unto him, and unto him alone, all praise and honour and glory? Do you say with the apostle Paul, 'God forbid that I should glory, save in the cross of our Lord Jesus Christ' (*Gal.* 6:14)?

12

The Supernatural

And the angel of the Lord spake unto Philip, saying, Arise, and go toward the south unto the way that goeth down from Jerusalem unto Gaza, which is desert (Acts 8:26).

In the story that has been unfolded to us in the first twenty-five verses of Acts chapter 8, we have seen how the gospel came to the people of Samaria through Philip, and how Peter and John arrived in the city and laid hands on the new Christians. We have also considered the story of Simon the sorcerer, and, finally, we have seen how Peter and John, on their way back to Jerusalem, preached in many Samaritan villages. Now we move on to verse 26, which is an important verse because it tells us that the gospel is now being spread yet farther.

We are going to consider the case of this Ethiopian eunuch, as he is called, this great man who was the treasurer of the court and of the government of the queen of the land called Ethiopia, which in those days was a great tract of Africa, including the Sudan and other parts that we are familiar with now. So here we are being told about the first African to believe the gospel and we are shown the gospel beginning to spread into the great continent of Africa.

Now this twenty-sixth verse is, of course, a simple historical statement, a statement of fact. It is a kind of introductory statement to lead us on to the dramatic account of the conversation between Philip and the eunuch, as a result of which we see this eunuch going on his way 'rejoicing' because a marvellous thing had happened to him and he had become a Christian. At first sight you would think that this verse is just a necessary connecting link. You do not suddenly start a story without giving some preliminary introduction to show how it came about. So this verse seems to be just a literary device. But it is much more than that, and I want to show you how it really tells us *why* this happened to the Ethiopian, and, still more important, perhaps, *how* it happened – all that is conveyed and implied in this one verse. It thus shows us some of the things of which the world is so ignorant. So we must examine it and I think I can show you quite simply that this verse, which appears to the casual reader to be just a bit of introduction, is really giving us some of the most fundamental principles of the biblical message, the principles behind the gospel of salvation of our blessed Lord and Saviour.

I want to show you, therefore, that the principles outlined here are of great value to all of us – to everybody who is a Christian and also to those who are not. Every Christian needs to be reminded of these principles; everybody who is not a Christian needs to be introduced to them. Here we are, the first Sunday night of a new year,[1] facing the unknown future. Who knows what lies ahead of us? What are the possibilities? They are endless. Some pleasant, some most unpleasant. And the great question for us is: How are we going to face it all? Are we ready for whatever may come?

Or let me put it in an entirely different way. Look at the world as it is today. We know the past history, we know what has happened in 1967, we know what is happening now. The question is: Is there any hope? Have you any hope for 1968? What are you pinning your faith to? What are you relying on? Surely these are the great questions that should be confronting us all. Why is the world as it is? What is the matter?

You see, we must constantly come back to these questions. We are living in an age when humanity is boasting of its ability and its power and understanding. All right, I grant that – it does have these things. Men and women are doing marvels. Pick up your newspaper almost any day and you will read of some new discovery and invention. All right, very wonderful. But still the question is: Well, then, if people have all these great powers, why is their world in such terrible trouble? And, still more specifically, if they are so wonderful, why are men and women individually so unhappy? Why are there such failures? Why are they having to

[1] 1968.

resort to various mechanisms and means of escape? These are the very questions that, I think you will all agree, should be uppermost in the minds of every thinking person on a night like this, the first Sunday night of a new year.

There are some things of which the world needs to be reminded. Yes, and there are some things of which the Christian needs to be reminded. I say this because the world is influencing us all. It is so insistent in its propaganda and so subtle in its teaching that we all need to be reminded of some fundamental principles. What are they? Well, the first is this: the reality of the supernatural realm. 'The angel of the Lord spake unto Philip, saying, Arise, and go toward the south unto the way that goeth down from Jerusalem unto Gaza, which is desert.' The angel of the Lord!

Now let us come down, as the common saying has it, to brass tacks. What is the matter with the world? And the first answer is that its chief trouble is that it knows nothing about the supernatural realm. I would say that that is the essence of the trouble. I think it is a waste of time to be arguing with people about the *details* of the gospel. If people do not believe in this realm of the supernatural, they cannot possibly believe in God, they cannot believe in the virgin birth, in miracles, in the atoning death and the resurrection. If you do not believe in the supernatural, in the spiritual realm, all that goes out. So this is the basic question, and that is why I start with it.

People who are not Christians think that this world in which we are living, the visible world, the material world, is all there is. That is the popular view today. Never has it had greater publicity than at the present time. It is the view held by what is called humanism or materialism. We hear it propounded in the Reith Lectures and by all these clever people who are given such prominence in the media. Radio, television, newspapers, magazine articles, are all proclaiming this teaching. It is the popular, the controlling view, characteristic of man in the twentieth century, this scientific age, when men and women have shed folklore and fancy and fantasy and at last have really come to know things as they are.

In its essence, the modern view holds that this is a material and mechanical universe that came into being accidentally. People do not all agree as to how – they have interesting debates with one another as to exactly how this happened – but they are all agreed that the world came about by chance and that everything in it is governed by brute, inanimate forces – power or energy. They will tell you about the energy in the atom. And, of course, that is true. Everything is in a state of tension; this tremendous power and energy is the basis of everything. But it is inanimate, there is no mind, it is all material, and it has all been operating accidentally. It produced the world accidentally, and everything has continued since in a blind manner as the result of these terrible brute forces, this power and energy.

And then this view goes on to tell us that the greatest thing that this process, this energy, has produced, is the human mind. This is the acme of its achievement so far. And we are told that this is a very wonderful achievement, because it is man alone who is capable of influencing these forces and factors that have even produced man himself. And so we are being told at the present time that man is in the position of a god, and that with his new scientific and biological knowledge, the understanding of genes and all the rest of it, he will be able to control life, and will be able to control even man, the physical frame. He will be able to manipulate life. He will be in the position of a creator. This process, this blind process, has thrown up a prophet that is able now, at last, if man only realized it and took advantage of it and grasped the possibility, to create new conditions and beings, banishing disease, making man great and strong and mighty. It is all here, the human mind is the greatest thing in the entire universe.

And so we are told that, of course, biologically there is nothing outside all this. There is no such thing as a supernatural realm. There are no powers greater than these powers of which we are aware; there are no forces beyond these forces that we can describe. And, therefore, the experts end by saying that there is no point or purpose in our looking for any interference in our world, any intervention from the outside. No, no, they say, this is quite impossible. Man's salvation and the salvation of the world is in his hands. If he likes to use the powers he possesses and the knowledge that he has now obtained and garnered, if he likes to harness it and to apply it, he can make a perfect world and perfect men and women to live in it. He has the power, he can make or mar this world and it is no use looking to anybody else. This old idea of some magical intervention, some kind of god – some *deus ex machina* who comes in – rubbish! Nonsense! Fantasy! Our fate and our future rest entirely with us. This is the popular view today; this is the view that makes most people reject the Christian gospel as being outdated, rather pathetic, and something that it is quite insulting to offer to modern people.

And this is the real explanation of why the world is as it is. This is the theory that has been controlling the minds of men and women for some time now, and we see a world that seems to be hurtling to calamity. As this teaching is propagated, we see increasingly clearly that crime and vice and a return to the jungle and the primitive are on the increase. We see that man is using his power for destruction, for selfishness, for greed and avarice. He uses it to make a beast of himself – to become expert at that. And we see that the main effect of the use of human ability and knowledge and scientific discovery has been the invention of bombs and other instruments of war that are more and more horrible. It all seems to be working up to some terrible climax of destruction and calamity. That is the position in which we find ourselves. And so the world today, owing to this view that entirely excludes the supernatural, is bankrupt. It is frightened, it is alarmed, and it is without any hope whatsoever.

Oh, it is tragic to see how men and women change in their allegiances! Once they trusted everything to the statesmen, the politicians; now they have become cynical about them and are looking to the scientists. Can you trust the scientists? Are they impartial, detached people inspired by pure reason, never moved by jealousy or envy or selfishness – is that true? My dear friends, if you believe that, you will believe anything! These are but men and women like all others, and they have this terrible power in their hands and you see what use is being made of it. And so the world, I repeat, is bankrupt and without hope.

So, then, why are we considering this in this church? We are here tonight because the view I have been describing is just a lie. The world is as it is because people believe that lie, and because they are totally unaware of what is mentioned here in Acts 8:26. Here is the answer: 'An angel of the Lord said to Philip . . .' What does this mean? It is the great message of the Bible from beginning to end, and I can put it to you like this: This world is not the *real* world, but is only the *visible* world, a passing world. There is another world, another realm. It is invisible. It is beyond our gaze. The new telescope in Sussex will not be able to see it any more than Jodrell Bank can. You can send people into outer space and they will come back and say, 'We haven't seen God.' Of course not! You can send them still higher but they will not see him. He is invisible, beyond. He is eternal, illimitable. It is the teaching of the Bible that there is a supernatural realm and that this is the true world and the realm that really matters, and that this invisible realm is actually controlling this present world.

Now the basic message of the whole of the Bible is that every one of us is in one of two positions. You either believe in this modern idea that the world is entirely self-contained and mechanical and material with nothing at all beyond it, or else you take the biblical position and say that beyond it, above it, all round it everywhere, is this other realm, which is the true and the real, and which determines what happens in this world. Take a famous statement of the biblical teaching given by the apostle Paul: 'While we look not at the things which are seen, but at the things which are not seen: for the things which are seen are temporal; but the things which are not seen are eternal' (2 *Cor.* 4:18).

And all that is introduced to us by this extraordinary statement: 'An angel of the Lord spake unto Philip.' What is an angel? Well, an angel is a spiritual being. There is quite a lot in the Bible about angels. Our Lord says about little children that 'in heaven their angels do always behold the face of my Father which is in heaven' (*Matt.* 18:10). The author of the epistle to the Hebrews, writing in his first chapter about angels, says: 'Are they not all ministering spirits, sent forth to minister for them who shall be heirs of salvation?' (*Heb.* 1:14).

I repeat that the whole case of the Bible is that over and above all that you and I see and know, there is another great realm, a spiritual realm, which intervenes in and controls this one. Further, this spiritual realm can be divided into two parts: there is the good section and there is the bad. The good section consists of the blessed Holy Trinity – God the Father, God the Son, God the Holy

Spirit – and it is peopled with angels and archangels, cherubim and seraphim, these great and glorious beings who are spiritual in their nature.

But we are told that there are other spiritual beings, which are evil: the devil and all his emissaries and all his servants. The apostle Paul always made a great deal of this. For example, in describing the world as it is without Christ, he says, 'And you hath he quickened, who were dead in trespasses and sins; wherein in time past ye walked according to the course of this world, according to the prince of the power of the air, the spirit that now worketh in the children of disobedience' (*Eph.* 2:1–2). Again, he says to the Ephesians, 'For we wrestle not against flesh and blood, but against principalities, against powers, against the rulers of the darkness of this world, against spiritual wickedness in high places' (*Eph.* 6:12).

The teaching is that there is a great conflict between the forces of God and of good, and the forces of the devil and of evil, and they are fighting for the mastery of this world in which you and I live. The whole business of the Bible is to tell us that you cannot begin to understand the history of the human race unless you begin to consider it in terms of these great, unseen spiritual powers that are surrounding us. We think we know everything and can see all things. But we cannot see the important things, these unseen influences round and about us. This conflict between God and the devil, the forces of light and the forces of darkness, is the whole explanation of human history.

The world is as it is because the forces of darkness and evil keep it in ignorance of this great conflict. That is the tragedy of the human race. Man thinks he is 'the master of his fate, the captain of his soul'; he thinks that he decides, and that with his scientific knowledge he can do this, that, and the other. He has always thought that – it is nothing new. Every generation has boasted of its knowledge and pitied everybody who has gone before. We are just a bit farther on. People in a hundred years' time – if there is a world in a hundred years' time – will think that we were more or less ignorant. So it continues and you see what man has made of his world. It is all because he is the dupe and the slave of these malign forces. 'We wrestle not against flesh and blood, but against principalities and powers.'

But the point is that there really is a supernatural realm. If this is a closed universe, if the future is in the hands of human beings, what have we to look forward to? What can we anticipate but a world that will get worse and worse, even as it has done during the years that are past? There is no hope at all. But let us remember that this is not true: there is another realm, there is the supernatural – 'the angel of the Lord'; 'an angel of God'. There are unseen possibilities; there are unseen powers. This is our hope, and our only hope.

So we start with the being of God: God over all. 'The angel of the Lord spake unto Philip.' Who told him to do so? I have already quoted to you Hebrews 1:14, 'Are they not all ministering spirits . . . ?' Angels are servants sent by God. It was God who sent the angel with his message to Philip. God is over all; this is the great message. This world is not man's world; it is God's world. The Bible does not hesitate to tell us things like this, so I do not apologize for saying them. It is the Bible alone that gives me a satisfactory explanation of this world. If you ask me to believe that accident and chance have produced all the perfection I see in nature and creation, I will tell you that I do not believe it.

I have often used an argument based on the perfection of the eye. Have you ever dissected a human eye? Do you know anything about its structure? It is just nonsense to believe that this is an accident. It is inconceivable that blind, irrational forces could produce this perfect instrument of precision. Impossible! There is only one adequate explanation: 'In the beginning God created . . .' (*Gen.* 1:1). God, a great and an eternal mind, bigger than the universe, existing without it, able to conceive of it and to bring it into being by the word of his *fiat*, he created the world.

And not only that, this great message is to the effect that God alone sustains the universe. Read the eighth Psalm or Psalm 104. The latter is a long Psalm of thirty-five verses. It begins with the words, 'Bless the LORD, O my soul. O LORD my God, thou art very great; thou art clothed with honour and majesty. Who coverest thyself with light as with a garment: who stretchest out the heavens like a curtain . . .' The Psalm goes on to say that God upholds and sustains everything: 'That thou givest them they gather: thou openest thine hand, they are filled with good. Thou hidest thy face, they are troubled: thou takest away their breath, they die, and return to their dust' (verses 1–2, 28–29).

A mechanical, controlled universe? Of course not! It is being controlled and sustained and kept going by God. He could withhold the sun, and if he did we would all die. He can withhold the rain and the snow and all the elements. Our times, our breath, are in his hands.

And, furthermore, God is the Lord of history: everything is under his hand. This is the teaching. Thank God for it! And he is a God of power. Not the limited power of men and women but endless, illimitable power. Thank God, too, that he is a God of holiness and of righteousness and of truth. Man is not so, and he proves it by his actions. The world proves it. But God is light, and justice, and truth. He cannot lie, and he cannot do anything wrong. And, on top of it all, he is a God of all knowledge, he is omniscient.

Do you not see how this comes out in this verse? Let me show it to you. This is wonderful. 'The angel of the Lord spake unto Philip, saying, Arise, and go toward the south unto the way that goeth down from Jerusalem unto Gaza, which is desert.' Now there is a very interesting phrase here. The Authorized Version says, 'Arise, and go toward the south', but there is an alternative translation that reads like this: 'Arise, and go about noon . . .' Of course, there is no contradiction because it is at noon that the sun is in the south. But interestingly the only other place in which this Greek word is used in the New Testament is in this same book of Acts, in chapter 22 and verse 6, and there it is translated 'about noon', and I believe that is the right translation here: 'Go south, go down at noon when the sun is due south; go at that particular time.'

'What is the point?' asks somebody. It is this: if Philip had gone down an hour earlier or an hour later, he would never have met this Ethiopian eunuch at all. But God knows everything. There were two roads that went from Jerusalem down to Gaza in the south; but God knew which of the two the man would be travelling on, and he knew the exact time, the exact moment. So he told Philip to go at the precise moment that would lead to the meeting between him and this man who was seeking salvation.

My dear friends, *that* is the sort of world we are living in. There is God above and around us, knowing all these things. He knows exactly all that we do and all that happens to us. The Bible is full of this kind of thing. So is the history of the saints of God throughout the centuries. The meeting between Philip and the Ethiopian eunuch did not take place by chance, it was not an accident, it was not a coincidence. No, no! It was the God who knows everything sending his servant at the critical moment so that the two would come together and this glorious thing happen to this man.

Oh, what a message to start a new year with! How I thank God that we are not living in a closed universe, and that I am not dependent upon what people are going to do in this coming year! There is God, and he knows all, and he is outside, and he is above, and he is illimitable in his power, in his omniscience and in everything else. And all his attributes are eternal.

But I want to tell you something of the plan of this great and glorious God, his purpose with respect to this world. That is the great theme of the Bible. That is why we have it, that is what it is all about. It is just to tell us about God, what he has already done with respect to this world, and what he is going to do. It tells us that he has a great plan, a great scheme, a great purpose. I do not know how people can live without this. My only hope at this moment is that God, the everlasting and eternal God, has not turned his back on this world of ours, but that, on the contrary, he is very concerned about it, and has a plan for its redemption, for its deliverance, for its restoration to the condition in which he originally made it. This message tells us that God interferes in this world, erupts into it, enters into it, and is most intimately concerned about it. 'The angel of the Lord said to Philip, Go . . .' What for? Oh, he has an errand, a message. Here is a man in need, in trouble – go! That is the great message of the whole of the Bible: God seeking lost man.

What are the characteristics of this plan and purpose of God with regard to this world? It is all here in this passage. Have you learned how to read your Bible, my friend? You do not look at words, you look at meaning, you look beneath the surface, you see the great principles coming out to meet you and they are a great proclamation. God's plan for this world is a redemptive plan. Why did he send his angel to meet Philip? In order to redeem the

Ethiopian eunuch. The man was in trouble; I hope to show you that. He was helpless and in need, and God's purpose was a purpose of redemption.

God is displeased with the state of this world today. He sees his marvellous creation marred, defaced, ruined and he sees man, the supreme creation of all. That is what astounds the psalmist in the eighth psalm. He says, in effect, 'When I look at the sun and the moon and the stars, and all these marvellous things that you have created, what is man, that you are mindful of him, and the son of man, that you visit him?' To God, who can contemplate the sun and the moon and the stars and the constellations, and the outer spaces, and the light suspended over the north, what is man? But God is concerned. It is incredible, but it is true – this all-powerful and everlasting God is interested in us and concerned about us. This world is not abandoned, it is not left to human beings and their ingenuity and ability and all their horrible plans and purposes. No, no! God is concerned, and his plan is a plan of redemption.

And the next point that I find here is that redemption is always the result of God's initiative. Can you not see it all! Where is your imagination? Look at this Ethiopian eunuch going down, in hopelessness, back to his home, expecting nothing. But suddenly he is confronted by a man. Who sent the man there? God sent him.

My dear friends, this salvation of ours is all of God – entirely. You must not bring yourself into it at all. If you do, you are denying it. It is all of God. 'By grace are ye saved through faith; and that not of yourselves: it is the gift of God' (*Eph.* 2:8). This is the whole message. God makes the world, makes man in his own image and gives him a perfect start. But man, like a fool, listens to the enemy and down he goes. There he is, in misery, hiding behind the trees! But God comes down into the Garden and calls him out and addresses him. God comes down! It is always God's initiative.

We saw this same principle when we were considering Acts chapter 7. Stephen, addressing the Sanhedrin, said, 'Men, brethren, and fathers, hearken; The God of glory appeared unto our father Abraham' (*Acts* 7:2). That is the whole story of the Jewish race. God approaching a man called Abram, who was a pagan in Ur of the Chaldees, calling him out and turning him into a nation. This is

God – God making a people in order that he can spread this news, God preparing for the coming, ultimately, of his own Son. The Old Testament is full of this preparation of God, how he made these people, how he blessed them. They sinned against him and rebelled and they would have been destroyed a hundred times and more. How did they persist? Oh, at the critical moment, God came in, God intervened, God delivered them: Red Sea, crossing of the Jordan – all these great deliverances. The Old Testament is full of it.

And then you come to the New Testament, and here is its message: 'God so loved the world, that he gave his only begotten Son, that whosoever believeth in him should not perish, but have everlasting life' (*John* 3:16). 'When the fulness of the time was come, God sent forth his Son' – into this world, from heaven, from the unseen, the supernatural – 'made of a woman, made under the law, to redeem them that were under the law' (*Gal.* 4:4–5). It is always God's initiative. Nobody was expecting him at that time. There had been four hundred years of silence after Malachi. The world was in a terrible condition when the Son of God came into it. God sent him down. From the beginning to the end it was God acting.

And look at the Son of God. There he is walking along and he sees a man called Matthew, a tax collector for the Romans, sitting at the receipt of custom – not thinking much, but thinking, perhaps, of how to cheat and make a little more money for himself by robbing his own fellow-countrymen. Suddenly he is arrested by Christ and the command comes, 'Follow me', and off he goes, a new man (*Matt.* 9:9). It was the same with Simon Peter, Andrew, all the rest of them: God calling, always God's initiative.

And one of the greatest men who appears in the New Testament is a mighty man called the apostle Paul. How did he become an apostle? Was it because he was always looking for Christ, because he was listening to him, ready to accept him? No, no, it was the exact opposite. Down he goes on the road to Damascus 'breathing out threatenings and slaughter' (*Acts* 9:1), utterly opposed and antagonistic. But suddenly the light, the face, the call! Invariably the initiative of God. There was a man living in a place called Philippi. He was the keeper of the prison, rather a desperate man, and God took the initiative with respect to him, and in his case it was an earthquake (*Acts* 16). There is nothing that God will not do. It is always God. This is what we see in the New Testament.

Come into church history – here it is again. Do you know why there is still a Christian church? Is it because of the brilliant doctors of the church, the bishops, archbishops and popes? Ah! They would have ruined it long ago, they have done their best to do so. There is only one reason why we are here – God has come in, in revival! The church would have perished long since were it not that God intervenes, sends down the Spirit and calls out his people. This is our only hope. Always the initiative of God.

But what I want to emphasize for you on this first Sunday night of a new year is God's concern for each of us individually. Is this not marvellous? Look at this man Philip: he has had brilliant success as an evangelist in Samaria, many converts, great joy, and these people need to be trained and built up. You would have thought that God would have left him there. No, no! God knows that there is this one man, this isolated, solitary person, who is in desperate need, and he takes Philip out of his success and prosperity and sends him into a desert way to meet this individual soul.

How glad I am that I can tell you that tonight, in an age that is talking about immense powers and energies, even the universe of power that is in an atom. You read of these great spaces and measurements, these light years, and you feel that you are small, you are insignificant, you do not matter, you are cannon fodder or just the sport of all these unseen forces, and you say it is hopeless. No, no! The God who has made everything, and who sustains everything, and who owns everything, and who controls everything, he knows you and he is interested in you, and he is concerned about you; and he will change events in order that you may be included. This is the staggering thing. The psalmist has seen it: 'What is man, that thou art mindful of him?' (*Psa.* 8:4). Yes, but I put it personally, 'Who am I, what am I, that this great God should be concerned about me?' But he is. 'The Son of God, who loved me, and gave himself *for me*' (*Gal.* 2:20).

The programme of God is not a social or political redemption and emancipation and improvement. It is individual; it is personal. The gospel is the good news that God takes hold of us individually and delivers us out of this present evil world, and translates us from the kingdom of darkness into the kingdom of his dear Son. Oh, the blessed gospel that tells you tonight, whoever you are and whatever you are, whatever your past may have been, however filled you may be with failures and disgrace and shame, that God is still interested in you, and is able to redeem you.

And then there is the marvellous unexpectedness of it all. You never know when it is going to happen. This Ethiopian eunuch was expecting nothing when it came to him. This is the romance of the Christian life. There are people in this congregation tonight who were not Christians twelve months ago. They did not expect twelve months ago that this mighty thing was going to happen to them. But it happened, though they did not expect it. You never know. Oh, my dear friend, the possibility is always there! The angels are around us, and God is over all, and he sees you, and he knows you. Do not listen to the pessimism, the hopelessness, and the despair of this materialistic age. Believe in this supernatural, miraculous, divine gospel, and the glorious character of all the provision that God has provided for us. This man knew nothing about it; he did not know what was going to happen.

Philip was able to tell the eunuch that it had all been done. He did not tell this man what he must do, but what God had done for him. He preached Christ to him. And he told him how God had sent his Son into the world to bear *his* sins, so that he could have free forgiveness at once. He had nothing to do; he had just to believe there and then. He did not have to go through a programme or through a great scheme. No, no!

Just as I am, without one plea.

Believe, be baptized, and there you are! Forgiveness and reconciliation to God are all God's free gift.

New life. That is what you need. You need a new nature, a new outlook, and you need a new beginning. You need a holy nature, a love of the light and a hatred of the darkness, instead of a love of the darkness and a hatred of the light. You need new strength and power. And it is all provided for you. The Spirit of God will come to dwell in you, and you will have a sure and certain hope beyond this world.

And here is the astounding truth – God prepared all this for us when we knew nothing about it. 'While we were yet sinners, Christ died for us' (*Rom.* 5:8); even while we were enemies of God and of his Christ, Christ died for us. Here it is, offered to you; forgiveness of all your past sins.

Today thy mercy calls us
To wash away our sin,
However great our trespass,
Whatever we have been;
However long from mercy
We may have turned away,
Thy blood, O Christ, can cleanse us
And make us white today.
Oswald Allen

And while you are still left in this world, whatever may happen in it, the very hairs of your head will all be numbered. He will care for you – he is your Father. He will watch over you. He will love you with a Father's love. He will surround you. He will be with you. He will lead you. He has said, 'I will never leave thee, nor forsake thee' (*Heb.* 13:5). He will take you by the hand. He will lead you on, come what may, and eventually he will land you in the everlasting and eternal glory.

That is the message. Are you aware of all this? Do you realize it? You are unhappy. You know that your life is a failure and you have no hope whatsoever. You have been trying to buoy yourself up, you have probably made new year's resolutions, which you have already broken, and you know the utter futility of trusting to some magical term, some new prosperity, or some new discovery, or the hope that the nations will suddenly burn all their armaments and embrace one another. You know it is nonsense.

No, what you need to know is that your real trouble is that you know nothing about the supernatural, you are earthbound. You are bound to the visible and the seen, the passing, the temporal, the evanescent, and you know nothing about this glorious universe that is surrounding us – angels and archangels; spirits of just men made perfect; God the Father, God the Son, God the Holy Spirit. It is around you. Have you seen it?

Let me close by putting it to you in the words of Francis Thompson who, at the moment of his extreme need and despair, suddenly became aware of it, like this man travelling down from Jerusalem to his house in Ethiopia.

O world invisible, we view thee,
O world intangible, we touch thee,
O world unknowable, we know thee,
Inapprehensible, we clutch thee!

Does the fish soar to find the ocean,
The eagle plunge to find the air –
That we ask of the stars in motion
If they have rumour of thee there?

Not where the wheeling systems darken
And our benumb'd conceiving soars! –
The drift of pinions, would we hearken,
Beats at our clay-shutter'd doors.

Listen!

The angels keep their ancient places; –
Turn but a stone, and start a wing!
'Tis ye, 'tis your estrangèd faces,
That miss the many-splendour'd thing.

But (when so sad thou canst not sadder)
Cry; – and upon thy so sore loss
Shall shine the traffic of Jacob's ladder
Pitched betwixt Heaven and Charing Cross.

You remember the story, do you not? Poor Francis Thompson had become a tramp and he was standing in a gutter in Charing Cross here in London selling matches to eke out a miserable existence, and this is the advice he gives, therefore:

But (when so sad thou canst no sadder)
Cry; – and upon thy so sore loss
Shall shine the traffic of Jacob's ladder

(The angels!)

Pitched betwixt Heaven and Charing Cross.

Yea, in the night, my Soul, my daughter
Cry, – clinging Heaven by the hems;
And lo, Christ walking on the water,
Not of Gennesareth, but Thames!

Wherever you are, in your hopelessness, in your despair, in the futility of the modern world and modern life, cry out, and suddenly the angel will appear and the message will be given, and you will be lifted out of all the horror.

And in spite of modern man and all his boasted learning and sophistication, this is still the verdict:

The angels keep their ancient places.

They are still there. Oh, the romantic, the glorious possibilities in this new year!

Turn but a stone, and start a wing!
'Tis ye, 'tis your estrangèd faces,
That miss the many-splendour'd thing.

Oh, my dear friend, just as you are and in your need, lift up your eyes. May God grant that this has happened to someone this evening! Has God sent his angel to you and have you heard the message? God grant that you may 'go on your way', like the Ethiopian eunuch, 'rejoicing' into 1968, whatever may follow, and end in the everlasting and eternal rejoicing of heaven and the glory of God.

13

The Religious Life, or the Christian Life

And the angel of the Lord spake unto Philip, saying, Arise, and go toward the south unto the way that goeth down from Jerusalem unto Gaza, which is desert. And he arose and went: and, behold, a man of Ethiopia, an eunuch of great authority under Candace queen of the Ethiopians, who had the charge of all her treasure, and had come to Jerusalem for to worship, was returning, and sitting in his chariot, read Esaias the prophet. Then the Spirit said unto Philip, Go near, and join thyself to this chariot. And Philip ran thither to him, and heard him read the prophet Esaias, and said, Understandest thou what thou readest? And he said, How can I, except some man should guide me? And he desired Philip that he would come up and sit with him . . . When they were come up out of the water, the Spirit of the Lord caught away Philip, that the eunuch saw him no more: and he went on his way rejoicing (Acts 8:26–31, 39).

Now this is one of the great New Testament stories. The Bible, amongst other things, has incomparable stories, and this is one of them. It is a story, of course, that shows us the essential nature of the Christian message, what it sets out to do, and how it does it. It shows us, therefore, the character of the Christian life and the effect that becoming a Christian has upon any individual or any group of individuals; and the thing, of course, that strikes us at once is the marvellous change that took place in this man's entire circumstances. From being miserable, he became a man who went on his way filled with a spirit of rejoicing.

This change is the great truth that is established by this famous story. It reminds us at once that the Christian life is something profound, and that when a person becomes a Christian, the truth about him is not simply that he is a little bit better than he was, or that he has been modified somewhat, or that he has added something extra on to what he had before. It just shows us that those ideas of what it is to be a Christian are totally inadequate. Becoming a Christian changes a person completely, and that is why the Bible talks about regeneration, or rebirth, or being created anew. No other term is adequate to describe this great and wonderful change.

That is what we find in this story, and thank God we have it, for we are living in an age when there are strange and curious notions with regard to what Christianity is and what it means to be a Christian. Some seem to have the impression that it is merely a question of 'Backing Britain'– at least, they seem to be preaching on that theme today, as if that were Christianity. But here we are given the true, the real, thing, and thank God that we have such records that we can consider together. How we ought to thank him that he ever caused his servant Luke to write this book and give us details such as this.

Has it ever occurred to you to ask why we have the story of how the gospel came to one particular man? Why do writers like Luke take the trouble to enter into all these details? And the answer is that this is the wisdom of God. Even at the very beginning there were misunderstandings with regard to Christianity, and they have increased since then. So God not only gives us the truth in the form of doctrine and teaching, but he also gives us examples and practical illustrations so that we are left without any excuse at all for not understanding. The Bible does not just make the statement that if a man believes in Christ he becomes a Christian. We know from experience that there are many difficulties and obstacles that trouble us. But, thank God, here we are given a case that we can follow from step to step and from stage to stage, and discover exactly what it is to become a Christian.

So here we are dealing with one particular case, and it is right that we should do so. But, remember, all cases are not identical. There are different types of persons with different types of temperament, different backgrounds, different abilities – there are extraordinary differences – and so we all become Christians in different ways, the details vary. But – and this is what I really want to emphasize – the great, essential centralities are all the same. I am simply making this point because I have known people to be in trouble, sometimes, because they have not had exactly the same experiences as somebody else. I once knew a Christian father who was a real hindrance to his own son because he was not satisfied that his son was a Christian at all. This was because his son had not had, in detail, the experience that the father had had.

The father said to me on one occasion, 'You know, he's not had the Damascus road experience.'

'But,' I said, 'why should he have it? That's not the test.' We are not concerned so much with how people become Christians, as with whether they are Christians – that is the question.

But you will find that while there are differences in the details of how a man or woman becomes a Christian, there are certain things that are absolutes and are always present, and it is these that really matter. Nevertheless, it is interesting to observe these differences, because as you do so you will find that you yourself are helped by one rather than by another. And that is why God has provided these different types for us – it is in order that somewhere or another, and somehow or another, taking them all together, we may all be covered and helped, even in the details.

So I am calling your attention to this passage for these great reasons: that we may examine ourselves in the light of truth, and know exactly whether these essentials are true of us. These things have been written for our instruction. We need to examine ourselves. Not every man who thinks he is a Christian is one. People have strange ideas as to what makes someone a Christian. So we must examine ourselves, we must make sure. This is the most vital thing in the whole of life. This is what determines not only how we live in this world but also how we die and how we are going to spend that unknown eternity. We cannot afford to take risks. Let us examine ourselves in the light of the teaching that we find here in connection with the Ethiopian eunuch.

Now here we have a very definite type. If you like, you can call him the intellectual type, the moral type, the religious type of person. That is what we are going to look at. So as we study the case of this man and his conversion, in addition to discovering these great essentials, as I call them, we shall, incidentally, be discovering something else, and this is what I want to emphasize in particular now. The conversion of the Ethiopian eunuch is too great an event to deal with in one sermon and I want tonight to deal with one particular aspect that this case, above every other in a sense, shows us: it is the difference between being religious and being Christian.

This is a vital distinction. In many ways, the greatest enemy of Christianity is religion; I do not care what type of religion it is. It was the greatest obstacle in our Lord's own time. His greatest antagonists were the religious people, the Pharisees, the scribes, the Sadducees. These were the people who opposed the apostles. This has ever been the great trouble throughout the centuries. So it is vital that we should know, beyond any doubt or peradventure, whether we are just religious, or whether we are truly Christian. And this man will help us.

So what do we find here? Well, there is one general point I want to make before I come to the details of this man's character. Can you read a story like this without being impressed by the greatness of life? Look at this great man; there he is going home in the condition I shall unfold to you, and yet everything changes. What a serious thing life is; what issues are involved; indeed, what a problem life is. Now this man shows us all that quite clearly, but he shows, too, what glorious possibilities life holds.

I was dealing with this in introducing the whole subject in the last sermon: the angel suddenly appearing to Philip; the eunuch, at the most unexpected moment, in the most unexpected place, suddenly being confronted by the very teacher he needs, and the great and glorious transformation of the whole of his life. It is a great tragedy that at this moment so many people fail to realize the greatness of life.

Just think how the average person spends Sunday evening. What are they doing? Do you not see the triviality, the superficiality, that is so characteristic of it all? The trouble is not only that people are not Christians, but also that they do not realize what a tremendous thing life is. They think it is a joke, something you can dismiss with a sneer, something you can be sarcastic and clever about. What a debased view of life!

No, no, even if I were not a Christian at all, I should protest against this. Life is not a joke, not something to be dismissed with a quip or a clever jibe. If this story does nothing else, it will enable us to look at a great man who realized what a great thing it is to live and the whole problem of existence; it is here on the surface. This is the note that is so characteristic of the Bible from beginning to end. There is no book in the world that gives such an impression of the immensity and the profundity of life as this book of God, and that is why we must read it and pay attention to it and try to understand it.

So let us begin to look at the details, let us look at this man – there he was in that chariot. What sort of man was he? Well, he was obviously a man in a great position. He was riding in a chariot, perhaps accompanied by other chariots, certainly surrounded by a number of servants. He was a man, we are told, of 'great authority' under the queen of the Ethiopians, 'who had charge of all her treasure'. Now in those ancient courts there were various courtiers and there was a type of man who was given the highest position, like the Chancellor of the Exchequer, if you like, but in those days this was a position that was even more important than it is today. The charge entrusted to such a man was very great indeed. The first thing you are immediately impressed by, therefore, is the fact that you are dealing with an important man. But that, of course, at once tells us other things about him, one of which is that he must have been a very able man. You did not get into such a position unless you had great ability. Further proof of his ability is the fact that he was able to read. Not everybody could read in those days, but here was a man who could. He was an intelligent man, an educated man, a man quite out of the ordinary in the gifts and the propensities and the faculties that he possessed.

In addition, it is quite clear that he was a moral man, a man of good character. No man was ever put into the position of handling great wealth unless he was reliable and trustworthy, unless he was known to be a man of wisdom, judgment, balance, utter honesty, absolute reliability. All that is quite clear of him in just these little glimpses that we are given here in this cameo that Luke paints to such perfection. But you have to search for these things and see them and realize the sort of man you are dealing with.

The Religious Life, or the Christian Life (8:26–31,39)

And the Ethiopian was obviously living the kind of life that people of his position lived in the courts in those ancient days. You have read about them in history books, or novels, or seen them, perhaps, on the television – the life of an ancient court in the first century. It had its interests, it had its culture, it had its drinking and dancing and feasting. We see it in royal courts today and a court then was even more magnificent.

But there are so many other things that I can tell you about this man, and the first is that he was dissatisfied with all that. He had ability and he knew it. All men of ability know it. It is a part of their ability that they should. And yet for all his ambition, and his high position, and his ability, this man was unhappy, dissatisfied. How do I know that? I know it in this way: we read that he 'had come to Jerusalem for to worship' (verse 27). These words tell me immediately that he had become a proselyte to the Jewish faith. He had ceased to be a pagan and had taken up the Jews' religion. Now this is a tremendous fact and we must realize its significance. Here was a man, a pagan by birth, who had been brought up in a pagan culture and tradition. But he had become so dissatisfied with this pagan background that he had forsaken it, probably at considerable risk, and had become a practising Jew.

So the great question confronting us is this: Why did this Ethiopian take up the Jewish faith? He was not the only one, as we see from Acts chapter 17. The ancient world was a very big world and the Jews, this little nation, this little people, stood out as different. They were surrounded by people in different stages and degrees of paganism, from the most primitive to the most cultured and exalted, such as you found in Greece, in Athens above all, among the philosophers such as the Stoics and the Epicureans.

Well, now, here in Acts 8 is a man who could obviously be compared very readily with those Athenians because, I repeat, he was a man of ability and knowledge. And we are told about him, just as we are told about the Athenians, that for all that they had, they were dissatisfied. Notice that pregnant statement about the Athenians: 'For all the Athenians and strangers which were there spent their time in nothing else but either to tell, or to hear some new thing' (*Acts* 17:21). Why were they always interested in something new? There is only one answer: they were not satisfied with what they had. The people were always rushing to the latest cult, to the latest teaching. In this way, such people always betray that they are dissatisfied with what they have. The people of Athens, like the Ethiopian eunuch, were profoundly dissatisfied.

In what respects were these people dissatisfied? Well, there was obviously intellectual dissatisfaction. This is the whole point of philosophy, is it not? They found themselves in this world, and they found it a world of contradiction and problems and difficulties, and they were trying to understand it, to understand man, to understand life and death and history. And their great minds grappled with all these problems. They divided up into rival schools, but all together they could not arrive at a solution and they ended with a question. They were great at asking questions, philosophers always are. The tragedy with philosophers is that they can never answer their questions. They are very good at propounding them and they can see the weakness in the other man's theory, but it all ends on the same level – they do not know. Intellectual dissatisfaction!

And so when a strange teacher turns up, as Paul did on that occasion in Athens, they crowd round to hear him: 'What will this babbler say?' In the first century there were travelling teachers who went round, set up their stands, and then began to speak. And there in Athens the Athenians would listen: 'Ah, he's got something new, what is it? This is strange; what's this new doctrine?' What a perfect description it is of this modern world – all the cleverness and the interest and the excitement. 'How intriguing,' they say, and they rush from one idea to the other, they hurry after the latest teacher, the latest novelty. Oh, let me say it again, almost every night, certainly regularly, three nights a week, your television feeds you with this apparent interest and excitement about the new. It is a manifestation of intellectual bankruptcy.

But not only was there intellectual dissatisfaction, there was moral dissatisfaction. This man in our passage, like any intelligent man looking on at the life of the court, could see the utter superficiality of it all. The glamour and the glitter, the affectation and the supposed sophistication – what a farce, what a charade it was! They were not real people, they put on masks. And there was all the sin, the dishonesty, the chicanery, that accompanied court life. This man, in his position, saw it all, he knew it all. He knew the private accounts of so many of these people and he saw through their outward show.

And then, on the lower levels, the debauchery, the drunkenness, the sexual orgies, and all the foulness, the perversions – he saw it all. This is all described in many notable passages in the New Testament. You need not even go there: read your newspapers and you will find it, look at your television and you will see it. That was the life; he saw it and he was disgusted.

But the question was how to overcome it, how to get out of it. 'Is there no rule?' he asked. 'Is there no code of conduct?' He was searching for something, for a liberating word; he was searching for moral power, a moral dynamic, something that could stand between him and ever falling into the same sin. The man wanted moral liberation and he could not find it in all his pagan teaching and all the law of the society in which he had been brought up.

And in the same way, and beyond it all, there was a religious dissatisfaction. Of course he was religious. Everybody is religious. There is no such thing as an irreligious person. Every man has a god and he worships it. In the ancient world they had all sorts of gods. Some people, of course, believed there were spirits in trees and even in stones; others worshipped the sun and the moon and stars; others created gods for themselves – Baal, and these various other gods, Jupiter, Mercurius, a god of peace, a god of war, a god of love. As Paul observed of the Athenians: 'In all things ye are too superstitious', which literally translated, means 'too religious' (*Acts* 17:22). Paul found Athens cluttered up with temples, and in these temples they worshipped their various gods, and they took their offerings and their sacrifices to them.

Now the Ethiopian eunuch had been doing all this. We do not know exactly what kind of paganism he had and what kind of god he had worshipped, but what we do know is that he had seen through it, he had seen the vanity of it all. He knew that these gods did not exist, that they were mere figments of men's imaginations, that they had no reality, they had no power, no being. He had discovered what those false priests had discovered when they were challenged by Elijah on Mount Carmel. They had cried out to their gods in their hour of need and found that there was no reply, nothing but dead silence (*1 Kings* 18). There is no Baal, there is no such thing; there is no idol; it is all the creation of man's mind. This man had seen through it all – the vanity of idolatry, the vanity of paganism. He was looking for a God worthy of his worship.

And they were doing the same in Athens. There is a fascinating statement in that seventeenth chapter of Acts where we read that Paul was particularly attracted by one particular altar. All the temples had the name of a god over the doorpost – Jupiter, Mercurius, Mars, and so on – but here was an altar with an inscription 'TO THE UNKNOWN GOD' (*Acts* 17:23). What does this mean? Oh, this was the attempt of the Greek philosophers to find the God who was at the back of all the gods. They knew it. They said, 'Our gods are not adequate; they don't explain sufficiently. There is a God behind them all.'

> *There's a divinity that shapes our ends,*
> *Rough-hew them how we will.*
> William Shakespeare: *Hamlet*

There is a Power over the powers and they were seeking him: 'If haply they might feel after him, and find him' (*Acts* 17:27), but they could not. That was exactly the position of this Ethiopian eunuch. All he had did not satisfy him, either intellectually, morally, or religiously.

And so he had done something about it, and what he had done, as I have reminded you, was to become a Jew, a Jewish proselyte. He had taken this great step. There were numbers of these Jewish proselytes at that very time, many of them in Egypt. It was for them in particular that the Old Testament had been translated into Greek, the translation that we call the Septuagint. These were pagans who had become Jews and had turned to the Jewish teaching and religion. Now when the Ethiopian eunuch took this step, it brought about a great transformation in his life. As I have told you, he was a serious man, a man who was concerned about his existence and his life, and the meaning of it all. How was he going to meet death? What lay beyond? He wanted to know and he could not get satisfaction. But here was a teaching that seemed to him to be satisfactory.

What was the teaching that this Ethiopian had taken up? It was the teaching of the Old Testament, the teaching of the Jews at the time of John the Baptist and of our Lord. He had undergone a great change in the matter of his belief, therefore. From believing in a multiplicity of gods, he had come to see that all idolatry was a lie, that idols were vanities, that there was nothing there, no life, no truth, no power, no understanding, nothing. But he had heard this teaching of the Jews and had come to see that it was right, that there was only one true God. More: this God was the living God. Here was the explanation that he had been seeking; here was the answer to his problem.

What is this truth? It is the great truth that is stated at the beginning of the book of Genesis: 'In the beginning God created . . .' There were theories about the origin of life even then, remember. These ancient philosophers speculated a great deal about the origin of life, even as people who believe the theory of evolution are doing today. They are doing nothing new today. They are just reverting to the old speculations, and theorizing about the origin of the world. But the Jew was unique and separate; he said dogmatically that he had received a revelation. This was what differentiated the Jew. Jews did not claim to be philosophers. The Greeks were the philosophers. The Jews were a simple people, an agricultural people. But they had received a revelation. They had not thought it out and arrived at conclusions; they had not been investigating and examining. No. They said, 'God has spoken to us; we know nothing apart from what we have received.'

And the teaching of the Jews was that this 'true and living God' had made the world and all that is in it – the very teaching that Paul expounded to those Athenians. Paul began by telling them – 'God . . . dwelleth not in temples made with hands' (*Acts* 17:24). 'Your gods do,' he said, in effect. 'They can even be put into a box because there is nothing there; but God cannot be confined.' Why? Because he has made everything, and all things consist and subsist as the result of the word of his power. Not only that; the Jews taught that this truth about God as Creator included, very particularly, the creation of man, whom he had made in his own image and likeness. The Ethiopian, therefore, had a new, an exalted, conception of man, who was linked in this way to the everlasting and true God.

The Jews went on to say that this great God had a purpose and a plan with respect to life in this world. The Jews could review history and the Ethiopian, too, was the sort of man who would know how to do that. They said that whatever a man might have done or might be doing – governments and clashes and wars and power struggles – whatever men might do was ultimately irrelevant. What really mattered, they said, was the great purpose of God. And the Jews were able to show this by taking people through their own history. They were forever telling people and reminding themselves of how God had created them as a nation out of that one man Abraham, and had done so because, as he said to Abraham, 'In thee shall all families of the earth be blessed' (*Gen.* 12:3). At last there is a light; God is behind it all; God is bringing his purposes to pass.

This was the teaching; the Jews claimed a uniqueness; and said that they had a message. Paul says this when writing to the Romans. Somebody had raised the question: If you, Paul, are saying that the Jew will need salvation as much as the Gentile, then what advantage has the Jew?

Ah, says Paul, 'Much every way: chiefly, because that unto them were committed the oracles of God' (*Rom.* 3:1–2) – that is the Old Testament, the Word of God, this great light on God and his purpose. Now the Ethiopian had come to see this and to believe it. Not only that, at last he had found, he thought, the moral guidance that he needed. He wanted to know how to live. All the Greek philosophers had speculated, but it was a notorious fact that their lives were loose, they were dissolute. Sexual perversions were commonest among the philosophers, even as suicide was to be found in a higher proportion among them than in any other single section of society. Some of the most terrible things happened among them, even in their very temples. So this man had not only become dissatisfied, he longed for a way of life, he longed for a rule, for a law.

At last he found it. The law of God – this same God, this holy, just, righteous God – as given to the nation of Israel, the Jews, through Moses. He had it – the Ten Commandments, the first table, the second table. Here he read that there was only one God who alone is to be worshipped. You must not bow down to any graven image, you must not take the name of this God in vain; you must respect the day that he has appointed for himself – one day in seven is to be given to him. Then the second table of the law. Thou shalt not kill. Thou shalt not steal. Thou shalt not commit adultery. Thou shalt not bear false witness. Honour thy father and mother . . . (*Exod.* 20:1–17). Ah, said this man. This is the very thing I have been looking for. Here is morality. Here is the way to live. Here is holiness. Here is justice. Here is righteousness. He had not been able to find it anywhere, but at last he had heard of it here. This was the way to live, keeping the Ten Commandments. So he accepted it and became a Jew.

And likewise with regard to worship. He had seen through that pagan way, and at last he was told what he regarded as the only true way. God had to be worshipped by means of sacrifices. He had to be approached 'with reverence and godly fear' (*Heb.* 12:28). You had to have a priesthood, and a high priest over them all. And there were rules and regulations; lambs had to be offered, hands placed on the head of bullocks which were then killed. Then the blood had to be taken, and sprinkled before an ark and presented to God; burnt offerings, sacrifices, meal offerings.

This was the only way to approach God. The ordinary man had to stay in the outer court, the priests could go a little bit farther into the Holy Place. Then there was a curtain and behind that the Holiest of All, where only the high priest could enter, and even then only once a year. And he could not go in except with blood, and it was a momentous occasion when he did. Would he come out?

This holy God! This Shekinah glory that shone down upon it all. Here was the way to worship. And the Ethiopian recognized it, and he submitted to it. The priesthood and the sacrifices, the tabernacle and the temple, and all the ceremonial and the Jewish way of worship described in the Old Testament and in the New.

And so the Ethiopian had taken up all this. With all his might he was living this kind of life – not eating certain types of meat, observing certain special days, certain festivals, submitting to the regulations, washing his hands continuously when he came from the market before he sat down to eat, tithing 'mint and anise and cummin' (*Matt.* 23:23), washing cups and pots and pans. There were 614 regulations, and he did his utmost to keep them and to carry them out punctiliously. That is what had happened to him. The man had ceased to be a pagan and had become a Jew.

But I want to show you something further about this Ethiopian eunuch: he had not only taken up Judaism in a legalistic manner, he had taken it up with great spiritual thoroughness. Have you observed the zeal of this man? He was highly religious. He did not wear his religion, as it were, just on Sunday or keep it in a bag. No, no, this man's whole life was involved, it was the biggest thing in his whole existence. I can give you proof of that – he had gone up to Jerusalem. Read the passage again. Look up your atlases. It was a long journey, especially in those days, and a very hazardous one. It involved an extended absence from his work and from his office. That did not matter, he had to go.

Yet he was not satisfied, even then. He wanted further instruction and further knowledge. There were authorities up there in Jerusalem whom he could not find in Ethiopia, so he wanted to go to the headquarters, he wanted to listen to the greatest Pharisees. Ah, he said, if I could listen to these men, they would give something more. So he took this hazardous and difficult journey in order to find out something further, because, though he had changed his religion and had taken Judaism up with great thoroughness, still he was aware of further need. He had not found rest, he had not found peace. So he took his journey up to a religious festival in Jerusalem.

And on top of all that, he did something else: he took the vital step of buying a copy of a certain part of the Scriptures. He had bought a copy of the book of the prophet Isaiah: as I say, he was an able man and able to read. And he said to himself, 'Of course, I haven't the advantage that people living in Jerusalem have of hearing these great authorities whenever they like Sabbath by Sabbath or on weekdays, and of going to the teachers and putting my questions. I will buy their very Scriptures, the Scriptures they expound and I will read and study them for myself. He was taking it all so desperately seriously; he realized the momentous character of these decisions. He wanted the answer, he wanted light, he wanted knowledge, he wanted peace, and so he took these vital steps. And the picture we are confronted with is that of a man in trouble, a man who was terribly burdened.

Now the details are really very interesting and important. The Ethiopian deliberately chose to go home by the 'desert' road. I have reminded you that he had the choice of two roads for his journey home. There was another route that did not go through a desert way, but he chose the desert route. Why do you think he did that? I have no difficulty at all in answering the question. He wanted time to think. He was an important man and if he had gone on the other road, wherever he stopped to have a meal or to refresh himself, people would have come and talked to him, gossiped with him, asked his opinion on political questions and other issues, and he did not want it. Others would have been anxious to entertain him and make a fuss of him because of his great position, they would have considered it an honour, but he did not want it. He did not want the adulation of men, their praise and their conversation and chit-chat. Oh, all this to him was irrelevant and unimportant. Oh, the great question of the soul and of eternity! So he chose the desert road to have peace and rest from all the noise and clatter and chatter of the world and its trivialities. It was because he was in trouble, because he was not at rest, because, in spite of visiting Jerusalem, he still had not found satisfaction.

And, further, I see his spiritual earnestness in the extraordinary fact that even while travelling in his chariot he was reading the Scriptures; he could not wait until he got home, but started at once. He had only just left Jerusalem, it did not matter; this was the burden, this was the problem. He was in an agony of soul as he looked for something he could not find. He had changed his religion, he had better things to believe than he had ever had before, but still he could not find rest and peace. So even on the way home, he started reading the Scriptures he had bought. Travelling through the desert way, he had more time to concentrate. And do you not see this troubled, burdened condition even in his very voice and accent and in the terms he used?

Philip ran to him and put his famous question: 'Understandest thou what thou readest?'

And he said, 'How can I, except some man should guide me?'

Do you hear the note of despair, the note of hopelessness? The man was still seeking, in spite of all that he had done. There is the position. Have I been dishonest in handling it? Can you show me my error? These facts are staring us in the face as we look at this man.

But now I want to call your attention, as I close, to the tragedy of the Ethiopian's position. The tragedy of this man, of course, was nothing but the tragedy of all the Jews who rejected the gospel. The tragedy is this: something had already happened in Jerusalem that had the full and the perfect and the complete answer to his every question and to his every need, but he had not heard it. In Jerusalem, just outside the wall of the city, the thing had happened that would give him complete satisfaction. And he knew nothing about it. That was the trouble with all the Jews.

Had this man – now this is a bit of interesting speculation – heard about the Lord Jesus Christ on his visit to Jerusalem? We do not know. But we can be fairly sure of this: as a Jewish proselyte, he would have moved in circles where, if Jesus had been mentioned at all, it would have been in order to criticize him, to denounce him, to dismiss him as a blasphemer. And the Ethiopian eunuch would undoubtedly have accepted such teaching. And the result is that he went back to his home as dejected, as dissatisfied and hopeless, as when he had left.

And this is just the tragedy of all people who are merely religious. It is one of the best descriptions in the whole of the Scripture of the tragedy of the religious man or woman. What is this? Let me put it to you in a few words. The apostle Paul has said it all in Romans 10. He says: Look at my fellow-countrymen, 'I bear them record that they have a zeal of God, but not according to knowledge' (verse 2). They were most zealous, they were very keen, they were most punctilious, but 'not according to knowledge'. They were in ignorance. They did not have the light. They did not have the only thing that could give them satisfaction. Zeal without knowledge is the greatest waste of energy; it is sheer folly. Listen to Paul's great words:

Brethren, my heart's desire and prayer to God for Israel is, that they might be saved. For I bear them record that they have a zeal of God, but not according to knowledge. For they being ignorant of God's righteousness, and going about to establish their own righteousness, have not submitted themselves unto the righteousness of God (Rom. 10:1–3).

And what Paul means is this: Here they are, half killing themselves with all their rules and regulations and offerings and sacrifices and hair-cutting, and all the rest that is involved, and they do not realize that it is all utterly useless. They are 'going about to establish their own righteousness'. Why do they do that? Because they are ignorant of the righteousness of God. This was the position of the Jews and of the Ethiopian eunuch. This is the position of all religious people. They say, 'If only I say my prayers regularly, if only I go to church regularly – and of course if I go very early in the morning I am so much better than the people who only go at eleven o'clock – if I do not do certain things, if I do good, if I avoid certain sins, if I give a certain amount of money – if I do this, that, and the other, if I am wholly religious and zealous, then I must satisfy God.' And what a business it is, all expressed in the words 'going about' – compassing land and sea and hill and dale. But it is all utterly useless; they are ignorant of God's righteousness.

What does God demand of us? Is your bit of religion and mine enough to satisfy him? Is your morality sufficient to put you into the presence of the holy and the absolute and the eternal? No, no! What does God demand? Well, the Ten Commandments have told you. There is all the difference in the world between accepting the Ten Commandments with your mind and living them. Paul tells us that, does he not? He thought he was keeping the commandments perfectly, and then he understood the meaning of the word 'covet', and he suddenly found that he had never kept them at all (*Rom.* 7:7–11).

No, it is not a matter of law, it is not a matter of externals, nor of negativities. God says, 'Thou shalt love the Lord thy God with all thy heart, and with all thy soul, and with all thy mind, and with all thy strength' (*Mark* 12:30). God demands absolute perfection, and anyone who fails in one detail of the law has failed in it all. The Jews did not know that, and it was because they did not know what God demanded in terms of righteousness, that in their folly they were 'going about to establish their own righteousness'. But it cannot be done, as this poor Ethiopian had really discovered. He had new knowledge, higher knowledge, but it did not put him right; he was failing. 'For not the hearers of the law are just before God, but the doers of the law shall be justified' (*Rom.* 2:13).

And so that brings us to the final tragedy of these people – of this poor Ethiopian eunuch and all the Jews who thought as he now thought. Their supreme tragedy was that 'going about to establish their own righteousness' and half killing themselves, they refused the offer of God's righteousness in Jesus Christ his Son. That is what Philip went on to explain to this poor man, as I hope to have the privilege of explaining to you. All he was searching for was available. He did not know it at this time, but there was a man just round the corner, a simple man called Philip, not a great man, not someone holding a high and exalted position, a mere nobody, but someone who knew, who had the answer.

There is no need to ascend into the heaven, there is no need to go down into the depths: 'The word is nigh thee, even in thy mouth, and in thy heart' (*Rom.* 10:8). And Paul continues: 'If thou shalt confess with thy mouth the Lord Jesus, and shalt believe in thine heart . . . thou shalt be saved' (verse 9). It is justification by faith only; it is this blessed message that God has done for us what we could never do for ourselves, this message that 'God so loved the world, that he gave his only begotten Son, that whosoever believeth in him should not perish, but have everlasting life' (*John* 3:16). Everyone will perish apart from him. He is the only way of salvation. Human righteousness is never enough, we need a righteousness from God. That righteousness God has provided in his own Son, and offers to us as a free gift.

Here is the tragedy of the Ethiopian eunuch. He had been up to Jerusalem but he had not met the Christian church and they had everything he needed. Oh, but God is a God of love and mercy and compassion, and all that this man had not discovered, in spite of his efforts and striving and travelling, God sent to him by sending his servant with this simple, glorious message: 'Believe on the Lord Jesus Christ, and thou shalt be saved' (*Acts* 16:31). The poor pagan is hopeless, and the Jew, though in a better position, is still hopeless. There is no difference between the Jew and the Gentile, 'For all have sinned, and come short of the glory of God' (*Rom.* 3:23).

My dear friend, the question for you is simply this: Have you got as far as this Ethiopian eunuch? Are you serious – or are you dancing and walking and drinking and drugging your way through life? Have you seen the greatness of the possibilities? Have you considered the problem? Do you know there is a soul in you that is immortal? Have you faced it as this man faced it? This is the way. Have you come to the realization that this man had reached? Even this is not enough, but have you done anything? Have you realized your precarious position before the holy God before whom you will have to stand? Do you know anything about eternal torment and the damnation of hell? How are you living? Are you ready to die? Are you ready to face God? Look at this man, look at his story, follow him, emulate him, and be as ready as he was to listen to the glorious message of salvation in Jesus Christ our Lord.

14

Beyond Human Understanding

And Philip ran hither to him, and heard him read the prophet Esaias, and said, Understandest thou what thou readest? And he said, How can I, except some man should guide me? And he desired Philip that he would come up and sit with him (Acts 8:30–31).

We are advancing now to a further – a third –consideration of this wonderful story of the conversion of the Ethiopian eunuch, the treasurer of the court of the queen of the Ethiopians. It is an amazing story in itself but I call your attention to it because of the light that it throws on the message of the gospel, on the nature of the Christian church and the way this message comes to us; in other words, how one becomes a Christian. There is no question but that these records are given to us by the inspiration of the Holy Spirit in order that they may serve that very end. They are here to remind us of the history. Here we are in a Christian church, but what is a Christian church? There has been a lot of talk about the church this week – this 'Week of Christian Unity', as it is called – but the tragedy is, of course, that all this talk about unity goes on without people asking that first question: namely, What is an individual Christian church?

And it is because we have an account here of the beginning of the church that we are dealing with the history that is to be found in the early chapters of this book of Acts. You and I may have our ideas as to what the church should be, but I suggest that that is not very honest. If we talk of the Christian church, then let us make sure that we are in line with and correspond to what we read here about the origin of the church. The New Testament provides the only authentic account that we have. We do not rest upon traditions; we know that human traditions can be false as well as true. We have no authority apart from this, and that is why we are dealing with it.

Now here, in this particular story about the Ethiopian eunuch, we are told what it is to be a Christian, and how one becomes a Christian. And in a wonderful way, we are shown many of the difficulties that beset people who are concerned about this, and many of the stumbling blocks that stand in their path and obstruct them. We see here the issues and questions that have troubled people throughout the centuries with regard to this matter, and still trouble them. And this, again, is something for which we should thank God. We are not just told that Philip was sent to meet this Ethiopian, and that, as the result of a bit of a conversation between them, he believed the gospel and was baptized. No, thank God, we are given details; we are shown the problems, the pitfalls, and so, when we come across the same difficulties in ourselves or in others, we have some guidance as to how we can deal with them.

Now we have already considered two great stumbling blocks that stand between many people and their becoming Christians. The first is the failure to realize the reality of the supernatural realm, and the second is religion. Now some of you may be surprised to hear that second reason being given from a Christian pulpit. You may say, 'But I thought that Christians were religious people.' In a sense, of course, they are, but the point is that, like the Ethiopian eunuch, you can be religious without being Christian.

But now we come to another difficulty and perhaps, at the present time, this is the commonest of all. Look at this man. He had found the inadequacy of paganism, even paganism at its best, as represented by Greek philosophy; he had found the inadequacy of Judaism. So what did he need? And the answer, of course, is this: he needed the great message of the Bible concerning salvation. And this is the most interesting and dramatic point, in a sense, in this whole story. That is what he needed, and here we are told that he had it; he was actually reading it; he was reading one of the great evangelical passages in the book of the prophet Isaiah. So what, then, was the trouble?

Well, the trouble came out in the question that Philip put to him and in his own answer to that question. Here was a man actually looking at the very message that he needed; it was in his hands; he was reading it aloud. But Philip, knowing the difficulties, knowing what he had passed through himself, and filled with the Spirit and the enlightenment that the Holy Spirit alone can give, knew also that a man can look at the message and not see it, he can be reading it without apprehending it. So Philip put his question: 'Understandest thou what thou readest?' You are reading the very thing you need, my friend, do you understand it? And the man gave his pathetic answer – 'How can I, except some man should guide me?' And, we are told, 'He desired Philip that he would come up and sit with him.'

Now here in this preliminary conversation between Philip and the Ethiopian eunuch, we are face to face with one of the commonest difficulties that people experience in this whole question of the Christian faith – perhaps, even, the greatest stumbling block of all. This difficulty is in the very character of the Christian truth and the Christian message. Let me put this central matter to you in three propositions.

I start by laying down the dogmatic assertion that the Christian message cannot be understood by the natural man. If we had nothing but this one case of the Ethiopian eunuch, it would be enough to show us that. I have reminded you already of his character. He was a very able, erudite man, a man who could read. As a sort of Chancellor of the Exchequer to the Queen of the Ethiopians, he was in a prominent position, a position of trust and authority. He was a man who represented human culture at its very best, and yet this was the very man who said, 'How can I understand this, except somebody teach me?' Give him statistics, he would read them as an open book; give him philosophy, he could follow it; give him all these matters that interest men, he was equal to anybody else.

But here he was reading these words, and he said, 'I don't understand it.' He wanted to, he was very keen and zealous, he was an honest, sincere man. As I have reminded you, this man had taken the trouble to travel from Ethiopia up to Jerusalem, with all the attendant discomforts of a journey in those times, and yet he admitted quite frankly and honestly that he did not understand what he was reading.

Now here is the stumbling block for so many, for most people claim that they have the right, and the ability, to understand. This is, I suppose, of all the obstacles, the one that keeps most people outside the Christian faith, and never more so than at the present time. For we are living in an age, as you all know perfectly well, that places unusual confidence in man and his powers. I do not trouble to point out the utter contradiction that is involved in all this. The world is in greater trouble than perhaps it has ever been, yet man is more confident than ever in his own power and ability and especially the power of his understanding. That is the inconsistency that is ever characteristic of man in sin. In a way, I suppose it is quite natural; man really has done astounding things during the last century. It is nonsense to dispute that. The advances in science, in medicine and other realms and departments of science are phenomenal, and these discoveries that have come one after another, even in the years since the last war, are, of course, quite staggering.

But the result of all this is that man claims that he has the competence to understand anything and everything. So he takes up the position of saying that he will not believe anything unless he can understand it. Then he says that he does not understand the Christian message, so he rejects it; that is the reason he gives. He says, 'I don't follow this, it seems to me to be quite wrong and irrational and ridiculous.' He dismisses it all, simply because he cannot follow it, simply because it does not fit in with his canons of judgment and of reason. Now this attitude is very apparent today. You read it in your newspapers, you hear it on the television. People are always saying such things. Indeed, on those grounds alone most just dismiss the whole of Christianity without even arguing about it.

But there is something much more serious, something that, to me, is the great tragedy of today, and the greatest problem of all. It is that this attitude does not only characterize people who are avowedly not Christians and are outside the church, but there are also many inside the church who are raising the same objection. There are many teachers in exalted positions in the church who do not hesitate to say, 'It's no use preaching the message of the Bible as it has been preached for so many centuries.' They say that modern men and women cannot possibly accept it. People today have scientific knowledge; they are cultured and informed of things that people were not aware of in the past. So if you go to them with your New Testament as it is, with a lot about miracles and the virgin birth and subjects like that, then you are just a fool. You must not expect people to believe it, they cannot possibly. So these church teachers and leaders say that we must trim our message and get rid of everything in the Scriptures that is offensive to modern people in order that we may present them with a message that they can accept and believe. And so, of course, these teachers are doing that.

I have often reminded you of a popular movement on the continent of Europe, a movement that talks of 'demythologizing the gospel'. This is the teaching of a man called Bultmann and it is the very rationale of this whole movement. Bultmann says: If you want – as you should – to influence the modern man in the direction of Christianity, then you must take out of it everything that is offensive to him, and present him with a message that will appeal to him, one that he can accept and understand.

But that is just another way of saying that the message of Christianity is intelligible to the modern man, to man as he is. It says that the message of Christianity can be understood, and that the measure of the message is to be man and his outlook and mentality. And so proponents of this view do not hesitate to take parts and aspects out of the Scriptures and say they do not believe in them. So not only do they take out the early chapters of Genesis and the whole teaching on the origin of the world and of man, but they also say that we should accept what science teaches at the moment. She may not teach in a hundred years what she is teaching now, but science must be the standard to which everybody must submit.

Now this is a most serious matter. I repeat that it is just another way of saying that man is capable of understanding the message, and that what determines what I or anybody else may preach from a pulpit is the modern mind, modern knowledge, the modern attitude formed by this scientific age in which we live.

And then, of course, there are other teachings that express this view even more crudely. There is a popular teaching going round that says that if only the message is presented in a reasoned and reasonable manner, men and women are bound to accept it. The argument is that the trouble has been in the method, and that our methods have been wrong, so they must be changed and modified. But that, again, is just another way of saying that the Christian message in and of itself can be understood and received by the natural man, and I want to show you that all that is denied completely by this story.

But Acts 8 is not the only evidence we have that the natural mind cannot understand the gospel. The modern attitude towards Christian truth is a denial of the teaching of the whole of the New Testament. Take, for instance, our Lord's words in Matthew chapter 13. He says that the natural man cannot understand this message and that he deliberately taught in parables. People have the curious notion that parables are just illustrations that we use to make things easy. But our Lord said that he spoke in parables in order that people could not understand and should not understand, that they might be under condemnation. 'It is given unto you', he says, 'to know the mysteries of the kingdom of heaven, but to them it is not given' (*Matt.*13:11). The whole tragedy of the Pharisees and the scribes was they never understood it, never at all; they were incapable, in spite of all their learning and authority.

But then our blessed Lord himself gave us a still more explicit statement. Matthew writes:

At that time Jesus answered and said, I thank thee, O Father, Lord of heaven and earth, because thou hast hid these things from the wise and prudent, and hast revealed them unto babes. Even so, Father: for so it seemed good in thy sight. All things are delivered unto me of my Father; and no man knoweth the Son, but the Father; neither knoweth any man the Father, save the Son, and he to whomsoever the Son will reveal him (Matt. 11:25–27).

Could you have anything more explicit or categorical? No one can know the Father, except the one to whom the Son has revealed him. And our Lord thanks his Father that these things have been hidden 'from the wise and prudent', and have been revealed unto babes.

The Scriptures are full of this. Consider again the famous confession of Peter at Caesarea Philippi. Our Lord put the question to his disciples: 'Whom do men say that I the Son of man am?' And he got various answers: some say this, some say that. Then he asked, 'But whom say ye that I am?' and Peter stepped forward and said, 'Thou art the Christ, the Son of the living God.' Then notice our Lord's comment: 'Blessed art thou, Simon Bar-jona: for flesh and blood hath not revealed it unto thee, but my Father which is in heaven' (*Matt.* 16:13–17). It was not 'flesh and blood', it was not human ability, it was revelation. It was God who had revealed this.

Then in the last chapter of Luke's Gospel we are told that our Lord meets the two men walking disconsolately along the road to Emmaus. They are cast down because Christ has been crucified and they say, 'We trusted that it had been he which should have redeemed [restored the kingdom to] Israel' (*Luke* 24:21). But they have taken him and they have crucified him. They have buried him. It is the end!

'O fools, and slow of heart', he says, 'to believe all that the prophets have spoken' (*Luke* 24:25). He is saying, in effect, 'You have read your Scriptures but you have not understood them. You are blind, you are fools, you are simpletons, you are ignoramuses in spite of having your Scriptures.'

And then all that we find in the first letter to the Corinthians, especially in chapters 1, 2 and 3, really deals with little else; this is the whole point that the apostle is making. 'Which none of the princes of this world knew,' he says, 'for had they known it, they would not have crucified the Lord of glory . . . But the natural man receiveth not the things of the Spirit of God: for they are foolishness unto him: neither can he know them, because they are spiritually discerned' (*1 Cor.* 2:8, 14).

So the whole of Scripture is opposed to this view that the gospel should be intelligible to the natural mind. Paul again puts it in explicit terms in his second letter to the Corinthians. Writing about his fellow-countrymen the Jews, who were rejecting Christ and the gospel, he says, 'But their minds were blinded: for until this day remaineth the same vail untaken away in the reading of the old testament; which vail is done away in Christ. But even unto this day, when Moses is read, the vail is upon their heart' (*2 Cor.* 3:14–15). Paul is saying that these Jews are like that poor Ethiopian eunuch who, travelling on the road home from Jerusalem, was reading the Scriptures and not understanding. They are looking at words but they do not get their meaning. They cannot; there is a veil over their eyes and they are helpless. And then, still more openly and plainly, Paul goes on to say, 'But if our gospel be hid, it is hid to them that are lost: in whom the god of this world hath blinded the minds of them which believe not, lest the light of the glorious gospel of Christ, who is the image of God, should shine unto them' (*2 Cor.* 4:3–4).

Now this is surely perfectly plain and clear; so my answer to the modern man or woman who says, 'I want to understand', is this: My friend, as long as you are trying to understand, you will remain what you are. You will not only remain a non-Christian, you will remain confused and a failure; you will not understand yourself, nor life, nor death; you will not know where you are. Because you are trying to do something that is impossible, you will remain outside.

The first thing people must do is stop talking about 'modernity'. We have this marvellous idea that because we have split the atom, because we can get up into outer space, we know! The modern man with all his knowledge, says Bultmann, cannot possibly receive your three-tier view of the world. But the simple answer is that he could not accept the gospel in the first century either, before they knew that there was such a thing as an atom, let alone splitting it. There is nothing new about this rejection of the gospel. It is the oldest problem of all – man in the pride of his intellect trying to understand the incomprehensible. That is why people remain outside the Christian faith. And here it is in Acts chapter 8, put before us in this most interesting and dramatic manner. There is nothing new. There is no new knowledge that the 'modern man' has that makes the slightest difference to whether or not the gospel is believed. It always has been, it always will be, entirely beyond human understanding. So I lay that down as a dogmatic proposition. Let me give you some reasons for doing so.

Why is it that the natural man cannot understand this message? And here let me get rid of a preliminary matter. There are some people who say that the whole difficulty is that of understanding the language. This is a common view at the present time. It is said that the main reason why people are not Christians is because Christians still go on using that Authorized Version, and people do not understand it. They do not understand your words – justification, sanctification, glorification, regeneration. So the argument is that all we need to do is to have a new translation. Have a translation in the modern idiom, using modern terms. And the moment people can comprehend the language, they will understand and believe the message.

Well, in reply to that, I need only say that new translations are tumbling off the presses. Do they make people believe? Is the obstacle to belief the archaic language of the Authorized Version? Is it that this priceless language, this Shakespearean Elizabethan language, is not comprehensible to people nowadays – is that the trouble? Is the only problem just that of words? How utterly ridiculous such an argument is!

And, of course, there are other arguments, and these I find still more pathetic. There is an epidemic now of addressing God in prayer as 'You' instead of 'Thou'. It is all right, I do not waste time on a thing like this, but I am interested in why this is happening. The reason given is that people today do not use 'Thee' and 'Thou' and so when the preacher still prays to God using these terms, they cannot follow and are bewildered rather than helped. Is it not pathetic! As if just to make that little change and address God as 'You' is going to make people understand the message of the gospel and make them Christians.

Do not misunderstand me. I am not here to defend archaic language. I know that there are words whose meaning has changed since the Authorized Version of 1611 – by all means change them. But what I am saying is that when you change them, you will find that people will be as blind to this message as they were before. It is not a problem of linguistics. You can change all your words and people will still remain what they were. No, the problem is much deeper. There is something childish about this excitement over new translations – as if once we have everything in this sort of 'kitchen sink' language we will all be Christians. Oh, what utter nonsense! What a failure to realize this great matter.

So let me put it before you. Why is it that men and women by nature cannot understand the gospel? Why was this poor Ethiopian eunuch in this sad condition in which he had to say, 'How can I, except somebody teaches me, and explains it to me?' What is the matter? Well, the first answer is the very nature and character of the truth itself. This is what is forgotten. I do not stay with this now because we have already considered it, but let me remind you that when you come into a church like this you are doing something that is altogether different from anything you do in the world.

Now that is not a criticism of the world; I am simply saying it is different. When you go to a political meting, you use your abilities to assess and evaluate. That is all right. When you go to a lecture on philosophy, you do the same, and so it is with history, art, music or any other subject you choose. But when you come here, it is not the same. You are dealing with a type of truth that is altogether different. Why is this? Well, it is not only that the gospel is not secular. I want to go beyond and say that it is not merely human. All these other subjects are human. Poets at the height of their poetic inspiration are still only human beings. A genius such as Mozart was only a man. I agree, his powers were accentuated and developed and stimulated; they were at their height. But you are nevertheless not outside the realm of the human.

But the moment you enter this building, you are in an altogether different realm. Look at the language that is used; look at our Lord himself. This was the whole trouble, was it not, with Nicodemus? Nicodemus was trying to understand what our Lord was saying. When he went at night to seek that interview, he said, 'Rabbi, we know that thou art a teacher come from God: for no man can do these miracles that thou doest, except God be with him.' And he was about to put his questions; he wanted to understand this and that. But our Lord interrupted and said, 'Verily, verily, I say unto thee, Except a man be born again, he cannot see the kingdom of God.' And you remember Nicodemus' response? He did not understand. He said: 'How can a man be born when he is old? can he enter the second time into his mother's womb, and be born?' It seemed ridiculous, monstrous.

And in reply our Lord said, 'Verily, verily, I say unto thee, Except a man be born of water and of the Spirit, he cannot enter into the kingdom of God.' Then the explanation: 'That which is born of the flesh is flesh: and that which is born of the Spirit is spirit. Marvel not that I said unto thee, Ye must be born again' (*John* 3:2–7). My dear man, our Lord said, in effect, I am not talking about natural human birth; that is 'flesh', that is nature. I am talking about the Spirit, the realm of the supernatural. That was the whole trouble with Nicodemus, as it is with people today. They do not realize that there is a realm that is altogether different.

And so our Lord said again to the disciples and others: 'Verily, I say unto you, except ye be converted, and become as little children, ye shall not enter into the kingdom of heaven' (*Matt.* 18:3). In every other realm you start where you are and you go on. But not so here; you go down, then you start again. You become a little child, you are 'born again'. Why? Oh, I say again, you are in a different realm, the realm of the supernatural.

Notice again the term that the apostle Paul used in the second chapter of 1 Corinthians:

Howbeit we speak wisdom among them that are perfect: yet not the wisdom of this world, nor of the princes of this world, that come to nought: but we speak the wisdom of God – that is the term – *in a mystery, even the hidden wisdom, which God ordained before the world unto our glory: which none of the princes of this world knew: for had they known it, they would not have crucified the Lord of glory* (1 Cor. 2:6–8).

The term is 'mystery', something beyond human reach and grasp, the realm of the eternal. So you must not approach this gospel as you approach everything else. That is the first fallacy of people who insist upon understanding. They show that they have not even an awareness of the nature of the truth that they are considering, and that is the most elementary and fundamental blunder. You cannot get any further.

But that is not the only reason why natural people cannot understand the gospel. It is not merely that the character of this message is different, but its content also is such that a human being cannot possibly understand it. What is it about? Now Paul summed it up in one phrase when writing to the Corinthians. He says, 'And I, brethren, when I came to you, came not with excellency of speech or of wisdom' – what was he doing? – '*declaring unto you the testimony of God*' (*1 Cor.* 2:1), which somebody has translated like this: 'declaring unto you the attested truth of God, the attested truth about God'.

So what is the content of this message? Now come along those of you who want to understand it as you understand geometry or physics or chemistry or some human proposition about politics, what is the subject matter, what are we dealing with? And the answer is that we are here primarily not to talk about ourselves, still less to talk about the economic problems of this country and 'Backing Britain'. That is not the theme of the Christian church. We are not even here to be talking perpetually about the church, and the unity of the church. No, no; what am I here to talk about? About God! The blessed Holy Trinity! God in three Persons – Father, Son, Holy Spirit. Look at this man Philip here in Acts 8. We are told: 'Then the Spirit said unto Philip . . .' (verse 29). A holy Spirit! That is the teaching – that God is in three Persons, co-equal, co-eternal, without any admixture, with all their attributes absolutely perfect.

Tell me, is it reasonable, is it sensible, to try to understand that? Do you not see that modern men and women are fools? Those who attempt to do something that by definition is impossible are nothing but fools. You say, 'I want to understand this question of the Trinity.' Who ever asked you to understand it? Whoever suggested to you that you could understand it? Understand it! The apostle Paul, who knew more about these things than conceivably any human being has ever known, puts it like this: 'great is the mystery of godliness' (*1 Tim.* 3:16). Mystery? Of course! We are dealing with infinities, with absolutes, with eternities, and to try to pit our pygmy minds against this is sheer irrationality, it is the height of folly. Yet that is what people are doing.

And then the gospel goes on to deal with God's great plan and purpose for humanity and for this world. And what a plan it is! Who can understand it? 'O the depth of the riches both of the wisdom and knowledge of God!' says Paul, 'How unsearchable are his judgments, and his ways past finding out!' (*Rom.* 11:33). Understand? You cannot understand yourself, and do you think you can understand God? Don't be foolish! Stop and think what you are saying.

And then consider how God has put his plan into execution – and here we stand and look at the blessed person, Jesus of Nazareth, born in a stable, laid in a manger, working as a carpenter, not even trained as a Pharisee, still less trained as a philosopher in the Stoics' or Epicureans' schools of thought. No, no, an ordinary workman – and yet he stands before them and says, 'Before Abraham was, I am' (*John* 8:58). He says, 'I and my Father are one' (*John* 10:30). 'He that hath seen me hath seen the Father' (*John* 14:9).

He is claiming that he is God as well as man, that he has two natures in one person. The modern man says, 'I can't understand that; two natures in one person and yet unmixed? I don't follow it.' Follow it! Are you telling me that you are mad enough to try to understand something like this? My friend, this is mystery: 'the mystery of godliness: God was manifest in the flesh' (*1 Tim.* 3:16)! Understand it? You do not try to, you just glory in it, you are amazed at it, lost in wonder as you contemplate it.

And then consider the atonement, the way of salvation – a stumbling block to the Jews and foolishness to the Greeks (see *1 Cor.* 1:23). The message is that God has laid on this Son of his your sins and mine, and has punished them in him.

'What?' you say. 'This is immoral. I don't follow it. It's wrong that another should suffer for me; I bear my own sins.'

Do you? If you do you will go to hell, and you will bear them and their punishment to all eternity. But if you have the sense to see that you can never atone for your sins and will go on suffering eternally, then you will look at the blessed Son of God, who, because he is God as well as man, and because he is perfect, is big enough to take your punishment, to go through with it and to finish it, and to rise again and ascend into the presence of God and to intercede on your behalf. That is the message.

And, too, there is the blessed work of the Holy Spirit – regeneration! I have already mentioned it in connection with the case of Nicodemus. He tried to understand it. Understand being 'born again'? Of course you do not! Nobody has ever understood it. All you know is that it happens to you. And you go on being increasingly amazed at it, and amazed at yourself. And you look at yourself and you say with Charles Wesley:

And can it be, that I should gain
An interest in the Saviour's blood?
Died he for me, who caused his pain;
For me, who him to death pursued?

You are amazed at yourself. You find yourself enjoying the Bible, enjoying prayer, and the company of people who may be unknown to the world, but are saints. And you get more from them than you do from the greatest intellects in the land, or in the whole universe or in the whole of history, because they know God and are children of God. You are amazed? Of course! It is a part of the mystery.

But that is the content of this message and that is how we know that the Ethiopian eunuch was a very honest man – because he said, 'I don't understand.' But he wanted to! Do you? Or are you still standing on your great modern knowledge, as a twentieth-century man or woman? Oh, my dear friend, can you not see that you are fooling yourself? Or rather that the one who makes you do it is, as Paul says, 'the god of this world'. He it is who 'hath blinded the minds of them which believe not, lest the light of the glorious gospel of Christ, who is the image of God, should shine unto them' (2 *Cor.* 4:4).

Well, there is my second reason: the whole realm with which we are dealing is different, and the very content of the truth makes it transcendent. 'Canst thou by searching find out God?' asks Job. Of course not. But listen, in the third place, and quite apart from all that: the state and condition of men and women, by birth and by nature, renders them quite incapable of understanding this message. Why? Because at best they are finite and limited, and their knowledge and capacities are limited. That is why they are always advancing from one idea to another, having to deny today what was taught dogmatically a few years back. It is also why they always despise the past, not stopping to think that those who come after them will also despise them and say that they knew nothing and that they were ignoramuses and how amazing it was that they could be so confident in their ignorance! But people still go on full of self-confidence. They do not realize their finitude and the obvious limits to all their knowledge.

> *There are more things in heaven and earth, Horatio,*
> *Than are dreamt of in your philosophy.*
>
> Shakespeare: *Hamlet*

Men and women are not only finite and limited they have also lost the spiritual faculty, they are dead in trespasses and sins. 'For what man', asks Paul, in one of his great questions, 'knoweth the things of a man, save the spirit of man which is in him? even so the things of God knoweth no man, but the Spirit of God' (*1 Cor.* 2:11).

Now that, being translated, means this: 'How does a man know a man? How do you have a conversation? How can you and someone else discuss together these questions and problems? The answer is that you have the same spirit in you. A man understands a man in a way that a dog cannot. There is a correspondence of spirit, an interchange, we are on the same wavelength, if you like. 'Even so', says Paul, 'the things of God knoweth no man, but the Spirit of God.' Man has lost the spirit, the faculty, that enables him to understand the things of God and to commune with God. Man started with that but he has lost it, and while he has lost it he can never understand these things.

But on top of that, man, as the result of sin and the Fall, is even opposed to the things of God. 'Because the carnal mind is enmity against God: for it is not subject to the law of God, neither indeed can be' (*Rom.* 8:7). Every man, by nature, is a hater of God.

'But,' you say, 'I've never hated God; I've always been religious. I've always prayed to God.'

Yes, but I would like to know the sort of God you have prayed to. Is he the God of the Bible. You have never known the God of the Bible. You cannot, in and of yourself. You have conjured up a figment of your own imagination, you have postulated a god; but he is not God. Again, as Paul says in 1 Corinthians 2:14: 'The natural man receiveth not the things of the Spirit of God: for they are foolishness unto him: neither can he know them, because they are spiritually discerned.'

Men and women today are so prejudiced against God that they can never know these spiritual truths. Prejudice is blinding. You can have the truth before you, but you will be blind to it. 'All looks yellow to the jaundiced eye,' wrote Alexander Pope. People hate the gospel and explain it away and they think they are clever. They are not open to it and so they do not understand it or receive it.

If you want to see all I have been saying in a nutshell, you find it in the apostle Paul himself. Here is this man we always think of as the great apostle and preacher, but listen to what he says about his past life: 'I thank Christ Jesus our Lord, who hath enabled me, for that he counted me faithful, putting me into the ministry; who was before a blasphemer, and a persecutor, and injurious: but I obtained mercy, because I did it ignorantly in unbelief' (*1 Tim.* 1:12–13). Why did Paul persecute Christ and the church and try to exterminate it? It was because of prejudice. He was blinded – 'ignorantly in unbelief'. He hated the very Saviour whom he came to love and to revere and for whom he laid down his life. Prejudice!

But, lastly, this truth and this message are beyond human understanding because of the wisdom and the love of God. Have you anticipated me? Do you know what I am going to say? What do I mean? Well, read again that second half of the first chapter of Paul's first letter to the Corinthians. Begin at verse 17 and go on to the end; and then read that second chapter. And you will find Paul saying that God has adopted this plan of salvation in order that he might humble the pride of the natural man. That is his wisdom. The man of the world does not understand it, the Jew and the Greek both reject it, but, Paul says, this is God's way. And then he puts out that great challenge of his:

Where is the wise? where is the scribe? where is the disputer of this world? hath not God made foolish the wisdom of this world? (verse 17).

And then he puts it in this great statement:

For ye see your calling, brethren, how that not many wise men after the flesh, not many mighty, not many noble, are called: But God hath chosen the foolish things of the world to confound the wise; and God hath chosen the weak things of the world to confound the things which are mighty; and base things of the world, and things which are despised, hath God chosen, yea, and things which are not, to bring to nought things that are.

Why?

That no flesh should glory in his presence (verses 26–29).

He humbles the whole of humanity. In the face of God's salvation, your wise, your prudent, your philosophers, your thinkers, your scientists, are like babes; they are fools; they are helpless; they are nothing, nobodies. God humbles the pride of man in a salvation that is beyond the understanding even of the greatest and the highest. There is the wisdom of God.

But I said also that the gospel cannot be understood because of the love of God, and I show you that in this way. If this salvation were something that could be understood, if people received it because they understood it, it would of necessity be a salvation for VIPs. It would be a salvation for philosophers, for scientists, for men and women who have been born with good brains and who have primary, secondary, college education and have done research work; people with great brains would have a priority over everybody else, and the vast majority of us, who cannot read philosophy, and know no science, would have no hope at all. And so we would be lost eternally and just a select handful of humanists would be saved.

Now do you see it? Oh, the wisdom of God! Nobody can understand it, and therefore everybody is on an equal footing. Nobody has priority here. It does not matter who you are, or what you are. You are a sinner, you are lost, you are helpless, you are hopeless, you do not understand. We are all in the same position. And therefore salvation comes of God and is the power of God, 'Which none of the princes of this world knew: for had they known it, they would not have crucified the Lord of glory . . . but God hath revealed them unto us by his Spirit' (*1 Cor.* 2:8, 10). Paul writes to the Romans, 'I am not ashamed of the gospel of Christ' – why not? – 'for it is the power of God unto salvation to every one that believeth' (*Rom.* 1:16).

It is the wisdom of God. It is the power of God. It is the grace of God. It is the free gift of God and anyone can receive a gift. So there is as much hope today for the greatest ignoramus, the vilest, blackest sinner in London, as there is for the great philosopher and the paragon of all the virtues. What a gospel! What a salvation!

But, obviously, because it is such a gospel, it is something that no one can understand. What is needed, therefore? The answer is simple: What is needed is the very thing that happened to the poor Ethiopian eunuch. He needed help, he needed instruction and guidance, but he also needed a willing and a ready mind, a readiness to listen and humility to be taught. And that is what God supplies.

God sent Philip. The angel said, 'Go', and he went. The Spirit said, 'Go near, and join thyself . . .' The Spirit! God! Here was the man filled with the Spirit. He could teach, he could expound, and God sent him. And then the Spirit worked in the Ethiopian himself and he was ready to listen to his teacher.

And that has been God's way throughout the running centuries. I would not dare to stand in this pulpit unless I had been sent, unless I had been called. I do not expound my own theories and ideas; I simply hold before you, and divide, as I am enabled by the Spirit of God, the words, the message of God. But it will mean nothing to you until you have become as a little child and have realized your helplessness, your hopelessness, your ignorance, and your impotence, and yielded yourself to the influences of the Spirit of God and are ready to listen.

Have you yet arrived at the statement made by the great Blaise Pascal: 'The supreme achievement of reason is to bring us to see that there is a limit to reason'? Have you seen that? Have you used your reason sufficiently clearly and cogently to realize that here you are in a realm beyond your reason, where you just submit to the revelation of God as a little child? Isaac Watts says:

Where reason fails with all her powers,
There faith prevails, and love adores.

Do you agree? Charles Wesley says:

'Tis mystery all! The immortal dies!
Who can explore his strange design?
In vain the first-born seraph tries
To sound the depth of love divine:
'Tis mercy all! let earth adore,
Let angel-minds inquire no more.

Do you agree? It is the mystery of God, but it is the salvation of those who, as little children, submit themselves to it, and ask God to make it clear to them. Have you done that?

15

The Message

Then Philip opened his mouth, and began at the same scripture, and preached unto him Jesus (Acts 8:35).

We take now a further step in our study of the Ethiopian eunuch's conversion. Judged from any standpoint whatsoever, this is a very important matter. It is a part of the general history of the spread of the gospel and the growth of the Christian church at the beginning. The church started in Jerusalem, as was inevitable, and then began to spread out first through Judaea, and next to Samaria. And here is yet another step; here is the first African we hear of believing in Christ.

But we are not merely interested in this story from the historical angle. We are, of course, interested in it in that way, for, let us remember, the history of the church is all important. The church is very old – it did not begin in this century! – and we should be clear about the history. I would emphasize, again, that most of the troubles, it seems to me, in connection with the Christian faith and the church at the present time arise from the fact that people divorce themselves from history. They seem to think that they know what Christianity is. They dismiss the past and set up their own ideas and conceptions, and, of course, they are quite wrong. But, in any case, it is dishonest. As the church is historical and has a continuous history, it is our duty, if we are concerned about these things and understand them at all, to be aware of the history; and that is one of our reasons for going back to this account that we are given here at the beginning of the book of Acts.

But in addition to that, we are particularly concerned to do this because Acts is, after all, the standard and the pattern and the norm with respect to these matters. Would you know what Christianity is? Well, come back here. Would you know what the church is? Come back here. Would you know what a Christian is? Look at these people. And, especially, would you know how one becomes a Christian? Well, that in particular is dealt with in the story of the Ethiopian eunuch. As I pointed out last time, there are differences in the details of the way in which people become Christians. No two stories are identical. But though there are differences in the details, there are certain fundamental facts that are invariably present, certain absolutes without which one is not a Christian at all.

Now if you look at Christians in general you might think that they are very similar to certain other people, some of the devotees of the cults, for instance. How do you tell the difference between a Christian and someone who, on the surface, looks very similar as the result of some other teaching? And there is only one answer – it is that the Christian always conforms to what we find here. That is why it is essential that we should emphasize these basic principles that are invariably held in common by every Christian.

Why is it that there are so many people in the world who are not Christian, especially at a time like this with the world in such trouble? The answer is that people stumble at certain difficulties, and we have been examining these one by one as they are put before us here – the whole question of the supernatural; the danger of confusing Christianity with religion; and then the character, the nature, of Christian truth. Now all these are what I could call preliminary difficulties, the difficulties that beset us in the mere introduction to a consideration of the gospel, but they are vital. These truths are axiomatic. Christianity is supernatural, it is divine, it is beyond human comprehension. That is the character of the truth; that is the realm with which we are dealing. It is altogether different from everything we know in the world. As we saw, our Lord summed it all up by putting it like this: 'Verily, I say unto you, Except ye be converted, and become as little children, ye shall not enter into the kingdom of heaven' (*Matt.* 18:3). This is an absolute essential and without seeing it, we cannot proceed at all.

Now, then, that brings us to the next step. If that is the character of this truth, what is its content, its specific message? This is clearly quite crucial and it is what this thirty-fifth verse brings before us in a very striking manner. Philip has now climbed into the chariot. The preliminaries are ending and the work is really beginning. We come to the actual message of the gospel. I want to consider it with you in terms of this thirty-fifth verse, which, again, gives us a wonderful key to the understanding of all the difficulties that so many people find in connection with this matter of believing and accepting the Christian faith. Now you notice what this verse tells us: 'Then Philip opened his mouth, and *began* at the same scripture, and preached unto him Jesus.' I emphasize the word 'began' because I want to put before you the vital importance of where Philip began, and what he proceeded to do.

Let me put this to you in this way. What was the difference between the Ethiopian eunuch and Philip? I suppose if you analysed them from the standpoint of ability, it might very well be that the Ethiopian eunuch was the abler of the two. As we have seen, most of these early leaders of the Christian faith were untrained men, derided by the Sanhedrin as 'unlearned and ignorant men'. So doubtless Philip had not had the educational advantages of this great treasurer at the court of the Ethiopian queen. He was not as well versed in such subjects as philosophy, human learning and lore – I do not know, though probably what I am saying is the truth – but I would ask you again: What was the difference between the two men?

Here was this great eunuch; he had bought these scriptures in Jerusalem and was reading them there in his chariot because he wanted to know, but he did not understand. Then Philip approached him and put his question: 'Understandest thou what thou readest?' And the man, immediately detecting something about Philip, 'desired Philip that he would come up and sit with him'. And now Philip, we are told, 'opened his mouth, and began at the same scripture, and preached unto him Jesus'. Why was it that Philip could help him? How was it that he could do so? Philip was in no difficulty; the Ethiopian eunuch was in tremendous difficulty. What was the difference?

Now we are struck at once by the fact that Philip had no problem here. He could explain the passage that was so perplexing to the Ethiopian, and meant nothing to him, in spite of all his learning. Why was that? Now this, again, is a most essential point. Philip at once began to expound the verses and it is clear that he was giving a very definite message: 'Philip opened his mouth, and began at the same scripture, and preached unto him and told him the good news about Jesus.' That is what verse 35 really means. In other words, Philip was in no difficulty because he had a message; he knew exactly what it was and he was able to state it.

What is a Christian? Well, here he is in the person of Philip. Christians are people who know what they believe and can tell somebody else exactly what that is. Let us get this clear: Christians are not people who are searching for the truth. That has been the whole tragedy, especially in this present century. Christians have been represented as seekers, those who go out on a great intellectual quest, who dabble in philosophy and are 'seeking', wanting to know. But that view is monstrous. It is an utter contradiction of what it is to be a Christian. If Christians were but seekers, Philip would not have been able to help this man. All he could have said when he got into the chariot was, 'Well, I see that you are seeking and searching for the truth. You know, I am also, shall we do it together? Let us have a look at this passage now, and see if we can make something of it. I have been struggling myself and I see you are, so we will go on together and see what we can find.' The great intellectual quest! And week after week the books come tumbling out. An 'insight', a 'new view'. What an utter travesty of the Christian faith! No, no! The Christian message is clear; it is plain; it can be stated simply, directly, in terms that can be followed and understood.

Now I am urging this point because in this century the idea is once more current that Christianity cannot be defined, that it is something very beautiful and wonderful that cannot be put into words, that can be felt but never stated. This view that Christianity is some sensation, some feeling, some kind of attitude that you cannot describe, is sometimes called mysticism. I have often dealt with this teaching from this pulpit because it is found so frequently.

And I say again that it is the exact opposite of the truth. The Christian message is a perfectly clear message, it is well defined and can be stated in propositions and categories.

Now are we all clear about this? There is something almost ludicrous about the way in which people behave. I have known men who have taken this modern view of the Christian message, the Christian faith, and have talked in this vague mystical way about it, and then in their churches each Sunday they suddenly get up and invite people to join with them in reciting the Apostles' Creed or perhaps the Athanasian Creed or the Nicene Creed. You see the contradiction? In their sermon, in their speaking, they have said, 'Christianity cannot be defined. It is a vague sensation, a feeling you get, something wonderful.' Then they recite the Creed. There was a slogan a few years back that put it like this: 'Christianity is caught, not taught.' Caught! Christianity, they say, is a spirit you catch, a spirit of fellowship, a spirit of mutual help and aid, and always something you 'get'. You mix with people and you catch it from them but you cannot state it, you cannot define it.

But I repeat that that is the exact opposite of the truth. What are the creeds? They are simply statements of the truth. They are definitions, propositions. All the great creeds were drawn up for only one reason. From time to time, owing to certain false teaching, the people in the early church would become confused, and begin to say, 'Well, then, what is the truth? What is the Christian faith? Is it this or is it that?' And the Fathers of the church would be led, I believe by the Spirit of God, to meet together in great councils where, under the guidance and direction of the Spirit, they would draw up these creeds. And in the creeds they said, 'The Christian faith is this and it is not that.' They described it, they defined it – it can be done. You need not be in any doubt as to what the Christian faith is; you need not be in any doubt as to whether or not you are a Christian. It is a concrete, well-defined truth that can be stated in propositions and contrasted with error and with heresy.

Now all that comes out here. Philip immediately expounded the truth to the Ethiopian. We must be perfectly clear about this. It is a point that is made constantly in the New Testament. You did not have the problem in the early church that you have today. All these apostles and preachers preached exactly the same message. The apostle Paul often uses this as an argument. He says: The message that I preach, the others are preaching also. There is no difference between us. We are all saying exactly the same thing. And they were – there is no question about this. And that is why, when somebody began to say something else, they could tell the people not to listen to him. Indeed, they put this very strongly at times. The apostle Paul deals with it, for instance, in writing to Timothy. There were certain false teachers who were casting doubt upon the truth by going around saying that the resurrection was past already. And Paul says to Timothy: Don't be disturbed by these things, 'Remember that Jesus Christ of the seed of David was raised from the dead according to my gospel' (2 *Tim.* 2:8) – *my* gospel! Is this conceit? Is this arrogance? No, no, what he means by that is, 'the' gospel. How was he so sure it was the right one? The answer is that he never created it, it was not his good idea. He had 'received' it and all the other apostles had received it, too.

But the apostle Paul goes even further when he writes to the Galatians. The members of the churches of Galatia had been troubled by certain false teachers who had insinuated themselves amongst them and were bringing in heretical teaching. And Paul says to them, 'Though we, or an angel from heaven, preach any other gospel unto you than that which we have preached unto you, let him be accursed' (*Gal.* 1:8). What a strong statement! Says Paul, in effect, 'If I ever come to you again and deny what I have already told you, or if an angel from heaven should appear before you and contradict what I have said to you, let him be cursed.' How does Paul dare to say such a thing? There is only one answer – he knows exactly what the gospel is. There is no difficulty, no question. They can test every teacher that appears amongst them by the gospel that he (Paul) had already delivered to them, and through believing which they had become Christians and had entered into the Christian church.

So here is the first thing that is obvious about Philip. When he climbed into the chariot, he was not in difficulty, he was not nervous and he was not saying to himself, 'What shall I say to this man, because I really don't know myself, but I am hoping . . .?' No, he sat down with confidence knowing exactly what he had to say because he had this message that all the early church preached.

And the second thing that is equally obvious about Philip is that he had received that enlightenment, which the Holy Spirit alone can give, that enables a man both to understand this message and to be able to teach it to others. So that was the difference between Philip and the Ethiopian eunuch. Philip was not uncertain, he was not frightened, he was not hesitant. He climbed into the chariot, and he began. He 'opened his mouth', glad of the opportunity. He had the message, he could give it – he had authority.

On what was this authority based, or whence did it derive? And here it is again as plain as anything can be. This was an authority that was derived from the Scriptures alone. At that time, of course, Christians did not have the New Testament, as we have, they only had the Old Testament, but that was enough. Philip's only authority was the Scriptures. The Ethiopian was reading one of the books of the Old Testament, the book of the prophet Isaiah. And Philip dealt with this.

This, again, is vital. What is this Christian message? The first point we must be perfectly clear about is that it is not any human thought or concoction. Peter says in his second letter, 'We have not followed cunningly devised fables, when we made known unto you the power and the coming of our Lord Jesus Christ' (*2 Pet.* 1:16). Look here, says Peter, I am reminding you of the things I have told you.

Peter was getting old, he was about to die, so he said he was going to go on repeating these facts in order that after he had gone they might have them always in remembrance. He was not recounting 'cunningly devised fables'. Now that is what man does, is it not? Man concocts his theories. He may put them in the form of stories or allegories; he may put them in the form of poetry. It does not matter, they are always 'cunningly devised fables' that man has produced. That is what philosophy is – speculation. It is clever and 'cunningly devised'. Oh, yes, there is no difficulty about that. And it is plausible and wonderful when you look at it on the surface. But that is not what the preacher has, that is not what Philip had to do and to give, that is not what Peter had. He says: 'It is not cunningly devised fables', it is something else.

So Philip did not just go and have a discussion with the eunuch – or 'dialogue', as it is called now. Philip did not have a dialogue with him about this problem and that situation. They did not have 'an exchange of views', with the Ethiopian saying, 'Well, it seems to me to be like this', and Philip replying, 'But, I don't quite see it like that.' They did not then begin to speculate about life and its meaning and the import of what was happening. No, no! It was teacher and pupil. It was the man who did not know listening and the other man speaking with authority.

But, secondly, the message of the gospel is not merely the relating of experience. Let us also be clear about this. What did Philip do on this occasion? What so many, it seems to me, would do today is something like this: being invited to join this man in the chariot, Philip would have said to him, 'I see you are looking rather troubled and unhappy. You know, I was once like that, but not any longer. I've had a marvellous experience and I'm absolutely different now.' Of course, he could have said all that, it was true of him, but the point is that that is not what he said. He did not sit down by the Ethiopian eunuch and share his experiences, or relate the story of his conversion and talk about it and leave it at that. No, no!

Christian people are sometimes at fault at this point in always talking about themselves and their experiences. That is not the preaching of the gospel; that is not evangelism. We must be very careful about this. Some people are always relating their mystical experiences. Others tell about this great change that took place in their lives and say, 'You can get this. I want you to get it. What has happened to me can happen to you.' Philip did not do that. Of course, being a Christian involves all this; it is true of the Christian, but that is not how one becomes a Christian. Philip's primary concern was not so much for this man to have a particular experience as that he should come face to face with the truth that could do for him everything that he needed. So I emphasize these negatives.

What, then, did Philip do? He did, of course, what the preacher should always do – he expounded the Scriptures. 'Philip opened his mouth, and began at the same scripture, and preached unto him Jesus.' He started with the passage that the Ethiopian was reading, he worked it out with him and showed him what it meant. In other words, Philip was not giving his own opinions about life and death and eternity, he was dealing with the scripture that was there in front of him. The point that I am establishing is that the Scriptures are our only authority. I have no other authority as I stand in this pulpit. The authority of the cults is the authority of experience. Members of the cults talk about and recommend experience, that is what they have to offer. But that is not the case here. Here there is exposition of the truth. Indeed, let me put it as plainly and as simply as this: standing in this pulpit tonight on 28 January 1968 I am doing nothing different from what Philip did with the Ethiopian eunuch.

'But wait a minute,' you say, 'surely the position is not identical now with that in the first century? All the knowledge that has been garnered, all the advances in science, all that humanity has produced – is all this nothing?' I do not hesitate to assert it – it is absolutely nothing. I have no advantage over Philip, none at all. The modern Christian has no advantage over the Christian of the first century. Why is this? It is because we all have the sole authority of the Scriptures; we know nothing apart from this. Modern philosophy does not help me; modern science does not help me. They do not even hinder me: they leave me exactly where I am. The great fundamental questions have never changed; they are still there. The Ethiopian eunuch had the same problems as modern people and the answer is the same; there is no difference. We are dealing with the authority of the Scriptures.

Why do I say that Scripture is our only authority? Well, I have already shown you that human understanding and philosophy do not help us. There is no authority to be found there. Scripture is the authority because it makes a unique claim, a claim to be a revelation from God. In other words, this book must be put into a category that is different from all others. All others are the productions of men and women. They may be able, they may be great, they may have poetic inspiration, or unusual insight as philosophers – all right, grant them anything you like, but they are still only human beings. They are seeking, they are searching, they are trying to find; that is the highest they can ever do. But here is something that starts on an entirely different, a unique, basis because it claims to be a revelation from God.

That is the claim that is made throughout the Bible. And that is why I do what Philip did. That is why I do not stand up here in the pulpit and tell you a few stories or try to affect you by having different coloured lights and other psychological means and mechanisms, with appropriate singing to get results and make you feel happier. That would be a travesty of my task. My task is that of Philip. I have a book and here it is open and I say, 'Do you understand it?'

You say, 'I don't.'

'Very well, listen,' I say. Why do I say that this is the Word of God? I do so because these biblical writers say it. You will find the prophets in the Old Testament all saying it. They do not say, 'I have just had a brilliant idea.' What they say is, 'The word of the Lord came unto me.' It came in a remarkable manner and they knew God was speaking. Some of them, like Jeremiah, will tell you at times they did not want to deliver the message because they knew it would get them into trouble. At times, they could not understand it themselves. But God was speaking and the pressure was upon them. They felt it in their bones and they had to speak, come what may. Jeremiah was thrown into a dungeon for proclaiming God's message; others were put to death. It did not matter, God had given them a word. They spoke from God, and they had to speak, regardless of the consequences.

And notice what is said in the New Testament: 'For the prophecy came not in old time by the will of man: but holy men of God spake as they were moved by the Holy Ghost' (2 *Pet.* 1:21). Peter also says, 'Knowing this first [I would have you understand], that no prophecy of the scripture is of any private interpretation' (2 *Pet.* 1:20). What he is saying, in effect, is this: 'Now, you good people, I do not have long to be with you' – Christ had quite clearly given him an intimation that his end was at hand – 'I'm soon going to put off this my tabernacle, I'm going to die, but I want you to hold on to what you have heard from me.'

On what grounds does he say this? Is it just arrogance? Of course not. As we have already seen, he says, 'We have not followed cunningly devised fables, when we made known unto you the power and coming of our Lord Jesus Christ' (2 *Pet.* 1:16). And then he tells them what happened. He says: I remember a day when James and John and I were taken up by the Lord on to the top of a certain mountain, and there a most amazing thing happened. A cloud gathered and a brightness, and suddenly, in our very presence, he was changed. He began to glisten. His clothes began to shine. A radiance came streaming from his face. We had never seen anything like it and were almost blinded by the sight. And we heard a voice from heaven saying, 'This is my beloved Son, in whom I am well pleased.' Listen, I am not asking you to believe these things because I, Peter, am saying them. No, I heard the voice from heaven. I am an eyewitness of his majesty. I heard a voice from the everlasting Glory. I would not dare speak to you if I had not heard it. It is not cunningly devised fables, it is fact (see 2 *Pet.* 1:13–18).

But, Peter adds, it is not only that: 'We have also a more sure word of prophecy; whereunto ye do well that ye take heed, as unto a light that shineth in a dark place, until the day dawn, and the day star arise in your hearts' (2 *Pet.* 1:19). And he goes on to tell them that 'no prophecy of the scripture is of any private interpretation'. It did not come as the result of human will or energy or understanding, or insight. No: 'holy men of God spake as they were moved by the Holy Ghost' (2 *Pet.* 1:20–21). It was God's revelation. It was God who was giving them the message, telling them what to say, guiding them in the saying of it. That is what Peter says.

So this is why we say there is no other authority. And the apostle Paul gives exactly the same teaching in his second letter to Timothy: 'All scripture is given by inspiration of God' – perhaps a better translation would be: 'All scripture is God-breathed' – 'and is profitable for doctrine, for reproof, for correction, for instruction in righteousness: that the man of God may be perfect, throughly furnished unto all good works' (2 *Tim.* 3:16–17). It is not man but the revelation of God.

What else? Well, I could keep you for a great length of time as I told you the arguments for believing that the Scriptures are the Word of God. Read the Bible for yourself. Look at the transcendent nature of its truth; look at the way in which it is expressed; look at the glories that belong to it that belong to no other literature.

But something that emerges clearly in Acts chapter 8:35, as I hope to unfold to you, is the unity of the message. Have you ever considered this? We read: 'Then Philip opened his mouth, and began at the same scripture.' But he did not finish there, he only began there. He began with the scripture that this poor fellow was trying to understand and could not. And he explained it and expounded it and that led on to other passages, which led on to others, and, as he did so, he was preaching, expounding the good news concerning Jesus.

But do you see the point? Some people have described the Bible as 'a library of books'. There are sixty-six different books in the Bible – written, many of them, by different men, written in different ages, in different centuries, in different circumstances, and yet – and this is the astounding thing – there is only one message in the whole book from beginning to end. One message! The same message always, put in different ways, with different emphases: one continuous running message from beginning to end, in spite of all this diversity of writers and conditions. And that explains why Philip was able to begin where the Ethiopian was reading. You can start wherever you like in this book and you will always arrive at the same message. You begin, as they began on this occasion, in Isaiah 53, but you can begin anywhere you like in this book and you will always arrive at the same end. There is this solidarity, this unity, this essential oneness in the whole position.

And the unity comes out, of course, in many different ways. They were reading the book of the prophet Isaiah, yet out of that Philip was able to preach Jesus. In other words, we see here one of the greatest proofs of all that this is the Word of God and the book of God – the amazing phenomenon of prophecy. Is not this astounding? These words that the poor eunuch was trying to understand had been written by Isaiah eight centuries before these two men met together on that road – eight hundred years! And yet Philip, with extreme ease, was able to show that Isaiah had been writing about Jesus Christ, who had just lived and died and risen again.

Eight hundred years! Ah, but this is the wonderful thing about prophecy, and this is what no human ingenuity can ever explain away. How is it that men eight centuries before the time could not only prophesy the coming of the Son of God but could give us an amazing exactness of detail in telling us all about him? It is all here before us. This, I repeat, is the great fact that proves that this is indeed the Word of God. So I say again that our only authority is the

Scripture. And preaching, teaching, leading people to Christ, consist of expounding it, bringing it out and showing what it means.

So what is the message? And that, too, is all here. Oh, how Philip must have rejoiced when this man invited him into the chariot! He knew exactly what he was going to tell him; he knew the great message of the Bible. But, oh, it is put in so many different ways and there are so many ramifications that if you do not know the message, you will get lost, as this poor fellow was. But once you have seen this message, you see it running as a golden thread right through the Scriptures from the beginning to the very end.

What, then, is the message? It is the message that this world is God's world. It was not meant to be as it is now. It has gone wrong; it has gone astray, and it cannot put itself right. But God is still concerned, he is still interested and he has a plan and a purpose for its redemption. Before the very world was made, God had this plan. And this book is the account of that plan. It tells us how God has been revealing it in parts and portions, bringing it to pass in instalments and with increasing momentum. And the purpose is redemption, deliverance, salvation, the rescuing of people from the misery and the havoc and the despair into which they have fallen as the result of sin and listening to the devil, the enemy of God, the enemy of their souls.

God's great plan and purpose for the redemption of the world is the one great message of the Bible from beginning to end, and that is what Philip expounded to this poor Ethiopian eunuch. But notice again how it is put: 'Then Philip opened his mouth and began ["beginning" is a better translation] at the same scripture, . . . preached unto him [literally "stated the good news concerning"] Jesus.' Good news! The centre of the message is *Jesus*. This is where it all comes to a focus, this is where you see the great unity of this great book – these sixty-six books. This is the way to understand it; it is to see that there is a centre to it. Look at the other side of the centre – there is the Old Testament, which is just a book that tells you that he is going to come.

I never tire of saying this. I wish I had kept a record of how many times I have said it from this pulpit! I think I know exactly what Philip felt as he was stepping up into that chariot. He knew what he was going to say – and do you know what it was? It was this: Yes, you are in trouble, of course you are, everybody is in trouble, but listen to me, I have something to tell you. God caused that man Isaiah to write these words that you have been reading but cannot understand. Isaiah was not the only man. God started telling people what to say long before that.

You know, said Philip, God began speaking to the human race even in the Garden of Eden. It was there that man rebelled and sinned, and, listening to the devil, brought chaos down upon himself, and it would have continued until he had finally found himself in hell. But God came down, and God spoke, and God condemned man for his rebellion and sin and folly. But he did not stop at that, he gave him a promise. He told him that life was going to be what you and I know it to be, a strife and a conflict between the seed of the serpent and the seed of the woman. But God also said that the seed of the woman would bruise the serpent's head (see *Gen.* 3:15). That is the first promise of the coming of Jesus Christ. With these words God was beginning to prepare the people. He would send one, who would be the seed of the woman.

Then you go on reading and you come to a man called Abraham. God said to that man – he was ninety-nine years of age and his wife was ninety – that from Abraham and Sarah he would produce one through whom 'all the nations of the earth' would be blessed (*Gen.* 22:18). It seemed utter rubbish, and when Sarah heard that she would have a baby, in her unbelief she laughed. But God promised that eventually out of the seed of Abraham this great and mighty Deliverer should come. And he did. Jesus Christ was a Jew, of the seed of Abraham. The promise was repeated to Isaac, and to Jacob; it was repeated even to Judah. He was told that the great Shiloh would come out of his loins, though he was an adulterer, among other things. It does not matter, it is God's plan; the Deliverer is promised, and all the Old Testament is looking forward to him.

Did you know, Philip said, that the very furniture and the decorations of the tabernacle are prophecies of Christ? The lamb being killed morning and evening, the burnt offerings and the sacrifices – all this is not mere Jewish ritual and ceremonial, it is prophecy. He is going to come and these are all foreshadowings of this mighty Deliverer.

Then you come to the writings of these great prophets, Isaiah, and all the rest of them. And Philip would have said that they were all pointing forward to this Deliverer. They are all saying, 'Comfort ye, comfort ye my people, saith your God . . . Prepare ye the way of the LORD, make straight in the desert a highway for our God' – for this mighty Deliverer – '. . . and all flesh [all eyes] shall see it together' (*Isa.* 40:1,3,5). This is the message of the entire Old Testament. It is waiting for the coming, and giving details about the eventual arrival, of this blessed Deliverer.

Then Philip came to the birth of Jesus – all the details that were later written down in our New Testament – he is here, he has come. And Philip, we are told, 'preached unto him Jesus'. What did he say? He told the Ethiopian the facts about Jesus. He told him first how he was born. He told him about an archangel visiting Mary, his mother, and about all that preparation and how it was a virgin birth – this extraordinary child, this mystery, this marvel. It is a part of the story. 'And he preached unto him Jesus.' Jesus, yes; but Jesus was only a man, you say, and only a carpenter. No, no! This is the whole point. Jesus is the Son of God.

And how do you know that he is the Son of God? Well, it was his birth, to start with, and then his extraordinary life, his teaching – 'Never man spake like this man,' said the officers (*John* 7:46) – and his miracles – 'The blind receive their sight, and the lame walk, the lepers are cleansed, and the deaf hear, the dead are raised up' (*Matt.* 11:5). Jesus! Miracles! Power! Manifestations! Storm calmed! Raging waves and billows silenced – all down in peace! And then his extraordinary death in apparent weakness, his burial, the tomb, the stone. And yet the stone removed, the empty tomb! The resurrection! His appearances! The ascension! That is what Philip preached.

You see, you must take all this – the Scripture prophesying, the facts fulfilled, the verification, the events, the history. Not 'cunningly devised fables' but facts, apostolic witness and testimony, witnesses to the resurrection. And then there is his own prophecy that he would send upon the apostles the Holy Spirit after he had returned to heaven. And then that tremendous event that happened at Jerusalem on the day of Pentecost when the Holy Spirit suddenly came upon them and they were transfigured and transformed, and spoke in other tongues and had a power and an amazing ability to work miracles. This is the message! The Old Testament looked forward to him; the Gospels unfold him. They tell us he came. Then the book of Acts looks back to him: 'In the name of Jesus Christ of Nazareth rise up and walk' (*Acts* 3:6). And the epistles expound him, and show the meaning of his life, his death, his teaching and everything else.

And finally the book of Revelation, the last book in the Bible. What is this? Well, here is a book that still tells you about him: he is the centre of every book in the Bible. The book of Revelation tells you that he will come again, that he will destroy every enemy. He will have victory. He will reign from pole to pole and shore to shore. 'That at the name of Jesus', said Paul, 'every knee should bow, of things in heaven, and things in earth, and things under the earth; and that every tongue should confess that Jesus Christ is Lord, to the glory of God the Father' (*Phil.* 2:10–11). 'He opened his mouth, and beginning at the same scripture, preached unto him Jesus.' Philip told the Ethiopian the good news of Jesus.

What is the point of all this? Who is he? What is he? What has he come to do? And the answer is that it is good news. It was given to old Zechariah, the father of John the Baptist, to state it first: '[God] hath visited and redeemed his people' (*Luke* 1:68). Our Lord said it himself: 'The Son of man is come to seek and to save that which was lost' (*Luke* 19:10). 'And Philip preached unto him Jesus.' He said: You are lost, you are helpless, you admit it. Do you know that he has come to save you, the one Isaiah was writing about? He is Jesus, and he has come to give you light, understanding, knowledge, forgiveness, all you stand in need of. The good news of Jesus!

That, my friends, is the content or the message of the Scriptures. That is the Christian message – whoever you are, whatever you may have been, whatever you may have done, it does not matter. You are a sinner, you are lost, your are hopeless, you are as helpless as this poor Ethiopian eunuch.

You can change from paganism to Judaism, you can change from a vague pantheism to the highest that the Greek philosophers have got to give you, and you will be as blind at the end as you were at the beginning.

But there is one who can give you light, who can give you life, who can assure you of the forgiveness of your sins, who can introduce you to God and make you a child of God, who can change you from a miserable seeker into a confident and rejoicing disciple, for the last words we read about this eunuch are these, 'He went on his way rejoicing.'

16

The Heart and Centre of the Gospel

The place of the scripture which he read was this: He was led as a sheep to the slaughter; and like a lamb dumb before his shearer, so opened he not his mouth: in his humiliation his judgment was taken away: and who shall declare his generation? for his life is taken from the earth. And the eunuch answered Philip, and said, I pray thee, of whom speaketh the prophet this? of himself or of some other man? Then Philip opened his mouth, and began at the same Scripture, and preached unto him Jesus (Acts 8:32–35).

We are considering this story, let me remind you, not only because it is very important historically, but also because it teaches us exactly what the Christian message is, how one becomes a Christian, and what it means to be a Christian. This is most important because, though this happened in the first century and we are here in the twentieth century, the situation we are in has not changed – and neither has the message of the gospel. We are concerned with an everlasting gospel and the message that Philip preached to the Ethiopian eunuch is the message that is needed in this world today. That is why we are interested in it. There is considerable confusion today as to what Christianity is and what the church is. Well, here is the answer, and the only answer.

We have already considered many reasons why people are not Christians and now we come to the actual message. So let us do what Philip did. Here he found this Ethiopian reading a portion of Scripture and this is what he was reading: 'He was led as a sheep to the slaughter; and like a lamb dumb before his shearer, so opened he not his mouth: in his humiliation his judgment was taken away: and who shall declare his generation? for his life is taken from the earth.' This is from the fifty-third chapter of the book of the prophet Isaiah and it is a description of a man undergoing terrible suffering. This man is as innocent as a lamb. He does not speak up for himself. He does not defend himself. He is quite passive though he is treated in an abominable manner.

And when Philip had sat down in the chariot, the Ethiopian put a very good question to him. Indeed, he asked the vital question: 'I pray thee, of whom speaketh the prophet this? of himself, or of some other man?' He was perplexed by these words. He was studying this chapter and he could not make head nor tail of it. It was clear that somebody was suffering, but who? Was the prophet talking about his own suffering or about the suffering of somebody else? What an excellent question that is!

So Philip took the opportunity he was given. The answer is that Isaiah is not talking about himself but about somebody else. Who is he talking about? Then we read, 'Philip opened his mouth, and began at the same scripture, and preached unto him Jesus.' That is the one of whom Isaiah is speaking; that is the one who is suffering. Not Isaiah, not the nation of Israel, but the Lord Jesus Christ. So Philip preached to this Ethiopian eunuch on the suffering and the death of Jesus of Nazareth; and that is what I want to speak about now.

Why do I do this? Because it is the heart and the centre of the Christian message. This is the very nerve of the Christian gospel. You need not take my word for that. Philip spoke about it here, and Peter had already done so on the day of Pentecost in the first sermon ever preached under the auspices of the Christian church. That sermon was an exposition of the meaning and the purpose of the death of Jesus of Nazareth, the Son of God. This is the great theme running right through the book of Acts, and you find it emphasized in the epistles and in the Gospels; it is everywhere.

The apostle Paul is never tired of emphasizing this. He says to the Corinthians: 'We preach Christ crucified, unto the Jews a stumblingblock, and unto the Greeks foolishness' (*1 Cor.* 1:23). 'Christ crucified.' And a few verses later he puts it still more strongly: 'For I determined not to know any thing among you, save Jesus Christ, and him crucified' (*1 Cor.* 2:2). Here was Paul on the way to this cosmopolitan city of Corinth. It was a typical Greek city, a seaport and yet a place of learning, too. It engaged in trade and business – indeed, it had a bit of everything, it was a kind of London in the ancient world. So the apostle was about to enter the city, and he tells us that he deliberately decided, in advance, what he was going to preach about: it was to be nothing but 'Jesus Christ, and him crucified'.

Later on Paul tells the Corinthians why he had made this resolve. It was for this reason: 'For other foundation can no man lay than that is laid, which is Jesus Christ' (*1 Cor.* 3:11), and, remember, 'and him crucified'. In the fifteenth chapter of that first great epistle, Paul reminds the Christians in Corinth how, at the beginning, he had preached to them 'first of all', 'how that Christ died for our sins according to the scriptures' (*1 Cor.* 15:3). The first thing always gets priority. He reminds the Galatians that he had 'placarded' Christ to them (*Gal.* 3:1). He says: I am a sort of bill-poster, and when I came amongst you I put up a poster, 'Jesus Christ crucified! The death of the Son of God!'

And remember this: the apostle did that deliberately, as did all the other preachers. Though they knew that this message was unpopular and infuriated many people who heard it, it made no difference. The death of Jesus is the central message of the gospel. It is the only message of salvation. Philip was concerned about this man's soul. He wanted to help him and the Ethiopian wanted to be helped. So Philip expounded to him the meaning of the death of the Son of God.

But, of course, to natural men and women the message of Christ crucified is the greatest obstacle to their believing the gospel; it is the greatest source of offence. The apostle speaks, again to those Galatians, about 'the offence of the cross' (*Gal.* 5:11). And it is an offence, and I know it is; and that is why I am dealing with it now in this manner. You know, everything about the Lord Jesus Christ was surprising. People do not realize this. They would like him to be someone whom they can understand, they want him to fit into their categories, but there was nothing about him that fitted into any ordinary category.

Now this very fifty-third chapter of Isaiah that the Ethiopian eunuch was reading and that Philip expounded to him tells us this: *Who hath believed our report? and to whom is the arm of the* L*ORD* *revealed? For he shall grow up before him as a tender plant, and as a root out of a dry ground: he hath no form nor comeliness; and when we shall see him, there is no beauty that we should desire him*(verses 1–2).

What a perfect account of the effect that the coming of the Son of God, Jesus of Nazareth, had upon his own contemporaries; he surprised them in everything. He was 'a root out of a dry ground'. What does that mean? Well, you do not expect anything to grow in dry ground, do you? But here was something suddenly sprouting in dry, barren ground. Astonishing!

Of course, the Jews thought that when the great Messiah, the great Deliverer, would come, he would be born in Jerusalem, born in a palace, born the son of a king, and would be outstanding in appearance and in every other respect. But, again, the reality was the exact opposite. He was not born in a palace but in a stable. He was not born amidst pomp and ceremony but in the midst of straw and cattle and laid in a manger. He was born of a virgin, an unknown virgin. You could not explain him in ordinary human terms. And then there he was, born in lowliness, brought up in lowliness; indeed, in poverty; and, instead of being a great philosopher, he worked as a carpenter until he was thirty years of age. Now to the world this was simply astounding. The world does not think of deliverers or messiahs or benefactors in these terms. It can understand a benefactor being a great military personage or a great king, a great teacher of philosophy or a scientist. But a carpenter, a lowly person, a root out of a dry ground?

Everything about our Lord is always surprising, and people look on at him and say, 'He hath no form nor comeliness; and when we shall see him, there is no beauty that we should desire him' (*Isa.* 53:2). They think they can recognize greatness when they see it. Yet the Son of God came and they saw nothing in him. 'Who is this fellow?' they said. His very person did not fit in to human categories and canons of judgment.

But what always surprised everybody about him was that he refused to become a king. They realized that there was something distinct and unique about him, and they could not understand why he was not going up to Jerusalem and setting himself up as a king, and why he was, instead, spending most of his time in Galilee preaching to ordinary common people: 'The common people heard him gladly' (*Mark* 12:37). Even his own brothers remonstrated with him about this and said, 'Why don't you go up and declare yourself?' (see *John* 7:3–4). One day a large crowd of people tried to take him by force and make him a king (*John* 6:15). That is the world's idea of how it is to be saved – there will be some great man, great in human esteem, great in human understanding, great according to our canons of judgment. But our Lord would not do what they wanted. He always amazed and even shocked his contemporaries.

But if that is true of our Lord in general, it is particularly true about his death. The Jews misunderstood his death. It was the final shock. And it has always been the greatest scandal of all. It has always been misunderstood. So it is not surprising that the poor Ethiopian eunuch could not understand it. The natural man has never understood it – never. The Bible is full of this.

Our Lord, remember, was born as a Jew, and the Jews, of all people, were those who were waiting for and looking for the Messiah. Their Old Testament Scriptures had taught them to do this and at first when our Lord came they were interested. They could not dispute and deny his miracles, though they tried to. They had their legalisms – 'You should not be doing these things on the Sabbath' – and their pettifogging little criticisms, but the miracles were not the main trouble. The final scandal was his death upon the cross. We are told in the Gospels of how, when he was hanging on the tree, they were there – the Pharisees and scribes and Sadducees, the leaders of the Jews, the religious and moral leaders – standing there and mocking him and jeering at him. 'He saved others; himself he cannot save . . . let him now come down from the cross, and we will believe him' (*Matt.* 27:42). To them the cross was the final proof that he was an impostor. A Saviour dying! The Deliverer being put to death in weakness and ignominy and scorn! This was, as Paul says, 'unto the Jews a stumblingblock' (*1 Cor.* 1:23). This was the final proof to them that this man was no Messiah, in spite of all his arrogant claims.

And they thought this because of their utterly false ideas of the Messiah. The Jews were politically minded, and what they wanted was to be a great nation again, a separate nation, above everybody else, having conquered everybody else. They had this nostalgia, as it were, for their great past, particularly under David, and the Messiah was to be the son of David, so when he came he would come as a great regal person, conquering the world. But here was one who did the exact opposite, and was even killed in utter shame, as a felon, between two thieves on a cross on a hill called Calvary. It was monstrous!

But the Pharisees and scribes were not the only people who were offended by his death. His own followers, his closest, innermost circle of disciples, were also. The Scriptures are very honest, and they tell us this. There is a great statement to this effect in Matthew chapter 16. When our Lord was with his disciples at a place called Caesarea Philippi, he asked them:

Whom do men say that I the Son of man am? And they said, Some say that thou art John the Baptist: some, Elias; and others, Jeremias, or one of the prophets. He saith unto them, But whom say ye that I am? And Simon Peter answered and said, Thou art the Christ, the Son of the living God.

Marvellous!

Jesus answered and said unto him, Blessed art thou, Simon Bar-jona: for flesh and blood hath not revealed it unto thee, but my Father which is in heaven.

Peter has understood; he is all right. But wait a minute:

From that time forth began Jesus to shew unto his disciples, how that he must go unto Jerusalem, and suffer many things of the elders and chief priests and scribes, and be killed, and be raised again the third day. Then Peter took him, and began to rebuke him, saying, Be it far from thee, Lord: this shall not be unto thee. But he turned, and said unto Peter, Get thee behind me, Satan: thou art an offence unto me: for thou savourest not the things that be of God, but those that be of men (Matt. 16:13–23).

Peter objected to his dying. 'No, no,' he said, in effect. 'I have seen you are the Son of God, but you must not die, that is to finish everything.' He did not understand it. It was an offence to him.

And our Lord's teaching about his death continued to be an offence to the disciples. Every time our Lord mentioned it, even his closest followers were troubled. So he had to say to them, 'Let not your heart be troubled: ye believe in God, believe also in me' (*John* 14:1). But they stumbled at it every time. Even after his resurrection they still stumbled. Look at the two men on the road to Emmaus, commiserating sadly with one another – Oh, we had thought that it had been he, but he is dead, buried; it is the end (see *Luke* 24:21). And then, as Paul reminds us, our Lord's death was, of course, 'unto the Greeks foolishness' (*1 Cor.* 1:23). This idea that a man by dying as a felon is saving the world is just sheer nonsense. The saving act is to be an act of thought, something that has to be taught. It is the philosopher who will save us. What we want is a man who can teach us, who can give us the word. Then we will rise to it and save ourselves and the universe. That is the way of salvation! As for a man dying in weakness, a Saviour coming out of a place like Palestine, a little country like that – rubbish! Palestine has no history of thought or of understanding or of greatness, and that carpenter . . . the very idea is just ridiculous! 'Foolishness to the Greek' – unutterable nonsense.

Well, my dear friends, there it is, that is how they took our Lord's death in his own day. But what I am concerned to show you is that it is still the same today. There are many people in the world who say that they admire Jesus of Nazareth, and think he is the best man who has ever lived. They admire his teaching and are ready, they say, to put it into practice. We must all do this, they say. The world needs to apply the Sermon on the Mount. Then the war in Vietnam would end. Jesus said, 'Turn the other cheek'; that is Christianity. Do this and all will be well.

But when you tell people that what they must do is believe that it was by his dying on the cross that Jesus Christ saves, they turn away, often in anger, and with derision and sarcasm. They say, 'That's monstrous!' And if they do not do that, they explain his death away as the death of a pacifist. They say, 'Yes, he died on the cross, but what he was doing was showing the way we ought to meet the brutalities of war and the cruelty of man to man. He's the supreme example of passive resistance. He said, "All right, I will not fight, do as you will with me", and he just allowed them to kill him.'

Or there are those who say: No, his death was just another example of the world not understanding its own great men. They killed Socrates, they've killed many a leader, many a man who was ahead of his time, and Christ was just one such man. He was a leader, a great teacher, but, of course, they could not take his teaching at that time – they were not as advanced as we are now. Today we are ready to accept this teaching, but they were not.

Because they misunderstood him, they killed him. Or people will explain the cross away in terms of a tableau, a great dramatic representation of the love of God. They say, 'There he is, the world does not understand him and it crucifies him.' But what is happening there? 'Oh,' they say, 'it's God telling the world that though we've done this to his Son, he still loves us, and is still ready to forgive us. The death of Jesus is God saying, "I forgive you anything. No one will be punished, all of you will go to heaven, and there is no hell."' So the cross, according to this view, is the supreme manifestation of the love of God.

But now, here is the question: What really is the truth about this death? What do you think Philip said to the Ethiopian eunuch? Tell me, what is your attitude to the death of Jesus of Nazareth? Is this crucial to you? Is it vital? Or was it an accident, just one of those unfortunate, tragic events that take place from time to time?

According to the New Testament teaching this is the most vital question of all, for it is by our attitude to the cross that we show whether or not we are Christians. It is by our attitude to the death of our Lord that we are saved. We cannot afford to be uncertain about it. So we must do what Philip did when he took his seat on the chariot and the man put his excellent question, 'Of whom speaketh the prophet this? of himself, or of some other man?' Exactly as Philip did, you and I must take that fifty-third chapter of the book of the prophet Isaiah, and we must see in it the gospel of Christ, the gospel of salvation, the way of deliverance. It is, I repeat, the very heart and centre of the gospel. According to this message, the Lord Jesus Christ saves us not by his teaching only, nor by his example – no, he saves us by dying on the cross. So as this is central and vital to salvation, what is the truth concerning it?

Now here is a fact of history: Jesus of Nazareth was crucified between two thieves on Calvary's hill, so how and why did it happen? The first thing we must say is that it was not an accident. This is, to me, of supreme importance. As I understand the message of the Bible, from beginning to end, our Lord's death was the focal point, the vital moment, of God's plan and purpose of redemption.

So I want to prove to you that it could not have been accidental, and that if it had been accidental it would not be saving. We know that our Lord's death was not accidental first, because it was prophesied in the Old Testament. Here was this man seated in his chariot reading the fifty-third chapter of Isaiah. And here Isaiah says that the Messiah will be 'a man of sorrows', he will be 'acquainted with grief', he will be 'smitten' and 'stricken'. And Isaiah wrote these words eight hundred years before these events took place!

But this is only one scripture. Philip only started with this. I have no hesitation in telling you what he did. Philip did with the Ethiopian eunuch precisely what our Lord had done with the two men on the road to Emmaus who were in the same sort of befuddled condition. Christ had died, and was in the tomb, they thought, and that that was the end of all their hopes. But our Lord said to them, 'O fools, and slow of heart to believe all that the prophets have spoken: Ought not Christ to have suffered these things, and to enter into his glory?' And then we read, 'And beginning at Moses and all the prophets, he expounded unto them in all the scriptures the things concerning himself' (*Luke* 24:25–27).

And later on, when our Lord suddenly appeared in an upper room in Jerusalem where the disciples were gathered together in fear, he did exactly the same thing: 'Then opened he their understanding, that they might understand the scriptures, and he said unto them, Thus it is written, and thus it behoved Christ to suffer' (*Luke* 24:45–46). The point he was making was precisely that his death was the fulfilment of prophecy. So he said: 'These are the words which I spake unto you, while I was yet with you, that all things must be fulfilled, which were written n the law of Moses, and in the prophets, and in the psalms, concerning me' (*Luke* 24:44).

So our Lord's death was no accident, and the proof is that it had been prophesied. It is in the whole of the Old Testament – Moses, the Psalms, the Prophets. Go back to Genesis 3:15. God said to Adam and Eve in the Garden of Eden that there would be warfare between the seed of the serpent and the seed of the woman. He said that the seed of the woman would bruise the serpent's head; yes, but the serpent would also 'bruise his heel'. That is the first prophecy of the death of the Messiah, Jesus of Nazareth, the Son of God. And then why was the offering of Abel accepted rather than that of Cain? It was because it was a blood offering, and not a mere offering of fruit or the produce of the ground (*Gen.* 4:3–5).

Do you remember the great story of Abraham being commanded to take his son Isaac, and build an altar and put Isaac to death as a sacrifice to God; and how at the last moment, when he has even raised his hand to strike Isaac, God stops him, and provides a ram for him to offer instead (*Gen.* 22)? What is that, do you think? Oh, it is only a great adumbration and illustration and prophecy of the day when that will happen to God's only begotten Son.

Come along, work your way through the books of Moses. Christian people, you must read them, they are full of the gospel. It is often because people do not know their Old Testament that they do not know their gospel. You say, 'I'm bored with all the instructions about the building of the tabernacle and the temple, and all the measurements and the colours, and all about lambs being offered and blood sacrifices and burnt offerings. What has it all got to do with me?' I will tell you what it has to do with you. It ought to show you that the death of Christ on the cross was not an accident. God was foreshadowing it, foretelling it, preparing us for it. That is what they all mean. All the teaching about sacrifice and offering is summed up in that momentous phrase in the book of Hebrews: 'Without shedding of blood is no remission [of sins]' (*Heb.* 9:22). There, then is Moses, and that is only a synopsis. I could keep you for hours working it out; the books are full of it!

But then the Psalms, says our Lord. Let me just give you one example. Read the twenty-second Psalm: 'My God, my God,' says the psalmist, 'why hast thou forsaken me? why art thou so far from helping me, and from the words of my roaring? O my God, I cry in the daytime, but thou hearest not; and in the night season, and am not silent. But thou art holy' – and on it goes. Do you know what that Psalm is? It is a perfect and exact description, in detail, of death by crucifixion! The hunger and the thirst, the crying out to God! Our Lord used these very words, and he used them not only because they were true, but also to show people that this was the fulfilment of what the psalmist said in that prophetic utterance, 'My God, my God, why hast thou forsaken me?' The Psalms!

And then the Prophets. Isaiah 53 is only one example And then you come to the last of the prophets. Who was this? John the Baptist. And what did he say? Well, at the very beginning of our Lord's ministry, John was standing one afternoon with two of his disciples when our Lord passed by, and John said: Wait a minute, 'Behold' – look at him, who is he? Look at this great teacher, look at this great personage, look at this great philosopher, look at this great . . . No! – 'Behold the Lamb of God, which taketh away the sin of the world' (*John* 1:29). There is the summary of the whole of the Old Testament. He has come! The one prophesied, predicted – God's Lamb! The fulfilment of all the other lambs and the types, the great antitype himself.

An accident? There never was an event that had been so prophesied and prepared for as the death of Jesus Christ on the cross on Calvary's hill.

But in addition to this, our Lord himself prepared his people for his death. I have already quoted to you what he said at Caesarea Philippi. And we are told that he began then to teach his disciples about his coming death, and he constantly did this. He said, 'As Moses lifted up the serpent in the wilderness, even so must the Son of man be lifted up: that whosoever believeth in him should not perish, but have eternal life' (*John* 3:14–15). 'I am the good shepherd: the good shepherd giveth his life for the sheep . . . I lay down my life, that I might take it again . . . No man taketh it from me, but I lay it down of myself.' There it is in the tenth chapter of John 's Gospel (verses 11, 17–18).

I repeat that this theme is to be found everywhere in our Lord's teaching. Perhaps the most striking and notable example of all is the one in the twelfth chapter of John's Gospel:

Jesus answered them, saying, The hour is come, that the Son of man should be glorified. Verily, verily, I say unto you, Except a corn of wheat fall into the ground and die, it abideth alone: but if it die, it bringeth forth much fruit. He that loveth his life shall lose it; and he that hateth his life in this world shall keep it unto life eternal . . . Now is my soul troubled; and what shall I say? Father, save me from this hour: but for this cause came I unto this hour. Father glorify thy name' (John 12:23–25, 27–28).

Do you see what that means? He was on the verge, the threshold, of his death upon the cross. He knew what it was going to mean, and he was tempted to say, 'Father, save me from this hour.' No, no! He said, 'I came into the world for this hour.' Accident? He left the courts of heaven in order to die on the cross. He later on told his disciples that he could easily escape. One of them pulled out his sword to defend him, but he said, 'Put it back.' And then he said: Do you not know that I could command twelve legions of angels if I so desired, and escape this death and go to heaven? No, no, I have come in order to die (see *Matt*. 26:52–54). Again, in Luke chapter 13, we read that some Pharisees came to him one day and said:

Get thee out, and depart hence: for Herod will kill thee. And he said unto them, Go ye, and tell that fox, Behold, I cast out devils, and I do cures to day and to morrow, and the third day I shall be perfected. Nevertheless I must walk to day, and to morrow, and the day following: for it cannot be that a prophet perish out of Jerusalem (Luke 13:31–33).

And then he expressed his sorrow over the city of Jerusalem.

I have said enough about this, have I not? Accident? It is the most deliberate event that has ever taken place in the whole course of history. It is central; it is crucial.

But let me take you to a second principle. Not only was our Lord's death no accident, it was the action of God himself. This is vital. The world, misunderstanding it, always regards it as the action of men. The world says, 'People did not understand him and were not worthy of him. They were foolish, they were mad, they were blinded and jealous.' That, of course, is true, but you see how wrong it is as an explanation of his death? It was not the action of man, and this is, of course, the crucial point. Did you notice how it is put in the very portion of Scripture that the Ethiopian eunuch was reading? Isaiah writes, 'Surely he hath borne our griefs, and carried our sorrows: yet we did esteem him stricken, smitten of God, and afflicted . . . the LORD hath laid on him the iniquity of us all' (verses 4, 6). This is the emphasis in this chapter. 'It pleased the LORD to bruise him; he hath put him to grief' (verse 10). The Ethiopian eunuch was reading that this one would suffer because he would be smitten by God. It would be God acting, not men. This is what Philip expounded to him This is the Christian message.

Now I want to prove this to you again. This is not only taught here in the book of the prophet Isaiah. In the Garden of Gethsemane our Lord knew he was about to be put to death, and he took with him three of the disciples, Peter, James and John. He separated them from the others and said, 'Now you stay here awhile praying, while I go on.' And he was praying there by himself in an agony; we are told that he was in such an agony of soul that he began to sweat great drops of blood. You have never sweated blood, have you? But it has been known that when people have been in extreme agony, they have begun to sweat blood.

What was the matter? He himself gave us the explanation; this is what he said in his prayer in the garden: 'O my Father, if it be possible, let this cup pass from me' – he was referring to his death, that is the meaning of 'the cup' – 'nevertheless not as I will, but as thou wilt' (*Matt.* 26:39). He was saying: 'Father, if it is possible that I can save the human race in any other way but this, oh, let me do it, show it me. At the same time, if this is thy will, if this is the only way, I surrender myself, "Thy will be done, not mine."' It was the Father's will. There it is in his own prayer.

And then I take you again to the teaching that our Lord gave those two men on the road to Emmaus; this is how he put it: 'O fools, and slow of heart to believe all that the prophets have spoken: Ought not Christ to have suffered these things, and to enter into his glory?' (*Luke* 24:25–26). Can you not see, he says, that this had to happen, that it was the will of the Father, that it was the Father's way? You are stumbling at it and cannot see it. You are blind, you are fools, you have not understood the teaching of the Scriptures.

But if you really want the most explicit statement of all about this, you find it in the sermon that was preached by the apostle Peter at Jerusalem on the day of Pentecost. Here he is, he has suddenly been filled with the Holy Spirit, the crowd has gathered and they say, 'What's this?' Listen, says Peter:

Ye men of Israel, hear these words; Jesus of Nazareth, a man approved of God among you by miracles and wonders and signs, which God did by him in the midst of you, as ye yourselves also know: him, being delivered by the determinate counsel and foreknowledge of God, ye have taken, and by wicked hands have crucified and slain (Acts 2:22–23).

Do you realize what that means? Peter is saying this: It was your 'wicked hands' that actually did it, you did it through the Romans, but, you know, you did not understand what you were doing, and neither did they. This was God's great plan and purpose coming into operation. It was God who was doing this to him through the instrumentality of ignorant men. It was the action of God himself.

And the disciples repeated the same message later: 'Of a truth against thy holy child Jesus, whom thou hast anointed, both Herod, and Pontius Pilate, with the Gentiles, and the people of Israel, were gathered together, for to do whatsoever thy hand and thy counsel determined before to be done' (*Acts* 4:27–28). He is the Lamb of God, slain before the foundation of the world. Accident? It was the action of Almighty God! It was not men who had smitten him, and stricken him, it was God. That was what Philip expounded to the Ethiopian eunuch, because that is what is stated in Isaiah chapter 53. This, as I say, is the focal point of God's plan and way of salvation: 'With his stripes we are healed'; 'he was bruised for our iniquities: the chastisement of our peace was upon him.' This is the whole explanation, and this is what Philip was able to expound.

Now this was explained later by the apostle Paul when he said concerning the death of Christ: 'God was in Christ, reconciling the world unto himself, not imputing their trespasses unto them . . . [God] hath made him to be sin for us, who knew no sin; that we might be made the righteousness of God in him' (*2 Cor.* 5:19, 21). This, my dear friend, is God's way of saving you! That is the meaning of our Lord's death. That is why he suffered.

Do you say you do not understand? I am not surprised. This is the greatest mystery of all time. This is the most amazing and astonishing fact. I am not asking you to understand it. God willing, I hope to give you the explanation that we are given in the Scriptures, but I want to assure you here and now that you need not wait even for that explanation.

This is a proclamation; this is an announcement: 'Believe on the Lord Jesus Christ, and thou shalt be saved' (*Acts* 16:31). Let me put it in our Lord's own words. Here he is, again in the upper room with those people. He has risen from the dead, and he appears to them, and Luke writes:

Then opened he their understanding, that they might understand the scriptures, and said unto them, Thus it is written, and thus it behoved Christ to suffer, and to rise from the dead the third day: and that repentance and remission of sins should be preached in his name among all nations, beginning at Jerusalem. And ye are witnesses of these things (Luke 24:45–48).

And it is my privilege to tell you just that – 'in his name'; 'repentance and remission of sins'. It is my privilege to tell you that though your sins be as scarlet, they shall be as white as snow; that though you have lived a life of sin until now, it does not matter. If you will recognize it, and believe that God has so loved you that he has given his only begotten Son to that death for you, has punished him for you, you will immediately receive remission of sins. Your sins will be forgiven, God will blot them out as a thick cloud. He will cast them into the sea of his forgetfulness. He will smile upon you and put his Spirit into you. You will become his child. You will get to know him, and you will begin to rejoice in him, and look forward to spending your eternity with him. This is the way of salvation.

I do not tell you to live a better life and to make yourself a Christian, or to try to put yourself right with God, or to save yourself by trying to follow Christ – you cannot do it. I am here just to tell you that he was 'bruised for our iniquities', and that it is 'by his stripes' – the stripes with which God smote him – that you and I are healed.

And all that you have to do, unless you have already done so, is what this Ethiopian eunuch did on that occasion on his way home from Jerusalem to Ethiopia, on the desert road between Jerusalem and Gaza. Just say, 'I see it! I see the explanation; I see the message of the Scriptures. I've been reading them but I did not understand, I could not make head nor tail of them. Now I see it all, it is all part of one great pattern. This Jesus who was crucified in Jerusalem is the Messiah, the Son of God! He is the Lamb of God. He died for me:

Just as I am, without one plea
But that thy blood was shed for me,
And that thou bidd'st me come to thee,
O Lamb of God, I come.

Charlotte Elliott

Thank God for such a gospel!

17

The Death of Christ

And Philip ran thither to him, and heard him read the prophet Esaias, and said, Understandest thou what thou readest? . . . Then Philip opened his mouth, and began at the same scripture, and preached unto him Jesus (Acts 8:30, 35).

The central message of the gospel, as we have been seeing, is the very one that is dealt with here in the story of Philip and the Ethiopian eunuch. This message is the great teaching about the death of the Lord Jesus Christ. So let us look at it again in terms of this story. What is necessary for all of us is, first of all, to understand the message, and, secondly, to see the relevance of that message to our own lives. Now you see the importance of these two points? This Ethiopian eunuch was not a kind of philosopher who was just interested in understanding a passage of Scripture. No, no, he was concerned about himself, and he had a vague feeling that this scripture had something to do with him and something to say to him. And it is necessary for us to come to this same point. Here is this message about the death of Jesus Christ and we, too, must know what it means. Yes, but still more important, in a sense, we must see what it means to us.

So let me ask you this question: Do you understand the meaning of the death of Jesus Christ? You heard me announcing a Communion service – what is the point of it? Are we just traditionalists here? Are we just doing this because it has been done for nearly two thousand years? Is that it? Has it any significance, any meaning? Is there any point in it in the modern world? Someone may say to me, 'Oh, you're going to preach on the death of Jesus Christ! What on earth has that got to do with 1968?

Look at the world we're in, look at what's happening in Vietnam! I want something to help me to live. I want something to give me understanding. What on earth has the death of Jesus Christ nearly two thousand years ago to do with me?'

Now if you are saying that, then you have obviously completely failed to understand the death of Jesus Christ. So I am here to do what Philip did. I am here to give you an understanding of this death, because it is the most important thing you can ever know. No one becomes a Christian without understanding something about it. It is crucial to salvation.

Last time I showed you how people misunderstand the meaning of the death of Christ. They are like this Ethiopian eunuch, and I am concerned to try to help those who still do not understand it. 'I can see the value of Christ's teaching,' they say, 'and I can see the value of his life, but you say the death is crucial and that I must believe in that death. I don't understand.'

All right, so let me help you. Let us go back again together to the passage that the man was reading – the fifty-third chapter of the prophet Isaiah. Now Philip, I repeat, did two things. He first of all expounded the meaning of the passage, and then he showed its relevance to this man. So let us start with the meaning of the passage itself, and Philip, as we have seen, explained to the Ethiopian eunuch that Isaiah was not speaking of himself but was making a prophecy. He was speaking of Jesus, and Jesus was the one Philip began to speak about. So you start with the person about whom the prophet Isaiah was writing. The whole of Christianity is about him. There is no such thing as Christianity apart from Christ. He is the beginning and the end: 'Alpha . . . Omega' (*Rev.* 1:8). He is everything. He is the centre. So you must start with him, as Philip did – 'and preached unto him Jesus'. He told him about Jesus of Nazareth, and what he told him was that he was the Son of God.

But here is the great problem, this is the mystery, this is what perplexes people: If Jesus was the eternal Son of God, why did he ever come into this world? This is a question that has baffled the ages. One important book on the subject had the title: *Cur Deus Homo? (Why Did God Become Man?)* Here is the central problem and it is the first thing that strikes you about the fifty-third chapter of

Isaiah. Here is this great and august person, yet you see him dying in a most terrible way. What is the meaning of this? Why did God become man?

Now, there is only one ultimate reason why anybody is in difficulty about the cross, about the death of Jesus Christ, and this is that they have never realized the depth of the human problem, the human situation. That is the whole trouble. And that is why it is always necessary to preach the law and to preach sin before you preach the gospel. It is no use saying to people, 'Come to Jesus', because they do not come. Why not? It is because they have never seen any need of Jesus. I repeat that people do not understand the cross, and cannot see why it is necessary, because they have never seen the depth and the profundity of the human problem.

'Yes,' people say, 'we're prepared to admit that we're not perfect, we're not all we should be. But surely it would have been sufficient to send teachers to us? Surely what we need is to be given instruction, we need an example? All right,' they concede, 'we'll even admit that we're sinners, and have sinned against God, but surely, even so, all that's necessary is that God in his love should forgive us. Why all this about the death and the crucifixion? And why do you say it's essential? We don't understand.'

Exactly! 'Understandest thou what thou readest?' asks Philip, because what you read is that the Son of God came into this world, that he humbled himself, that he left the courts of heaven, and was born in a stable. The world saw nothing in him. He lived as a man; he worked as a carpenter in poverty. The world did not understand him. It is all there in Isaiah 53. So here is the great question: Why did this have to happen? Why can we not be forgiven merely by God in his love saying, 'I forgive you'? That is the problem; that is the difficulty. And there is only one answer. It is obvious, is it not, that mere teaching is not enough, and that God (I say it with reverence) could not just say, 'I forgive you'? For it is clear that if he could, he would have done so. But that is not what he did. What I am told he did is this: 'God so loved the world, that he gave his only begotten Son' (*John* 3:16). He sent his Son into this world, and the Son came in this way. So what was he doing?

And it is here that you begin to understand the human problem. There is something about the problem of every one of us by nature that nothing can solve except the coming of the Son of God from heavenly glory into this world. God raised up prophets, he raised up teachers, he sent a law-giver and he gave a law: all that was done. But it was not enough. So, 'When the fulness of the time was come, God sent forth his Son, made of a woman, made under the law, to redeem them that were under the law' (*Gal.* 4:4–5). And he came into the world.

But what was the Son of God doing by coming? What was happening? He is God, eternal God, he is the Son. But he was born of a virgin, born of a virgin's womb. He was taking human nature unto himself. He was adding to his Godhead. He is God and man. And he was doing this to identify himself with us. So you find that paradox at the end of Isaiah 52 and running through Isaiah 53. You see there that you are obviously dealing with a very great person, and yet there are things about him that seem to make him very ordinary. Isaiah says, 'The kings shall shut their mouths at him' (*Isa.* 52:15). He is greater than all kings – and yet, 'He is despised and rejected of men' (*Isa.* 53:3). There is an apparent contradiction between this high and august person, and this man who is very weak. But that is the paradox of Jesus Christ. He is God; he is man. He is able to do anything – miracles are nothing to him – and yet he dies in weakness.

'Who is this man writing about?' asks the Ethiopian eunuch.

'Ah, he is not writing about himself,' says Philip, 'he is writing about Jesus.' So he tells the Ethiopian about Jesus of Nazareth, God-Man. So we come back to the question: Why did the Son of God come into the world? The answer is that he came into the world to identify himself with us, he came because of the human predicament, because of the state of the world and because of individual human beings. He himself says, 'The Son of man is come to seek and to save that which was lost' (*Luke* 19:10). That is what he was doing here, and he could not do this by telling us how to live and by giving us a list of things to do. No, no! He was identifying himself with us, and he did that by taking our nature upon himself.

But he did not stop at that. John the Baptist had appeared in the desert calling people to repentance, and preaching 'the baptism of repentance for the remission of sins' (*Luke* 3:3). And one day Jesus

Christ went to him and offered himself to be baptized. But John said, in effect, 'It is not for me to baptize you. You ought to be baptizing me. You have never sinned. You have no need to be baptized. You have no need of repentance.'

'Suffer it to be so now,' said our Lord to him. 'I must be baptized,' he said, in effect. 'I cannot do my work unless I take my place with these people' (*Matt.* 3:13–15).

The only way to understand this teaching is to see that this is the only way of salvation. It is not a mere word from God – it is the Son of God coming down in full identification of himself with us. So he took his place by our side as a sinner amongst sinners, though he had never sinned. And he said, 'I must be baptized', and he was baptized.

Still more amazing, we read that after his baptism he was subject to temptation in the wilderness for forty days and forty nights. Now you will read in the epistle of James that 'God cannot be tempted with evil, neither tempteth he any man' (*James* 1:13). This is obvious, is it not? It is axiomatic. 'God is light, and in him is no darkness at all' (*1 John* 1:5). It is inconceivable that evil could tempt God. But here was the Son of God 'in all points tempted like as we are' (*Heb.* 4:15). What is the meaning of this? It is just this identification of himself with us. He came into the world in order that he might be our representative. There is that about our condition which makes it essential that he should become one of us, as it were, and this is what he did. My friend, if he had not done this, we would all be damned, without hope, lost. We need someone who can take our burdens and problems and handle them, and this is what he has done.

Now there is the beginning, that is just a general view of this blessed person, which is held before us in the amazing portion of Scripture that this poor Ethiopian eunuch was reading there on the road. You are not so surprised now that he did not understand, are you? We none of us understand it by nature. All your scientific knowledge does not help you here; all theory is useless at this point. This is the mystery of mysteries, the mystery of godliness, the mystery of God. 'Understandest thou?' Of course not. All you can do is look at him and listen to the message concerning him, and here it is.

But let me go on: the next thing, of course, that really hits us in that fifty-third chapter of Isaiah is the suffering. It is a terrible picture of suffering, and the Ethiopian does not understand it. What does it mean? Well, what is clear everywhere in Scripture is the way in which our Lord suffered during his life in this world. That is how it is put: 'He is despised and rejected of men; a man of sorrows, and acquainted with grief' (*Isa.* 53:3). That is the picture. And, of course, it is the picture of our Lord in the New Testament Gospels. Listen, says Philip to the Ethiopian eunuch, the one who is being described there prophetically by the prophet Isaiah is none other than this Jesus. You heard of him when you were up in Jerusalem, the news of him has gone abroad. This is Jesus, look at him, this is the truth concerning him. He was 'a man of sorrows', and he was 'acquainted with grief'.

But why? He was pure, he never did any wrong, he never sinned. So why was he a man of sorrows? Has it ever occurred to you that we are never told that our Lord laughed? We are not even told that he smiled. Why not? Oh, it is the depth of the human problem. He came from heaven because the problem was so terrible that he must come! Laughing, joking? Unthinkable!

Look at him. Even as a boy aged twelve he was already beginning to feel the burden. It was the custom of Joseph and Mary to go up to Jerusalem at given times, and he, too, was taken with them. On their way back home, 'supposing him to have been in the company', they went a day's journey before they looked for him. But then they could not find him. So Joseph and Mary went back to Jerusalem to look for him and after three days they found him in the temple, arguing and reasoning with the doctors of the law – a boy aged twelve! Yes, but what was he doing? Joseph and Mary reprimanded him: 'What are you doing here? Why didn't you come with us?' And he answered them, 'Wist ye not that I must be about my Father's business [about the things of my Father]?' This boy aged twelve! This was not mere precocity, it was something beyond that. What was happening? Oh, 'my Father's business'. The burden of man in sin, the burden of the Fall, the burden of a world lost and going to destruction: 'the things of my Father'. All this worship, all this means of reconciliation, 'the things of my Father'. He was already, though a boy aged twelve, a man of sorrows, older than his years (*Luke* 2:41–50).

Indeed, at the end of John chapter 8 we are told about him that after he had said, 'Your father Abraham rejoiced to see my day', they said, 'You are not yet fifty years old.' Who was this man who could talk like this? They thought that he was approaching fifty, though he was just over thirty. It was this burden! These paintings of our Lord are all wrong; that is why you should never put them up. They are all imagination, and the imagination, generally, of artists who are not spiritually-minded men; they have got him wrong altogether. Isaiah says, 'His visage was so marred more than any man' (*Isa.* 52:14). He was not the type that is depicted in the pictures. No one should ever try to represent him. He was burdened, he was 'a man of sorrows, and acquainted with grief'.

But then consider the account of the temptation in the wilderness – it went on for forty days and forty nights. And here we are told a very interesting thing – that when the temptations ceased, 'the angels ministered unto him' (*Mark* 1:13). Why do you think that was? What do you think was happening there? Why was he in need of being ministered unto? My dear friend, this is the whole tragedy of the world. People think their problems are political and social: they are not. They are the problems of hell, they are the problems of principalities and powers, of the rulers of the darkness of this world, and spiritual wickedness in high places (see *Eph.* 6:12). He was struggling with the devil and the forces of hell; and though he was the Son of God in the flesh, the struggle was so tremendous that he needed the ministration of angels.

Our Lord went through all this so that you and I might be delivered, that you and I might be saved. He came 'to seek and to save that which was lost' (*Luke* 19:10), and this involved a conflict with these powers. We talk lightly about sin and falling into temptation, and we give up, and we go on sinning. But have you ever seen the power, the malignity, the awfulness! He met it directly. So here in Isaiah 53 you begin to see something about the depths of evil; that is why he was a man of sorrows. He looked out upon human beings and we are told that he saw them 'as sheep having no shepherd' (*Matt.* 9:36). Oh, how sorry he was for them! He said, in effect, 'There they are, they do not know, they do not understand, they know nothing about these powers that are manipulating them and playing with them as if they were but marbles and are nothing; they do not know it.' But this is the power that is ruling the world, this is what he has come to deal with. Here is the depth of the problem and it comes out there in the temptation in the wilderness. But it is seen everywhere.

Consider our Lord's ministry of healing; this is what we read in Matthew chapter 8:

When the even we come, they brought unto him many that were possessed with devils: and he cast out the spirits with his word, and healed all that were sick: that it might be fulfilled which was spoken by Esaias the prophet, saying, Himself took our infirmities, and bare our sicknesses (Matt. 8:16–17).

You know, I think we have not begun to understand all this. I plead guilty myself. I and all of us tend to look at him as the eternal Son of God with power and majesty and might who can cast out devils and deal with diseases. There is nothing he cannot do. But it was not as easy as that. 'Surely he hath borne our griefs, and carried our sorrows'; 'the LORD hath laid on him the iniquity of us all'; 'with his stripes we are healed'. Did you know that as he healed these people, somehow, in a way we do not understand, they became part of him, he bore them himself? Sin and infirmities and sicknesses are all the result of sin and of the Fall, and he came to deal with it, and it all became a part of him and he suffered? That is why he was 'a man of sorrows, and acquainted with grief'.

Take another example. You have read the story of how he healed the son of the man that came to him at the foot of the Mount of Transfiguration. Our Lord and Peter and James and John had gone up the mountain; and there he had been transformed before them, an amazing scene had taken place. But when they came down from the mount they saw a great concourse of people surrounding the other disciples, and a poor man was there with his boy, a boy who was having strange fits, and our Lord said, 'What's all this about?' Then the man said:

Master, I have brought unto thee my son, which hath a dumb spirit; and wheresoever he taketh him, he teareth him: and he foameth, and gnasheth with his teeth, and pineth away: and I spake to thy disciples that they should cast him out; and they could not.

Then, listen, this is what I read:

He answereth him, and saith, O faithless generation, how long shall I be with you? how long shall I suffer you? (Mark 9:17–19).

He had all power, he knew what he could do; yes, but it cost him, he was suffering. He was ever conscious of the power of evil.

Or take a final example. Our Lord was going one day, at the request of a man called Jairus, to heal his daughter, who was dying. A great crowd was round and about him and he was in a hurry to go to Jairus' house; but the crowd was so great that he was held up. Now in the crowd there was a poor woman who had an illness, and in a sudden flash she realized that he was so powerful that he could heal her without her needing to ask him. She said to herself, 'If I may touch but his clothes, I shall be whole.' I do not know the reason for the secrecy. There may have been an element of shame in her disease and she did not want anybody to know. So there she was, and she touched him. Our Lord was surrounded, literally thronged about by people, but suddenly he said, 'Who touched me?'

And our Lord's astonished disciples said, in effect, 'The whole world is touching you, and you ask, "Who touched me?"'

'Oh, yes,' he said, 'I am saying that.' He was aware that a particular individual had touched him, and Mark tells us how he was certain of this: 'Jesus, immediately knowing in himself that virtue had gone out of him' (*Mark* 5:25–34). You and I tend to think of him as this peerless, almighty Son of God who could do this and that – and he could. But, remember, everything he did cost him. 'Virtue'! Some power, some energy, something had gone out of him. That is what we are told in Isaiah 53. He was 'a man of sorrows', and 'acquainted with grief', and he suffered in this world.

Now let me bring you a commentary. We are twentieth-century people, are we not, men and women of great understanding? So I am going to ask you a question, the question that Philip put to the Ethiopian eunuch. I am going to test your understanding. The poor eunuch was dealing with Isaiah 53, which all expositors agree is an extremely difficult passage to expound. So we have every sympathy with him. But here is a very simple problem. I am asking you to expound a verse of two words, the shortest verse in the whole of the Scripture, 'Jesus wept' (*John* 11:35). Do you understand it?

'Oh, yes,' you say, 'it's quite simple.'

All right, what is it?

'Well,' you say, 'this happened at the grave of a man called Lazarus, a friend of the Lord Jesus Christ, who had been dead for four days. And it was there, standing by that grave, that Jesus wept. Next to him were Lazarus' two sisters – Martha and Mary – and there were other people weeping also and bewailing their loss. So the reason why Jesus wept was because he had lost a great friend. It is very natural that when one loses a bosom friend one should be filled with sorrow; and he was but a man, after all, and he wept as others weep.'

Yes, that is one proffered explanation.

'But not only that,' says somebody else. 'He wept also because of his sympathy with the sisters. They had lost this darling brother, and it was only natural that he should be sympathetic towards them.'

Well, I must not keep you, but those explanations are all wrong. I can prove that to you quite simply from John chapter 11. The first reason I would give is that when our Lord was first told about the illness of his friend Lazarus, instead of at once setting off to heal him, he delayed going – deliberately. Check the account for yourselves. He even gave the reason for not going. When the message of Lazarus' illness reached him, he said, 'This sickness is . . . for the glory of God' (*John* 11:4). So he deliberately did not go to save the man's life. And John says, 'When he had heard therefore that he was sick, he abode two days still in the same place where he was. Then after that said he to his disciples, Let us go into Judaea again. His disciples say unto him, Master, the Jews of late sought to stone thee' (*John* 11:6–8) – and so on. So there is the first answer.

But there is a greater answer, of course, which is this: when our Lord did go there to the grave, he knew perfectly well that he was going to raise Lazarus. This is what we read: 'Then said Jesus unto them plainly, Lazarus is dead. And I am glad for your sakes that I was not there, to the intent ye may believe; nevertheless let us go unto him' (*John* 11:14–15). He went in order to raise Lazarus from the dead. So if he knew he was going to raise him from the dead, why waste time in weeping because he was dead? Why waste tears in sympathy with the sisters when he knew that the next moment he would restore Lazarus to them? No, no, that is not why Jesus wept!

So why did our Lord weep? It is still the same reason; it is the reason why he was 'a man of sorrows, and acquainted with grief'. It was not natural human sympathy or concern about the loss of his friend. No, no, it was this terrible thing death, this thing that comes in and robs a man of his friend, and sisters of their brother, this thing that breaks people's hearts and spoils life – oh, this horrible thing! What is it? Is it the course of nature? No, it is sin, it is evil, it is hell, it is the devil; it is this thing that is fighting his Father. He saw it there and it made him weep. Not only that; he realized there that before he could deal with it he had to die himself.

So never interpret 'Jesus wept' sentimentally. I say again that it was this horror of sin, this horror of evil, this terrible problem of the human race that made him cry. It is there in the shortest verse in the Bible: 'Jesus wept.' And that was not the only time. I read in John 12, the next chapter, that when he was dealing with the whole question of his death, he said, 'Now is my soul troubled' (verse 27). Indeed, I should have pointed out to you that over this very question of the resurrection, or 'resuscitation', rather, of Lazarus, we read, 'When Jesus therefore saw her weeping, and the Jews also weeping which came with her, he groaned in the spirit, and was troubled' (verse 33). Why? Because he knew he was going to raise him? No, again, it was because of this terrible, evil problem, the thing that gets us down and makes us fools and the slaves of sin, and that causes death. It is this thing that has raised itself up against God and brought about the ruination of God's universe. He saw it, and knowing that he had to die, he said there again, 'Now is my soul troubled.'

Follow him on to the Garden of Gethsemane! What was the matter? He took Peter and James and John with him and said to them, 'Stay here for a while' – pray for me, I need your help. I am passing through an agony. And he went on alone. And there he was in such agony that he sweated drops of blood. But what is the meaning of this? Why this agony? Why this groaning? Why this breaking of spirit, as it were? What is it? That is what you must explain and understand. It all comes out in Isaiah 52 and 53 – 'His visage was marred.' He was passing through an agony, he was touching depths that no man had ever known; never has there been such suffering. It was this awful problem of sin, it was this awful problem of the human race that he had come to deal with. He had to feel the full force of it and he did. He is our Representative.

And so you come to this description of our Lord in Isaiah 53 where we are told, 'He is brought as a lamb to the slaughter, and as a sheep before her shearers is dumb, so he openeth not his mouth' (verse 7). The poor Ethiopian eunuch says, 'I don't understand this. I can't follow it. He's done nothing wrong, he's done no harm to anyone, there's nothing against him. Why doesn't he defend himself? Why doesn't he prove his innocence? Why does he allow all this to be said, and suffer in silence like a lamb brought to the slaughter? Why?'

There is only one answer to that question: he was not dealing with men, he was not dealing with human courts. He knew he was dealing with a vaster and a profounder problem. You remember what he said to Pilate? 'Pilate,' he said, in effect, 'don't talk to me about your authority, you have no authority except that which is given you from above. You do not know what you are doing. You are just signing a chit, this thing that gives them authority to crucify me. But, my dear man, you are nobody, you are merely a little scribe. You think you are a big man because you are a Roman governor but you are a nobody, a clerk, a mere official. *You* are doing nothing to me, it is God' (*John* 19:11)! So 'he opened not his mouth'. This was a part of what Isaiah had prophesied.

But come to the end of the story: look at him on his cross. What stands out? It is this exceptional suffering. 'As many were astonied at thee; his visage was so marred more than any man, and his form more than the sons of men' (*Isa.* 52:14). There has never been such suffering as that endured by the Son of God on the cross. 'I thirst,' he said. The thieves crucified one each side of him did not say that. But listen to him: he cried out in an agony, 'My God, my God, why hast thou forsaken me?' (*Mark* 15:34). Why did he say that?

There are some people who would have us believe that the death of Jesus Christ on the cross was the death of a martyr. Well, all I can say is this: if it was the death of a martyr, he was greatly inferior to the other martyrs. I have never heard of a martyr on his cross, or standing on a pile to be burned, or being hanged, crying out in agony, 'My God, my God, why hast thou forsaken me?' No, this is the story of the martyrs: there they are on the stake, the wood is all in position, they see the executioner standing with a flame in his hand, which has only to put to the wood for the flames to be lapping round their bodies and burning them and charring them, and they know the agony will be indescribable, but what do they do? Do they cry out, 'My God, my God, why hast thou forsaken me?' Quite the reverse. They smile. Some of them, like Cranmer, put their hands in first. They make great speeches. They thank God that they are accounted worthy. Complain? Never! They say, 'It's all right, I'm just being ushered into heaven.' They die gloriously. Why? Because God is with them, because he is upholding them, because he is sustaining them. They say, 'I'm not afraid; man can't do anything to me. I'm in the hands of God.' So they pass through the flames triumphing and glorying. But here is one who cries out in agony, 'My God, my God, why hast thou forsaken me?' And he was forsaken. It was true.

So this is the question you must answer: Why was he forsaken by God? Why the cry of dereliction? Then answer me another question: Why did he die so soon? Remember, crucifixion was a very slow way of dying. Yet the account tells us that when the soldiers came just to see how it was with these three who had been crucified, they were amazed to find that he was already dead. And then one of the soldiers thrust his spear into our Lord's side, and water and blood came out – which means blood clot and plasma. The blood had already separated into the clot and the plasma, the liquid, and the soldiers were amazed at this. 'Understandest thou what thou readest?' That is what you are reading of in Isaiah 53. You are reading of the most intense suffering that has ever been known in the world or ever will be known.

What accounts for it? He died, literally, of a broken heart, hence the clot and the plasma, the serum. What was the cause? There is only one answer and it is the whole answer. He was tasting death for every man (*Heb.* 2:9). He was dealing with this problem of man in sin. It was all on him – not his own sin because he was innocent, he was guiltless – but all human sin was on him. His Father had 'laid it all' on him. He was bearing all the sufferings of hell; in his own person he was bearing the full outpouring of the vials of

God's wrath upon sin. The agony, the suffering, was intense, it is inconceivable: 'The pains of hell gat hold upon' him (*Psa.* 116:3). It was, I repeat, the concentrated wrath of God upon sin.

That is the explanation of Isaiah 53. What suffering! 'Do you understand it now?' says Philip to the Ethiopian. This is not about Isaiah or about a man; no man could ever suffer like this. This is the Son of God suffering.

But why did the Son of God suffer like this? It was because this was the only way whereby you can be forgiven. 'The chastisement of our peace was upon him' (*Isa.* 53:5). 'My dear friend,' said Philip, in effect, to the eunuch, 'this is not merely of historical interest. Only this can save you from the punishment of hell.' Nothing else can. That is why he came; that is why he was 'a man of sorrows', that is why he was 'acquainted with grief', that is why he endured. He suffered all this that you might not suffer, that you might be reconciled to God, that all your sins might be blotted out as a thick cloud. But that is what it meant for him, that is what it cost him, that is what he came willingly to do. The Son of God so loves you that he did that for you! And it is the only way whereby any man or woman can become reconciled to God and receive the forgiveness of sins, and begin to live a new life in this world, and go on to the certain knowledge that they shall spend eternity in the glorious presence of the eternal God.

I leave you, then, with a question: Do you understand Isaiah 53? Do you understand the meaning of the death of Christ, the Son of God, on the cross? But still more urgently: Do you realize what it means for you? Can you not see that your whole eternal future depends upon your understanding and knowledge of this message that the Son of God has loved you, and given himself for you? If you believe and know this, then you are already delivered from this present evil world; whatever it may do to you, whatever may happen, it does not matter, you are a child of God, you are safe in life, in death, and to all eternity.

18

Why Christ Had To Die[1]

And Philip ran thither to him, and heard him read the prophet Esaias, and said, Understandest thou what thou readest? (Acts 8:30).

We have been considering together the difficulties that people get into about our Lord's death on the cross. We have seen that they do not understand it because they do not face it, they do not look at it, they are always idealizing it. They are doing the very thing that the apostle Paul says must not be done: 'For Christ sent me . . . to preach the gospel: not with wisdom of words, lest the cross of Christ should be made of none effect' (*1 Cor.* 1:17). People make it into something beautiful and wonderful. But it is not. The cross is offensive, and that is what comes out in that prophecy of Isaiah, which we have been looking at together – the terrible suffering. 'His visage was marred' (*Isa.* 52:14). The cross is ugly. It is foul. We notice the way in which our Lord's death on the cross is all prophesied there in Isaiah, and the way in which, when you read the latter chapters of the Gospels, you see that prophecy fulfilled in detail: the agony of our Lord, the agony in the Garden, the agony on the cross; the suffering, the intensity.

Now all this surely shows us at once that no superficial explanation of the cross is adequate – there is a great mystery here. Why did he have to suffer such terrible things? Why, I ask again, the cry of dereliction on the cross – 'My God, my God, why hast thou forsaken me?' (*Mark* 15:34). It makes him seem inferior to the martyrs, does it not? Yes, but you see that is a part of the suffering, it is a part of the message of the cross. There is something profound here, something desperate, something that demands that cry.

[1] This was the last sermon preached by Dr Lloyd-Jones as minister of Westminster Chapel before serious illness compelled him to retire.

Now that is the truth to which we address ourselves this evening. I said last time that obviously the cross happened because it had to happen. God would never have allowed it if the salvation of humanity could have been procured or effected in any other way. So the great question is: Why did that death on the cross have to happen?

Now it is because people do not understand the answer to this question that they are in trouble. But it is all here in Isaiah 53. The Ethiopian eunuch was already reading the explanation, though he did not yet understand it. Do you understand it? Do you know why the Son of God had to die in that terrible way? He was not your 'pale Galilean', not your aesthete, not your artist. No, no! Throughout his life he was 'a man of sorrows, and acquainted with grief' – why was that? Well, the answer is here, in Isaiah 53.

Or another way in which I can put it is this: the answer is really in the cross itself. But the trouble is that we talk about the cross instead of looking at it, instead of listening to it. The cross speaks. You remember that the author of the epistle to the Hebrews refers to blood 'that speaketh better things than that of Abel' (*Heb.* 12:24). There is a message coming from the cross, and we would hear it if we would but listen to it. But in order to do this we must not just turn it into something beautiful that we can all admire and seek to emulate. We must realize that it is unique, that it stands alone. So what is the meaning of the cross? Why did our Lord have to die in that way?

The first explanation of why our Lord had to endure and suffer all that he did is the state and the condition of man by nature. Here is the way we begin to understand it. He was innocent, yet he suffered, and he suffered because of us: 'He was wounded for our transgressions, he was bruised for our iniquities: the chastisement of our peace was upon him' (*Isa.* 53:5). I want, therefore, to put this to you. If you do not understand the meaning of the death of Christ upon the cross – why it had to happen, and why that death in particular was the means of salvation – then the main explanation of your lack of understanding is that you have never understood yourself, you have never realized the truth about yourself, you have never realized the condition in which you are by nature. This is always the first difficulty.

Now there are many different ways in which I could show you your true condition. It is, if you like, the whole tendency of modern man to start with the New Testament and not to be interested in the Old, and the moment you do that you are already wrong. The Old Testament is an introduction to the New. There is a sense in which you cannot understand the life and death of our Lord except in the light of the Old Testament. This was undoubtedly the very thing that Philip said to this Ethiopian eunuch. He said, in effect, 'This great message is all one. Eight hundred years before these events took place in Jerusalem, a man was given a preview of them – they are a part of God's great plan of salvation. Ever since the Fall of man God had been promising that he would send a great Deliverer who would deliver in a particular way, and this was the way.' 'He preached unto him Jesus.'

Yes, but the Old Testament will tell you why he had to come, and why, especially, he had to suffer. I am not surprised that people do not like this aspect of the message. It is what the apostle Paul calls 'the offence of the cross' (*Gal.* 5:11). The cross is offensive. If you let its message really come out, it will offend people. It did so at the time. Why did they jeer at our Lord as he was dying? Ah, it was because they caught something of this message. Paul says that the cross is 'unto the Jews a stumblingblock, and unto the Greeks foolishness' (*1 Cor.* 1:23).

What is the offence of the cross? The death of a martyr is not offensive. Indeed, we tend to admire it. There are those who try to imitate and to emulate martyrs; the world applauds them and admires them. Self-sacrifice! A man passively giving himself, not resisting! This is a message that people like. But they are taking away from the message of the cross, because the cross is always an offence. And the reason for the offence is found here in the answer to the question: Why did our Lord have to endure all this? That answer is in a little word that is so vital in the biblical message – the word *sin*. It is all due to sin. It is all due to our state and condition.

Let me divide it up for you. What is the condition of the human race? Why did the Son of God have to come into the world and why, especially, did he die on that cross? The first answer is that men and women are guilty before God. Now here is the beginning, here is the law, if you like. But people do not like the law, they want love, they say, they want a positive message. But you cannot understand the positive message unless you have first accepted the negative. Look at the words used in Isaiah 53: 'He was wounded for our *transgressions*, he was bruised for our *iniquities*. These two words, 'transgression' and 'iniquity' are vital words; they are key biblical words. And this is because they bring home to us the truth about ourselves. You will not understand the cross unless you understand these words and you will not understand yourself, either, or the state of the world today.

Griefs! Sorrows! That is the world we are in, is it not? But why are there griefs and sorrows? Why are there wars? Is there anything more superficial than that men and women should just make a protest about war? The thing we ought to be concerned about is what leads to it, what causes it. And are you asking an intelligent person to believe that this can be explained in terms of a particular president or a prime minister or some specific number of men? Of course it cannot. The problem is much deeper than that. To ask about the cause is to ask a profound question – it is the whole question of humanity in sin. Griefs and sorrows are the result of transgressions and iniquities. And what you and I need to do is to consider this message found in Isaiah 53 and not merely make our vapid anti-war protestations. These are not Christianity. They are almost a complete denial of Christianity. They are sad; they miss the whole point. They depict Jesus as a passive resister, as a pacifist, and they take the whole glory out of the cross as well as the horror and the terror and the ugliness of this visage 'marred more than any man'. No, no, that is too superficial.

Here is the real explanation. You can only understand the meaning of the terms 'transgressions' and 'iniquities' if you understand something about the biblical teaching concerning the law of God. God has made us; he has made us in his own image and placed us in this world. But having made us, and God being God, he told us that we must live in a certain way. God is the King, he is the ruler of the universe. It is his. Whether you like it or not, it is just a fact that the world belongs to God. And he has given us laws and has told us quite plainly that we will only be happy and only enjoy life in this world as long as we are obedient to, and conform to, his holy laws. And we can know what this law is because he has put it within every one of us; it is in our consciences. You can try to explain away the conscience in terms of psychology, but you cannot silence it; it is there. The law is written in the heart, says Paul (see *Rom.* 2:15).

But in addition to that, God has stated his law in an external, in an objective, manner through Moses and the children of Israel. Now that is where the Old Testament comes in. God made a nation for himself to witness to him. The world had gone wrong, and was in all the kinds of trouble that you find in the modern world. Read the account of civilization before the Flood and you might very well be reading about the mid-twentieth century: all the horrors of the world before the Flood are upon us today. Man, you see, has ceased to listen to his conscience. 'Every imagination of the thoughts of his heart was only evil continually,' says the sixth chapter of Genesis (*Gen.* 6:5). And so punishment came.

Then, after that, God took hold of a man called Abraham, called him out of paganism and turned this man into a nation. What for? Very largely in order to speak to humanity; he took this nation in order that he might teach. He gave them, as Paul reminds the Romans, 'the oracles of God' (3:2). We have already come across that in the seventh chapter of this book of the Acts of the Apostles. Stephen, in his great self-defence before the Sanhedrin, works that point out, you remember, in great detail. Refresh your memories by reading chapter 7 of the book of Acts. God did this in order that his laws might be perfectly plain and clear. So if we do not listen to our consciences, we have the Ten Commandments. There they are, the two tables of the law: man in his relationship to God, and man in his relationship to his fellow-man. The Ten Commandments are just an explicit statement, under ten headings, of how God intends human beings to live.

You only begin to understand the meaning of the cross when you start with the law, because the moment you look at that you see at once that humanity is guilty before God. This is the verdict, again, in Romans 3: 'There is none righteous, no, not one' (verse 10); and, '. . . that every mouth may be stopped, and all the world may become guilty before God' (verse 19). The whole world! Both sides of the Iron Curtain are guilty before God. It does not matter what political party you belong to, it does not matter what social class you belong to, it does not matter whether you are wealthy or poor: the whole world is guilty before God. This is what matters, not our superficial divisions and distinctions.

Why is the whole world guilty before God? Because it has not kept God's law. The epistle to the Romans is the great exposition of human sin and guilt, and I am certain that Philip, in his way, was giving the eunuch this same great doctrine that Paul works out there. This is the argument. The Jews thought that possessing the law put them right with God, but Paul says, 'Not the hearers of the law are just before God, but the doers of the law shall be justified' (*Rom.* 2:13). The fact that you know the law does not help you if you do not keep it, and the trouble is that the whole world has not kept the law of God. Thus sin is sometimes defined in the Bible as 'missing the mark', 'not coming up to the standard', 'falling short of the position in which we ought to be'. That is a part of the guilt.

But it is not the only part. We have not only failed to live up to the standards and the dictates of God's law, we have actually and deliberately broken it. That is the meaning of 'transgression' – deliberate flouting or breaking of the law; deliberately acting in an unrighteous manner. There is the law's statement. We have deliberately broken it. This is another source of guilt. But the most terrible cause of guilt is that, in doing all this, we have but been manifesting our rebellion against God.

Now here is the reason why the world is as it is tonight. 'The carnal mind is enmity against God: for it is not subject to the law of God, neither indeed can be' (*Rom.* 8:7). We have all gone our own way, says the prophecy here in Isaiah 53. We have gone astray, we have followed our own ideas, we have not listened to the way of God: 'All we like sheep have gone astray; we have turned every one to his own way' (verse 6), and this means deliberate rebellion against God.

My dear friend, you do not begin to understand yourself and your troubles and your problems and your unhappinesses and your griefs and your sorrows, you do not begin to understand the whole case and condition of humanity and this world in which we are living, unless you grasp that this deliberate rebellion was the original sin, the original rebellion of man.

Here was man, made in the image of God, in Paradise and enjoying life in communion with God, when the tempter came and asked: What has God said? Do you think it was fair of God to say that? Didn't God say this in order to keep you down, and to keep you as merely human? He knows perfectly well that if you only assert yourselves, you will be equal to him.

And man rose to the bait. Man still rises to this bait. He thinks he is God; he wants to be equal with God. He thinks he knows as well as God so he resents God's law and defies it and rebels against it. There is no greater sin than that sin of rebellion. And man is as he is today, and the world is as it is today, and the cross of Christ is as essential today as it has ever been, because man is guilty before God. Man's well-being consists of his being blessed by God and in the right relationship to him, but while he is a rebel and while he is guilty, he is not blessed by God.

Later on in the book of Isaiah, the prophet cries out in an agony, and he says to God: Oh, why are we as we are? What is the matter? And he gives the answer, 'Behold, the LORD's hand is not shortened, that it cannot save; neither his ear heavy, that it cannot hear: but your iniquities have separated between you and your God' (*Isa.* 59:1–2). This world was not meant to be like this; the world as it is today is a manifestation of the wrath of God against the sin and the unrighteousness and the ungodliness of human beings. God has said it everywhere in his law: 'The soul that sinneth, it shall die' (*Ezek.* 18:4). 'The way of transgressors is hard' (*Prov.* 13:15). It does not matter how clever and learned you are, how wealthy and sophisticated, if you are rebelling against God and flouting his laws, if you are guilty of transgression and iniquity, you will be miserable, you will be wretched. 'Grief and sorrow' – here it is! Guilt! Here is the problem.

But human guilt is not the only aspect of the problem. Man, I am told here in Isaiah 53, is not only guilty, he is also 'lost'. 'All we like sheep have gone astray; we have turned every one to his own way.' And here, again, is the whole message of the Bible. Man is not where he was meant to be; the world is not as it was meant to be. We all have this sense within us of being in the wrong place; it is a part of the restlessness we feel. But there is a misunderstanding as to where we are meant to be. Where the world thinks we are meant to be is this: that wars are banished so that we can all go on using our money to buy food and drink and sex and have a marvellous time. What a shame that Vietnam is spoiling it and causing trouble! That is the world's idea: it is not God's idea. We have gone astray; we do not know where we are, only that we are not where we were meant to be. The world is not enjoying fellowship with God, it is unhappy. 'Griefs and sorrows' sum up the whole of life today, do they not? The world does not understand itself; it does not understand life. It has no purpose; it has no sense of direction and no goal.

So the world has gone astray. It has 'missed the mark'. It has lost the route. It is in a wilderness. This is the whole tragedy and it is the very essence of the whole problem – life has become pointless, purposeless. What is the meaning of anything? What is the purpose of anything? Can you not see the confusion? Students! What do they do? What is the purpose of being a student, indeed, what is a student? The modern idea seems to be that students go to college to enjoy themselves, and it is the business of the taxpayer to fund that enjoyment. If they are not allowed to enjoy themselves they grumble and complain. Is that your definition of a student? But this is the modern idea. We are here to have pleasure and fun. That is a further indication that men and women have lost their sense of direction and do not know what they are doing or where they are going. All they want is a bit of ease. But then they realize that that is not enough because men and women cannot be satisfied with that. There is that in them which cries out for something bigger, something greater. But they cannot find it.

So there it is: 'We have turned every one to his own way.' What an extraordinary definition this is of the modern world! It is like the sheep who have gone astray. Can you not see the picture? Do you know anything about sheep? Have you ever seen sheep becoming wild, all rushing about, one in this direction, one in another, one going backwards, one going forwards? Is there anything more ridiculous than a crowd of frightened sheep? But that is the picture that is given here of humanity as the result of sin. Handel has caught this picture in the music that he wrote in order to depict this very verse. You can see in the music the silly nodding sheep rushing backwards and forwards with no purpose, no direction, no plan – in utter confusion. But is not that the world? The world is confused, the world is bewildered, but each person is trying to find a way out, each one is seeking a way of relief. There is humanity with all its learning and sophistication, but no direction, no answer, no solution.

What am I talking about? I am talking about the false religions, I am talking about the philosophies and the cults, I am talking about all human reasoning and all human ideas. One says this, the other says the exact opposite, and here are men and women completely bewildered and falling back upon drink and drugs. They cannot be bothered any longer; nobody understands; there is no sense in anything. Life is:

> *A tale told by an idiot, full of sound and fury*
> *Signifying nothing.*
> Shakespeare: *Macbeth*

'All we like sheep have gone astray.' Man is lost, as lost as foolish sheep, and in spite of all his civilization, all his educational efforts, all his striving, he cannot find the way out.

But, alas, not only is he guilty and lost, on top of that he is also miserable and sick. 'Griefs and sorrows'! Think again of this picture of the sheep. We read in the Gospel according to Matthew that when our Lord saw the multitudes, 'He was moved with compassion on them, because they fainted, and were scattered abroad, as sheep having no shepherd' (*Matt.* 9:36). That is how he saw life in this world; that is how he saw man. That is why he came into the world and later said, 'The good shepherd giveth his life for the sheep' (*John* 10:11). What does he mean by this? Well, this is his way of describing this 'grief and sorrow', this sickness – 'as sheep not having a shepherd'. You see the picture? Sheep are absolutely hopeless without a shepherd: it is a part of their foolishness. They do not have the understanding that the shepherd has. They do not know where to go to find pasture, so they are not adequately fed. They are thin and scraggy and are fainting because they do not know where the best pasture is to be found.

Not only that, sheep have no protection. Our Lord, again depicting himself as the good shepherd, says, 'I am the door: by me if any man enter in, he shall be saved, and shall go in and out, and find pasture' (*John* 10:9). There is the picture of the fold; the shepherd leads the sheep into the fold at night, and then, in order to protect them, he lies down across the entrance. He is protecting them against the wild dogs and wolves and other marauding beasts that used to attack sheep in these countries in the first century. But the shepherd keeps them safe: he takes them in, he takes them out. As well as giving them pasture, he also provides protection and care. And our Lord says: I have come to do that sort of thing. 'I am the good shepherd.' He sees humanity as sheep who are fainting for lack of nourishment and are being attacked by dogs and wolves.

What does he mean? Well, this is but a pictorial representation of life in this world. This is what life does to men and women and the world is fainting today. It has not got the food, the nourishment that can build it up and make it strong. As the General Confession in the Prayer Book puts it, 'There is no health in us.' Are we healthy, my friends? Are we full of vigour and life? Are you able to stand up to life? Are you conquering, are you gaining the mastery, are you full of the energy and power that we were meant to have? Human beings were meant to be God's representatives in the world, the lords of creation. Are we like that?

No, no, there is no health in us, we are fainting like these sheep. Moreover, we are attacked by the dogs and the wolves; we lose our chastity, our purity, we lose our peace; we lose our ideals, we lose everything that is ennobling. We sink into cynicism and perhaps into despair, and we say, 'What's the use of anything?' Or else we say, 'Let's eat, drink, and be merry, for tomorrow we die' (see *Luke* 12:19, *1 Cor*. 15:32). And the result is that like these poor fainting sheep, we are merely existing and not living. It is a miserable existence, a fainting existence. Have you ever seen sheep in this condition? You would not take them to market; you would not be proud of them; you would not take your friends to look at them. You would be ashamed of them and would try to conceal them. Why? Because they are not meant to be like that. They are meant to be well fed. They are meant to be full, and strong and vigorous.

'Understandest thou what thou readest?' asked Philip. The Ethiopian eunuch did not. 'Why should anybody suffer like this?' Oh, the answer is because of the condition of humanity! Guilty before God; lost, sick, miserable, unhappy. 'Grief' and 'sorrow'. Failure. Mere existence. We were never meant to be like this but we have become so. That is why the Son of God had to come into this world.

But wait a moment; even that does not complete the picture. On top of all this, man is perverted and depraved. What do I mean by this? Well, it is a part of the iniquity. He is in an unrighteous state; his heart is wrong. This is the most terrible thing about man. It is bad enough that he should be breaking God's law. It is bad enough that he should be transgressing, that he should be falling short of the pattern and of the standard. But, my friends, that is not the most terrible thing about us by nature. The most terrible thing about us is that even when we are offered salvation, we do not take it. We resent it. We reject it. Listen: 'Who hath believed our report?' (*Isa.* 53:1). Here is the question, and here is the 'report': 'My servant shall deal prudently, he shall be exalted and extolled' (*Isa.* 52:13). He will 'sprinkle many nations; the kings shall shut their mouths at him: for that which had not been told them shall they see; and that which they had not heard shall they consider' (*Isa.* 52:15). Here is the message – but, 'Who hath believed our report?' Less than ten per cent of the people of Great Britain. They do not believe it. Here is the trouble with humanity, and here in this rejection you see it at its very worst. Man is perverted; he has become depraved. He is offered a way of salvation, but he will not believe it or receive it. He still prefers to trust to his philosophies, to his own knowledge, his own efforts, his own understanding. Here is God's proffered way of salvation but, 'Who hath believed our report?'

'What?' says the modern man. 'You don't mean to say that you still believe that old gospel of salvation, you surely do not still say that we have to believe that Jesus of Nazareth is the Son of God, and that he saves us by dying on the cross at Calvary? Do you still believe this myth? It is really the best and funniest joke of all that anybody in the twentieth century should still be believing that!' But people have never believed it and they did not believe it in the first century. 'Who hath believed our report?'

But let us go on – the description is still more detailed. If you really want to know why the Son of God had to die on the cross, if you want to know why this, and this alone, can save you, here is the answer. You see it in the attitude of men and women to the Son of God who came into the world to deliver and save. What is that attitude? Well, first of all, they did not recognize him. Do you recognize him? Here is a question for you. Do you recognize Jesus of Nazareth as the Son of God? They did not recognize him when he came. Look at those Pharisees, those doctors of the law, those religious leaders in Israel. They looked at him and they said, 'Who is this fellow? Who is this carpenter who presumes to teach us?' They asked, 'How knoweth this man letters, having never learned?' (*John* 7:15). They did not recognize him.

And exactly the same, of course, is true of the Greeks who were so proud of their philosophy. Paul says of God's wisdom, 'Which none of the princes of this world knew: for had they known it, they would not have crucified the Lord of glory' (*1 Cor.* 2:8). Here is God incarnate! Here is the Lord of glory standing as a man amongst men, speaking such words as had never been heard before, words so amazing that the officers sent by the Pharisees to arrest him said, 'Never man spake like this man' (*John* 7:46). He was doing his mighty deeds, and yet they did not know him. The condition of humanity was such that when confronted by God in the flesh, they did not recognize him.

But it is even worse than that: 'He is despised' (*Isa.* 53:3). – they despised him. You have put your faith in human beings and in human understanding, human discrimination, human ability. You say that all that people need is teaching. If you put the teaching before them, they will rise to it. Give people a great example and they will follow it. But this has all been tried; the Son of God has been here and they despised him: 'He is despised and rejected of men.' Here is what you must understand and explain to yourself. The world chose a robber rather than the Son of God. Pilate, with a sense of Roman justice and equity, did not want to put our Lord to death. His wife had had a dream and she had warned him, and he, not knowing exactly what he was doing, had tried to save our Lord from crucifixion. But they had cried out, 'Away with this man, and release unto us Barabbas' (*Luke* 23:18). 'This man' – Son of God, Saviour of the world! 'Not this man,' they said.

'He is despised and rejected of men.' And unless you believe in him, you are rejecting him; rejecting his person; rejecting his death upon the cross. Here is the condition of humanity – here is the problem. This is what the world did with him. They ridiculed him, they spat at him, they laughed at him, they jeered at him; they mocked the Son of God who was bearing their sins.

This brings me to my final point, which is this: Man is completely unable to save himself. The cross proves this.

People say, 'What we want is teaching.' But I answer, 'You have had teaching. The law is the teaching of God.'

You say, 'What we want is to be shown the pattern; we want to be given the rules. Tell us how to live and we will do it.'

The commandments! There they are, but nobody could keep them. The apostle Paul has put this once and for ever in Romans 8:3: 'What the law could not do, in that it was weak through the flesh . . .'

It is no use giving us laws, we cannot keep them. 'This is the condemnation, that light is come into the world, and men loved darkness rather than light, because their deeds were evil' (*John* 3:19). Man knows what he ought to do but he cannot do it – that is the power of sin. 'I delight in the law of God after the inward man,' says Paul. 'But I see another law in my members' (*Rom.* 7:22–23), and this was dragging him down. It was more powerful than he was. The drives, the lusts, the passions, these are the things that make us break the law of God and that prevent us from keeping it.

Indeed, we know that the very Jews to whom the law of God was given misunderstood it completely. The apostle Paul is honest enough to tell us that he misunderstood it himself. He had once thought that he was absolutely perfect with regard to the law. He said, in effect, 'I did think that, but then I had not seen the meaning of this little word "covet"; and when I saw the meaning of this word, I knew I was lost' (*Rom.* 7:7–9). He had thought that as long as he did not actually, physically, commit adultery, he was not an adulterer, but then the force of the word 'covet' or 'desire' came in. 'Whosoever looketh on a woman to lust after her hath committed adultery with her already in his heart' (*Matt.* 5:28). It is not enough that you do not murder a man; if you say, 'You fool!' you have already murdered him in spirit (see *Matt.* 5:22). The Jews had misunderstood the law and they could not keep it.

No, men and women can never be saved by teaching. I repeat that they have been given the opportunity. They can never be saved by imitating and following an example. There is no greater folly in the universe today than that of being saved by 'the imitation of Christ'. Imitation of Christ? Should I, who cannot maintain my own standards, still less the Ten Commandments, talk about 'imitating Christ', the one who is sinless, perfect, absolutely holy! He condemns me more than anyone else. No, no, I cannot be saved by law, by instruction, by teaching, by example; my case is too desperate, my condition is too vile. I am guilty. I am lost. I am perverted. I am depraved. I am utterly helpless.

Is there no hope for me? Oh, yes, there is, and this is it: '*He* was wounded for our transgressions, he was bruised for our iniquities: the chastisement [the punishment] of our peace was upon him; and with his stripes we are healed' (*Isa.* 53:5). And so we have peace.

My dear friend, our Lord's death on the cross had to happen because of our transgressions, because of our iniquities, because of our utter helplessness and hopelessness. We cannot do anything. He had to come, and he has come, and, 'He hath borne our griefs, and carried our sorrows.' And the glory and the wonder of this way of salvation is that it does not ask me to attempt and to aspire to things that are impossible to me; it simply asks me to say this:

Not the labours of my hands
Can fulfil thy law's demands;
Could my zeal no respite know,
Could my tears for ever flow,
All for sin could not atone;
Thou must save, and thou alone.

Nothing in my hand I bring;
Simply to thy cross I cling;
Naked come to thee for dress;
Helpless, look to thee for grace;
Foul, I to the fountain fly;
Wash me, Saviour, or I die.

Augustus Toplady

I say again, he had to come. He had to die to bear the guilt and punishment of our sins, and he has done it.

That is what Philip said to the Ethiopian eunuch, and the man saw it. He said, 'I believe it. Can I be baptized?'

'You can' – and he was baptized, and then, 'He went on his way rejoicing.' And you will remain miserable failures with griefs and sorrows, iniquities and transgressions, until you likewise believe on the Lord Jesus Christ, and then, 'Thou shalt be saved.'

'Understandest thou what thou readest?' Have you seen and understood that it is by dying for you on the cross that he saves you and reconciles you to God?